ALSO BY BRAD LEITHAUSER

POEMS

The Mail from Anywhere   1990

Cats of the Temple   1986

Hundreds of Fireflies   1982

NOVELS

Seaward   1993

Hence   1989

Equal Distance   1985

PENCHANTS
& PLACES

PENCHANTS
& PLACES

ESSAYS AND CRITICISM

BRAD
LEITHAUSER

ALFRED A. KNOPF
NEW YORK
1995

THIS IS A BORZOI BOOK
PUBLISHED BY ALFRED A. KNOPF, INC.

Library of Congress Cataloging-in-Publication Data
Leithauser, Brad.
Penchants and places: essays and criticism / by Brad Leithauser.
p. cm.
ISBN 0-679-42998-0
I. Title.
PS3562.E4623P46   1995
814'.54—dc20   94-28629   CIP

Manufactured in the United States of America
First Edition

Most of the essays in this book have been previously published.
They appeared in the following publications, respectively:
"The Space of One Breath": *The New Yorker,* March 9, 1987.
"A Peculiarly Dark Utopian" *The New Criterion,* November 1986.
"No Loyalty to DNA": *The New Yorker,* January 9, 1989.
"Prose Prosodist": *The New York Review of Books,* September 29, 1988.
"Voices in the Clock": *The New Yorker,* July 8, 1991.
"Kasparov Beats Deep Thought": *The New York Times Magazine,* January 14, 1990.
"Dead Forms: The Ghost Story Today": *The New Criterion,* December 1987.
"Any Place You Want": *The New York Review of Books,* March 15, 1990.
"Demoniasis": *The New Yorker,* May 15, 1989.
"A Nasty Dose of Orthodoxy": *The New Yorker,* November 7, 1988.
"Alone and Extremely Alone": *The New Yorker,* April 22, 1991.
"Black Ships": *The New Yorker,* August 3, 1987.
"Irresistible Demons": *The New York Review of Books,* November 21, 1985.
"Severed Futures": *The New Yorker,* March 9, 1988.
"An Ear for the Unspoken": *The New Yorker,* March 16, 1987.
"A Hook Somewhere": *The New Yorker,* December 4, 1989.
"A Nonesuch People": *The Atlantic Monthly,* September 1987.

To my first critic,

GLADYS GARNER LEITHAUSER,

who, by example,

praised praise

Contents

ஜ

Preface

My mouth dropped, I was agog with admiration, the first time I watched an automated coin-sorter. Into its spout went a clangorous muddle of base coinage which, after a moment's digestive rumble, was excreted as trim columns of pennies, nickels, dimes, quarters. The machine seemed to have a keen eye for size, a delicate hand for weight—and a nose for money. A real taste for order.

No such sure and sweeping separations will emerge in the following pages. Still, I'd like to think that these "savings"—my first book of nonfiction, selected from some fifteen years of essay-writing and reviewing—are no jumbled heap of pocket-change either. I see this volume neither as a unitary whole nor as a collected prose, but as something in between. And if its contents stoutly refuse to be tagged and processed by the literary/critical equivalent of an automated coin-sorter, so much the better.

The book has two sections—a *Penchants* half and a *Places* half—each composed in turn of two subsections. Each subsection is meant to work as a counterweight to its partner. The first portion of *Penchants*—entitled "In the Era of Great Numbers"—explores the rational, natural, logical. It includes reviews of books by and about scientists and a long piece of reportage on computer chess, from which was born my novel *Hence*. The second portion—"A Mysterious Increase in Reality"—turns to the irrational, supernatural, mystical, and includes pieces about ghost stories, utopian novels, Salman Rushdie, Thomas Pynchon. In a similar opposition, the first portion of *Places* is devoted to Japan (a country populous, crowded, and powerful) and the second to Iceland (spare, empty, and—commercially speaking—all but powerless).

It is a truism—too often advanced by overly earnest critics—that every book is disguised autobiography. Even so, I can't resist saying that I feel toward this collection, in ways I haven't toward my three novels and three volumes of poetry, that this is where I've lived—literally so in regard to *Places,* spiritually so in regard to *Penchants.* These are the themes I'm forever taking up, the sites I keep returning to, the questions I keep fretting about. In the fourteen years of our marriage my wife and I have lived on three continents, in six countries—we've spent eight years overseas—with the result that our belongings, and often our wits, have been scattered. But this book reflects a steady rootedness—that of temperamental and artistic obsession. It feels like home to me. So it's with a proprietary tone, as though I stand on the threshold of a house I've recently been deeded title to, that I now say to my reader, *Thank you for coming.*

PENCHANTS

Introduction: In the Era of Great Numbers

My earliest professional ambition, as best I can recall, was to be a physicist. This was some years before I had any notion of the term's being connected to a discipline called physics. What I did understand, having received repeated assurances on this point, was that physicists were the people who dealt with the "biggest numbers": precisely the zone where I aimed to spend my time. There was a comfort, back then, in knowing *exactly* how many miles light travelled per second (to round off from 186,264 to 186,000 seemed a leap of wild irresponsibility; 264 miles per *second* was surely nothing to ignore) or how far the earth stood on average from the sun. And I enjoyed, particularly when whiling away time in the back of the car, doing multidigit addition and subtraction problems in my head.

Any genuine talent, as opposed to passion, that I might once have had for mathematics has so convincingly receded that nowadays I flounder when toting up an expense report or balancing a checkbook. My former obsession lingers only in stray pockets of the psyche—in a passion for prosody, I suppose, or in a slight, unfocussed vexation when the number of stairs in a long ascent fails to produce a multiple of four.

But since there is, for most of us perhaps, nobody we regard with more fond and tender indulgence than the Person We Might Have Been, I harbor an envious fascination with those men and women I meet, in life or in books, who have wed themselves faithfully to mathematical pursuits. I look upon them, whether or not I deserve to, as colleagues-once-removed. And for those modern writers whose creations are infused with a passion for the mathematical (Wells and Calvino are the writers I discuss in this volume, although I might well have taken up Lewis Carroll, Stanislaw Lem, Jorge Luis Borges, Primo Levi) my admiration often verges on the idolatrous.

In those Presbyterian Sunday school classes which, at the promptings of my devout mother, I attended regularly throughout my boyhood, I was informed that the very hairs on my head are numbered. From the start there was something unnerving to this notion. To be so *closely* overseen is, even for the child who has not yet stumbled upon any sins of the flesh, a claustrophobic sensation, and to the adolescent it is naturally horrifying. In adulthood, though, it's likely to take on a transformed sort of menace. The politics of our century have repeatedly demonstrated the perils lurking in the census-taker, the poll-tabulator, the statistician. We've come to shudder at the thought of functionaries in remote buildings—in credit-rating departments and police archives, in employment clearinghouses and intelligence agencies—knowing far more about us than we mean to present to them.

Simultaneously, and wholly inconsistently, another part of me is forever wishing that our information-seekers and -storers were a good deal more efficient than in fact they are. Surely there ought to be a place—if not in Heaven, then in the arid viscera of some megacomputer the size of the moon—where the hairs of one's head *are* numbered, for there is something disturbing to the notion that life in any of its intricate branchings is passing away unrecorded. When this mood settles upon me, I know that no number should ever be lost. All at once, I may find myself very much wanting to know how many people, across the entire globe, will lose a glove in a subway today—and lamenting the absence of any central data bank from which such information might be retrieved. Or perhaps wanting to know how many people at this exact moment are dutifully hunched over a piano practicing a Haydn sonata. Or how many good souls this week will read a poem by Henry Vaughan.

Precisely how many people the world over will tonight have their first go at incest? When did the very last Carolina parakeet die? How many people today will—as I did this morning—step on a Cheerio? What is the world record for human beings killed by a single shark? How many vegetarians are members of the Ku Klux Klan?

Such questions have a special poignancy and penetration in the domain of striking coincidences. It is here that the lack of any Recording Angel is most acutely felt. Is today the day when that crisp dollar tip you gave your taxi driver in New York, exactly a year ago, comes back in your wadded change when you buy take-out sushi in San Diego?

How many people this week will unwittingly pass on the street a child they once gave up for adoption? Is there a carrot right now decomposing somewhere in the ground which bore a firm resemblance to Teddy Roosevelt? Will a pair of boys be born today—one in Seattle and one in Edinburgh—who will alike be christened Spenser, and alike grow up to be red-haired, left-handed bank robbers?

Whether the coincidence in question is momentous or trivial, there's always an airy thrill in being let in on its existence: what is more irresistible than a glimpse at a one-in-a-million? At such times, the heavens open and we're vouchsafed a visual entry into the inner workings of the gods. And each such occurrence is potential grist for the fiction writer—or simple sustenance for any soul that craves a "good story."

Statistically, in a world of some five billion inhabitants even the most far-fetched, outlandish quirks and coincidences must be commonplaces—though the vast preponderance will go unnoticed. They will be lost. It's this image of a world in which, for all its pullulating multitudes, most of what is striking and funny and irregular and bizarre goes unremarked—the image, that is, of a planet spinning along a narrow rim of light, while in the encircling darkness the cosmos dances to rhythms and arrangements beyond our reckoning—that seems insupportably wasteful. It induces a sort of madness—though one suggesting we may be less in need of the analyst than the annalist. At such times, brandishing notepads and erasers, tripping over elementary computations, even the most math-anxious among us may venture forth in search of some safety in numbers.

THE SPACE OF ONE BREATH

Anthony Scherzer, who is the creator of BE-BE, the No. 3 seed at the Fifth World Computer Chess Championship, draws sharply on a cigarette. This morning's game is the second of five that BE-BE must undergo in pursuit of the world title. BE-BE has wrested an early advantage from CYRUS 68K, its opponent in this round, and should win easily, but these battles of computer versus computer can be protracted. The machines themselves will never admit defeat, and their human operators—seeking deliverance, if all else fails, through some malfunction in the opponent's computer—hesitate to call any game to a halt. Although things are looking up for him this morning, Scherzer seems more rattled than either David Levy or Kevin O'Connell, the operators of CYRUS 68K, who sit across from him at a table crowded with coffee cups, notepads, chessboards, and a running chess clock. In fact, Scherzer—who describes himself as a "born worrier"—appears more rattled than any of the other people seated on the long platform reserved for the operators and their machines. There are eleven tables in all, at each of which a computer is pitted against another computer. To anyone familiar with human chess tournaments, the Fifth World Computer Chess Championship presents a disorienting scene. There are no calls for silence, no restrictions on movement. Lodged in a corner of the vast Messe Rhine Halls of Cologne, West Germany, the championship is only one of the attractions of C '86, an international computer fair. The din and the flashing lights of the surrounding exhibits would subvert any human tournament, but the chess machines, each linked to the living only by a keyboard on which its operators punch in the opponent's moves, are wholly insensible to what is going on around them. The result is two nearly discrete worlds inhabiting the same space. In one, spectators drift about, chatting, analyzing, arguing, and the machine operators relax with beer and soft drinks, hot dogs and ice-cream bars. In the other—a contained, microscopic environment—machines are working indefatigably, processing electronic pulsings at speeds that beggar the human mind. During the four or five seconds that Scherzer inhales and exhales the cigarette smoke—the space of one breath—BE-BE analyzes almost a quarter of a million different chess positions.

This seems an astonishing feat when one considers that in the same amount of time a human grandmaster might well analyze one move, or merely some aspects of one move. But it is still more astonishing when one understands that Scherzer has good cause for fearing that his machine may be, in his words, "too darn slow." CRAY BLITZ, the reigning world champion by dint of its victory at the Fourth World Computer Chess Championship, held in New York City in 1983, is capable of examining a hundred thousand positions per second—more than twice what BE-BE can do. And CRAY BLITZ is only the No. 2 seed here in Cologne. The favorite, HITECH, which trounced all of its competition at the 1985 North American Computer Chess Championship, in Denver, can analyze a hundred and seventy-five thousand positions per second.

And yet Scherzer—who, in addition to being high-strung, is given to a likable modesty that often veers into humorous predictions of disaster for himself and BE-BE—has every reason to be hopeful about his machine; she has performed exceptionally well in the last few years. (BE-BE is a rarity among chess machines in that its maker always refers to it by the feminine pronoun.) She placed second among twenty-two teams at the fourth world championship. She also placed second at the last three North American championships. Furthermore, BE-BE has the advantage—at least by the topsy-turvy standards of the computer-chess world—of being old, and Scherzer can feel confident that in refining his machine over the years he has removed most of her hidden bugs.

Scherzer wrote his first chess program in 1979, at the age of thirty-three, and began work on BE-BE in 1981. As the president of SYS-10, a computer firm near Chicago which specializes in office systems, he is free to apportion his time as he sees fit, and BE-BE, which he regards as both a hobby and a source of business publicity, has taken up hundreds of hours over the past few years. Scherzer tells me that he came to Cologne hoping for "second place—*another* second place," but will be "quite happy with a third." First place is "almost too much to dream about."

The entrants at this championship can be divided into three categories, although the complexity of the machines ensures some degree of overlap. The most modest—and, in general, the least formidable—entrants are the "micros" and the "minis." These are machines so small and light—some weigh only a few pounds—that they can be transported easily to the tournament site. The second category consists of chess programs that run on a large mainframe computer, which often lies thousands of miles away and is "brought" to the tournament by way of a telephone hookup. CRAY BLITZ, for example, is hardly present in Cologne at all. Although Harry Nelson, one of its designers, has flown from California to West Germany to serve as its operator, its chief programmers, who are based at the University of Southern Mississippi, have remained at home, and the program itself is being run on an immense four-processor Cray X-MP/48 computer in Minnesota. In the third category are machines like BE-BE and HITECH, whose programs are adapted to run on what is called special-purpose hardware—costly, complex machinery designed exclusively to play chess. This hardware may be transported to the tournament site, as in the case of BE-BE (quite a chore for Scherzer, since BE-BE's hardware weighs almost ninety pounds), or it may, like HITECH, report in by telephone. Special-purpose machines are a comparatively recent development—the first successful one, called BELLE, emerged in 1978—but, as the high seedings of BE-BE and HITECH attest, they appear to be in the ascendant.

Scherzer says that much of the inspiration for BE-BE came from BELLE, which was created by Ken Thompson and Joe Condon, at Bell Laboratories, in Murray Hill, New Jersey. Scherzer refers to Thompson, the designer of BELLE's software, as a pioneer, and regrets that BELLE is not competing in Cologne, in what should be the strongest field of chess computers ever assembled. BELLE dominated computer chess from 1978 until 1983, when it lost the world title to CRAY BLITZ in the last round of the fourth world championship. Thompson has since turned his attention to other projects, but a few weeks before that tournament I went to see him and BELLE at Bell Laboratories. It was my first encounter with a sophisticated chess machine and I didn't know quite what to expect. At my request, Thompson confronted BELLE with the position that arose on Black's seventeenth move in

Bobby Fischer's game against Donald Byrne during the 1956 Lessing J. Rosenwald Trophy Tournament. In what has since become known as the game of the century, the thirteen-year-old Fischer stunned Byrne, one of the finest players in the country, with a winning queen sacrifice. To enter a game in the middle means confronting, in effect, a tableau isolated from an extraordinarily complex series of tensions, threats, expectations, and inducements, and thus perhaps is not a true test of skill; nevertheless, I wanted to see whether BELLE, too, would find what is perhaps the most famous move ever executed upon a chessboard. Thompson, of course, had tested BELLE with the problem before, but he did so again, for my benefit. We did not have to wait long for the answer: in seventeen seconds, BELLE made the queen sacrifice.

The rapid ascent of machines like BE-BE and BELLE has created enormous excitement and unease in America's chess-playing community. Only fifteen years ago, it was possible for most of the better tournament players to dismiss chess machines as mere toys or curiosities. Computers did not begin to participate in human chess tournaments until 1967, when MAC HACK VI, the brainchild of Richard Greenblatt, who was then an undergraduate at M.I.T., made a rather undistinguished showing in the Massachusetts Amateur Championship, drawing one game and losing four. But there are perhaps fewer than a hundred players in America today who can still speak condescendingly of chess computers. In 1983, BELLE became the first machine entitled to the rank of United States master, one rung below the top rank of senior master; HITECH became a senior master in the spring of 1986. The United States Chess Federation, which is responsible for rating players and running official tournaments in this country, has been obliged to set up a Computer Chess Committee and to establish rules governing the participation of computers in human tournaments. David Welsh, the chairman of the committee, reports that many tournament players, once they have adjusted to the idea, enjoy facing computer opponents, but there has been virulent opposition as well. A group called WOCIT (We Oppose Computers in Tournaments) was founded in 1983 with the goal, according to its president, Clifford Anderson, of "protecting our right to play a human opponent." WOCIT has been successful in having the rules changed to ensure that no one is compelled to play a computer in a U.S.C.F. tournament. Though the play of the earliest computers was marked by humorous indecision, shortsightedness, horrendous blunders, and frequent mechanical breakdowns, in recent years computers have demonstrated a prodigious tactical flair and a sound grasp of defensive structures. As chess machines have progressed from the laughable to the formidable, the U.S.C.F. and chess players generally have been forced to contemplate the possibility of a wholesale transformation of the chess world.

This is a transformation not necessarily limited to the world of chess. The designers of chess machines have long been insisting that their work has vast implications for all of modern society—a claim that grows increasingly convincing as their machines become more powerful. Donald Michie, chief scientist at the Turing Institute, in Glasgow, and one of the world's leading experts in the field of thinking machines, observed a while ago, "Scientific study of computer chess, which includes the technological work but goes far beyond that, is the most important scientific study that is going on in the world at present. In the same sense, if I were asked what was the most important study in progress during the First World War, I would say the breeding experiments on *Drosophila,* by Thomas Hunt Morgan and his colleagues at Columbia. The analogy is very good. The final impact of that early work in laying down the basic theoretical framework for genetics was just enormous—unimaginable. We see now the industrial consequence of genetic engineering, which is the final, delayed outcome for human society of the fly-breeding work. The use of chess now as a preliminary to the knowledge engineering of the future is exactly similar, in this respect, to the work on *Drosophila.*"

While it might seem that the challenges a player faces within the confines of a chessboard have little to do with the unpredictable difficulties one meets in the hurly-burly of modern life, the game offers the scientist a purified, manageable environment in which to study the complex nature of problem solving. The playing of intelligent chess, whether by man or machine, requires an ability to maintain a long-range goal (checkmate of the opponent) while working toward the incremental accomplishment of subordinate tasks (obtaining control of the center, building a sound pawn structure, securing an early haven for one's king, and so forth). It calls for fluid powers of evaluation as pieces are shifted or are removed from the board, a talent for rooting out weaknesses in configurations of apparent strength, and a capacity for envisioning and analyzing multiple contingencies that will probably never arise. These are clearly skills of a pervasive utility, essential to the successful running of a business or a government. Today's chess computers may well be the provincial, limited forerunners of hugely more intelligent machines that will oversee marketing campaigns or federal budgets.

Although the chess machine may eventually transform the organization of modern life, its greatest effect thus far has probably been a psychological one. Our society has grown accustomed to the ascendancy of machines in handling various sorts of drudgery—compiling and sorting customer lists, totalling debits and credits, switching telephone lines—but there is still something unsettling for us in the sight of computers excelling at play as well as at work. While non-chessplayers may view the game as a strictly mechanical, mathematical activity (in which case they will accept a grandmaster computer with little difficulty), serious chess players usually think of it as requiring a mystical talent, analogous to what a poker or bridge player means by "card sense." Chess literature teems with phrases like "artistic stroke," "feel for the game," "graceful thinking," and "intuitive genius." To the chess-obsessed, the board can serve as an arena in which nearly the whole of the human personality expresses itself. Much like literary or musical masterpieces, the finest games of the finest players are to be regarded as distillations of the human soul, and by playing through these games one can, in a sense, get to know each of the masters personally. Dr. Reuben Fine, who, being both a psychoanalyst and one of the century's greatest players, has a unique vantage on the game, ably set out this view in his book *The Psychology of the Chess Player:*

> An extensive psychoanalytic literature has grown up depicting the intimate relationship between the works of artists and their neurotic conflicts. It is to be expected that similar unconscious forces would be involved in chess, both in the way the game is interwoven into the character structure, and in the style which the player adopts. . . . In fact, just as any artist has a characteristically individual style which permeates his artistic works to such an extent that an expert can recognize that such and such a painting is a Degas or a Leonardo, so too the styles of the chess masters assume a highly distinctive cast and are readily identifiable by the experts.

Obviously, such a notion must run into difficulties when it encounters powerful chess machines. If one were to analyze, say, a selection of BE-BE's finest games, what could one discern about the "unconscious forces," the "character structure," of the cool, rectilinear assemblage that is BE-BE?

The chess machine, like chess itself, has a surprisingly long history. Although computers capable of playing a well-balanced, reasonably adept game were developed only in the last few decades, the lore of chess machines goes back more than two hundred years. In 1770, Baron Wolfgang von Kempelen, a thirty-six-year-old counsellor to the Royal Chamber of the Kingdom of Hungary, presented to the court of the Empress Maria Theresa an exotic wooden automaton, complete with turban, that he claimed could play skillful chess. This contraption, later known throughout the world as "the Turk," consisted of the upper body of a larger-than-life-size figure seated behind a maple cabinet three and a half feet long, two feet wide, and two and a half feet high. The Turk's gaze rested intently on a chessboard inlaid on the cabinet's surface.

Those familiar with von Kempelen's reputation for mechanical wizardry were disappointed on first glimpsing the Turk, whose "mystery" was all too easily explained: the cabinet surely contained a hidden person, probably a child or a midget. Yet von Kempelen had contrived a surprise for them—one that was demonstrated to skeptical audiences thousands of times over the next eighty-four years. Before play began, the cabinet and the Turk's torso were opened "completely," to reveal nothing within but the wheels, cylinders, and levers of a complex piece of clockwork. The cabinet doors were then closed, on the pretext that otherwise the machine could not operate properly, and the game commenced. The Turk moved his pieces himself, his left arm passing slowly over the board, and he would respond to an opponent's illegal move with a censorious shake of the head. Although it is now known that someone inside the mechanism selected the moves and operated the mechanical arm, no one knows precisely how this person was concealed. After a peripatetic career that included victories over Benjamin Franklin in France and Napoleon in Austria, the Turk was destroyed by a fire in Philadelphia's Chinese Museum, in 1854.

The Turk inspired numerous imitations, the most famous being the Moor Ajeeb, which was constructed by an Englishman, Charles Alfred Hooper, in 1868. Ajeeb drew huge crowds in Europe and America. His opponents included O. Henry, Sarah Bernhardt, and John Ruskin (who wrote of Ajeeb to a friend, "I get quite fond of him, and he gives me the most lovely lessons in chess"). Ajeeb was a creature of impressive and variable skills. He proved to be a world-class checkers player while the American champion Charles Francis Barker was his residing genius, and, later, an almost unbeatable chess master when Harry Nelson Pillsbury, perhaps the strongest player in the world at the time, was cajoled into the machine. Ajeeb's final resting place remains unknown. He served his last tour of duty in the late nineteen-thirties, travelling around the United States in a Cadillac on behalf of Magic Brain Radios.

Certainly the interiors of both the Turk and Ajeeb must have made ingenious use of false doors and sliding panels to create spaces far larger than the eye thought possible. One of the Turk's first inspectors came away convinced that the interior could contain no hidden space "of even the size of my hat." Others supposed there might be room enough for a legless man. The available space in Ajeeb appeared much too small for an adult of ordinary size, and Pillsbury found the work quite confining. He later recalled that "it was a pretty tight squeeze and not at all a pleasant duty, for I often played ten to fifteen games a day." Pillsbury's friend Albert Hodges, who also occasionally operated the automaton, attributed Pillsbury's premature death, at thirty-four, to too many hours inside Ajeeb: "I have always felt, from my own experience, that this strenuous work and the unhealthy environment of the chess figure must have to a great extent undermined his health and was the primary cause of his physical breakdown," he wrote in the *American Chess Bulletin*. At the very least, the job was an abject way to earn one's livelihood, and serves to remind us of the penury that even the best chess players could expect to suffer until recent times.

Hoaxes like Ajeeb and the Turk can tell us nothing about the functioning of true chess machines, but they do reveal much about the public's complex feelings toward artificial men. The chess automata enchanted the credulous and the skeptical alike. While some spectators fled the room, or even fainted, when an automaton began to stir, others would dispassionately study its movements in search of some scientific explanation of its powers. Edgar Allan Poe wrote a piece debunking the Turk, in part because it made occasional mistakes; Poe reasoned that a true chess machine would play flawless chess—a fallacy that has since come to be known as "the myth of the perfect machine." And Ambrose Bierce wrote a short story, "Moxon's Master," in which a chess automaton kills its master (etymologically, the perfect checkmate: the word derives from the Persian *shah,* meaning "king" or "master," and *mat,* meaning "helpless" or "defeated"). Chess automata have inspired plays and novels, and a couple of films as well. The allure of the Turk and Ajeeb may best be understood if they are viewed as siblings of Pygmalion's Galatea; of the gold and bronze servants of Hephaestus, the Greek god of craftsmen; of the Jewish golem and the alchemists' homunculi and Frankenstein's monster. Man's fearful but tempting dream of creating an artificial being appears to be timeless and irresistible.

When a genuine chess machine finally did appear, in a demonstration in Paris in 1914, it could hardly hope to kindle the public imagination as those colorful, head-shaking automata continued to do. Its inventor, Leonardo Torres y Quevedo, was no showman, and his machine played an unexciting and limited form of chess. It could handle only rook-and-king endings against an opposing king—an extremely elementary situation. However, Torres y Quevedo's machine accomplished what an army of unautonomous automata had failed to do: once set in motion, it played chess unassisted by any human intelligence. Torres was able to arrange this only by drastically reducing the moves open to the machine's human opponent, so that all possible developments could be provided for in advance. While the play of modern chess machines will often surprise their makers, there were no surprises in Torres' invention. In game after game, with an inevitability like that which Poe envisioned, it would steer the opponent's king into checkmate. Yet, primitive though his machine now looks, Torres was a revolutionary, who, in a 1915 interview in *Scientific American,* advanced a notion that came to dominate the modern world of thinking machines: "The ancient automatons . . . imitate the appearance and movements of living beings, but this has not much practical interest, and what is wanted is a class of apparatus which leaves out the mere visible gestures of man and attempts to accomplish the results which a living person obtains, thus replacing a man by a machine."

. . .

The modern era of chess machines dates from 1949, when Claude Shannon, an English mathematician then doing research for Bell Labs, presented at a meeting of the Institute of Radio Engineers, in New York, a paper entitled "Programming a Computer for Playing Chess." Shannon not only ingeniously foresaw many of the techniques by which today's chess machines operate but also identified a methodological schism that still divides the computer-chess world. He hypothesized that a computer could select its moves according to either of two methods. Machines of both sorts have since been constructed, and in acknowledgment of his achievements are usually called Shannon Type A and Shannon Type B machines. The Shannon Type A machine conducts what is known as a full-width search at some specified depth; that is, the machine will evaluate *all* possible positions that could arise after completion of the stipulated number of moves, or "ply." (Rather than the ambiguous "move," which can signify either a "full move," by both White and Black, or a "half move," by either player, programmers of chess computers use the term "ply"; a ply is always a half move.) To take a simple example of a full-width search, assume that a Shannon Type A computer with a two-ply depth of search is about to open a game. There are twenty possible first moves on the chessboard. This means that there are four hundred different positions (twenty times twenty) that can arise after each player has moved once. A Shannon Type A computer with a depth of two ply would evaluate each of these four hundred positions before settling upon the best opening move.

A Shannon Type B machine is designed to be more flexible. Its evaluations are not restricted to a fixed number of ply. If a particular line of play cannot be analyzed intelligently after a specified number of moves—as is true in "turbulent" positions, where many possible captures still exist—the machine will probe deeper, generating and evaluating the additional positions required for an informed analysis. Ideally, the Type B machine will also demonstrate time-saving powers of discrimination. Instead of analyzing *every* possible move, it will conduct a selective search of those lines of play which seem promising, and will examine them at a depth not possible for a machine conducting a full-width search. In its selectivity, the Shannon Type B is often referred to as an intuitive machine. I have also heard it called a "human machine," and the Shannon Type A a "mechanical machine"—a fair distinction, provided that one never forgets that the Type B machine is operating under mathematical principles no less exacting than those governing the Type A.

Each sort of machine confronts its own monumental obstacles on the road to skillful chess play. For a machine making a full-width search, as most of the entrants in the Fifth World Computer Chess Championship do, the chief problem is time. Tournament chess is performed under rigid time constraints, and a machine that devotes the bulk of its analysis to fruitless lines of play will not be able to analyze viable possibilities in sufficient depth. Given the dazzling speeds attained by computers in recent years, one might suppose that time problems would no longer exist for chess machines. After all, even in the complexities of the middle game, when the players have achieved maximum mobility for their pieces, neither side is apt to have more than thirty-five or forty moves to choose from. One must keep in mind, however, that the number of possible positions increases exponentially as a machine's search deepens. If a machine has thirty-five possible moves, and its opponent has some thirty-five possible replies to each of these, then the number of possible positions to be evaluated after only two ply is roughly twelve hundred. And if the computer then has, say, thirty-five possible second moves to each of its opponent's replies, the number of positions to be evaluated at a depth of only three ply jumps to over forty thousand. Even for HITECH, the fastest machine in the world, the numbers soon become impossibly large. It has been estimated that the number of different games that can be played is of the order of 25×10^{115}. This figure vastly exceeds the number of atoms in the known universe. Even at HITECH's lightning computational speed, aeons would unfold before the machine had evaluated all these possibilities. At its present search speeds, HITECH can conduct a full-width search to a depth of perhaps fifteen or even twenty ply in a simple endgame. While this is a far deeper analysis than most human beings can even dream of, it does not equal that of the top grandmasters, whose looser "selective searches" are apt to run some moves deeper still.

The principle behind a Shannon Type B machine sounds persuasive enough—after all, why should a computer waste so much time analyzing those "garbage moves" that preponderate in any full-width search?—but the programmer soon discovers that the task of instructing a computer to identify promising lines of play is fiendishly complex. Differences are often remarkably subtle in advanced chess, and a sound method of proceeding in one position will often prove disastrous in another that looks quite similar. This ability to distinguish subtle positional differences is one of the skills chess programmers are referring to when they speak of giving their machines more "chess knowledge." A human being's ability to identify and discriminate among such differences ultimately derives from the brain's astonishing powers of pattern recognition, which machines cannot begin to match. It has been estimated that a grandmaster can recognize some fifty thousand basic "building-block" configurations—small groupings of pieces by which the board's more complex structures are erected. Pattern recognition often requires an ability to identify essential similarities while ignoring extraneous differences. Of course, given the game's complexity, to formulate in advance any distinction between the "essential" and the "extraneous" which will cover all possible chess positions is remarkably difficult. Any distinction is necessarily going to be incomplete and imprecise, requiring chess players to rely on the guidance of "feelings" and "intuition," and here the very exactitude that is the computer's primary strength proves a shortcoming. The computer, for which such distinctions must be translated into the precise strings of binary numbers that are its only language, is not easily taught to "feel" or "intuit" accurately. To make the chess programmer's task still more herculean, his computer must operate with a very low margin of error. Advanced chess is not a game for any brain whose calculations are "mostly correct." Where a single misstep can be fatal, one simply cannot afford imprecision.

Twenty years or so ago, when chess computers were still operating at relatively primitive levels, the shortcomings of a selective-search machine were less evident—or, at least, less easily exploited by their maladroit machine opponents. MAC HACK VI, which was not only the first machine to participate in a human tournament but probably the first to play as well as the average U.S.C.F. member, employed a selective search. MAC HACK VI was probably the best chess machine in the late sixties, but by 1974, when the First World Computer Chess Championship was held, in Stockholm, it seemed clear that the future—at least, the immediate future—belonged to the "mechanical machines."

.   .   .

The deaf insularity of the combatants in the Messe Rhine Halls allows Michael Valvo, the tournament director, to offer on-the-spot analyses of every game. Equipped with a hand-held microphone, Valvo walks among the tables, commenting on the game positions, which are displayed on large magnetic chessboards mounted on the wall at the back of the platform. An international computer-chess tournament poses daunting problems of logistics and scheduling. For those machines— the majority—that are electronically linked to the tournament site, a reliable, unbroken line of communication must be maintained for each tournament round; computer-chess tournaments are often marred by communication problems—especially when overseas telephone lines are required. Many of the best chess programs are run on huge computers that serve a host of academic and business clients, and their programmers must ensure that computer time is reserved for the entire, unpredictable length of each game. This time can be frightfully expensive. Although the Cray Research company sponsors CRAY BLITZ without charge to the team of programmers at the University of Southern Mississippi, computer time on each of the four processors of a Cray X-MP/48 like the one that powers CRAY BLITZ is rented out at up to four thousand dollars per hour. At this rate, a chess game that lasts five hours—as many of them do—will run up a bill of eighty thousand dollars.

The site of a computer-chess tournament is perhaps best envisioned as the hub of a network, into and out of which coded information is continually being relayed. The isolation of the computers makes a computer tournament something unique in the chess world. Secrecy is—like silence—no longer necessary. A programmer will freely predict his machine's next move and openly admit disappointment when it falters, and programmers will often pool their wits in an attempt to discern the logic and direction of an evolving game. Although they are, through their machinery, competing with each other, they are psychologically detached from their machines. Once a game has begun, a programmer is prohibited from directing his program; he can only watch as the moves unfold. Chess is a game of violent passions and brutal subjugations (Larry Evans, one of America's top players, says of it, "The chess master today must have courage, a killer instinct, stamina, and arrogance"), and yet when it is played through the mediating presence of machines the sting of defeat is greatly soothed. For the most part, competitors in this tournament take their losses with a handsome, laughing grace.

Michael Valvo's job as an on-the-spot commentator is a taxing one, which demands a gift for making swift, precise evaluations and for juggling mentally the pullulating complexities of nearly a dozen different games—all this before an audience of programmers and chess buffs, who are quick to point out any looseness of thought, any overlooked threat or vulnerability. It is a task for which Valvo, an international master, renowned for his proficiency at both blindfold chess and speed chess, is well suited. Drifting from game to game, he lightens his detailed analyses with anecdotes about earlier tournaments and with occasional jokes. The most difficult judgments he must make arise not in his role as commentator but as tournament director. His is the chief voice in matching opponents for each round and in interpreting tournament rules, which—not surprisingly, given the newness of computer competitions—are often patchy and ambiguous. Valvo's judgment is called into play in the first minutes of the first day of the tournament, when it turns out that one of the operators has recorded an opponent's move incorrectly, resulting in his machine's wasting precious minutes evaluating a nonexistent position. Proceeding under what he calls his guiding principle—"Machines should not be responsible for human error"—Valvo orders the chess clock set back to the moment when the mistake was committed. The principle sounds lucid and fair enough in theory, but it is one that, because of the close and complex relationship between an operator and his machine, can prove extremely thorny in practice.

In his suit and tie, Valvo contributes a formal flair to an event marked by extreme informality; it is Valvo—rather than, say, Harry Nelson, in a pair of moccasins and a T-shirt that says "CRAY BLITZ: World Computer Chess Championship 1983"—who looks slightly incongruous in the exhibition hall. Not that anyone could look very much out of place in a scene of such happy diversity. The hall's energetic babble—English and German and Dutch and Swedish and French and Hungarian—confirms a geographical range that differences of clothing and physiognomy have already suggested.

Significantly absent in all this polyglot chatter is the sound of Russian. At the first world championship, in 1974, a Soviet program, KAISSA, pulled off a narrow victory in a field of thirteen contestants. At that time, it appeared that the Soviet Union, which had dominated human chess since the late forties, might be on its way to establishing a corresponding hegemony in computer competitions. The Soviet government had already shown itself devoted to chess at a level without historical precedent. Over the years, an awesome institutional network had been created to offer promising players supervisory scrutiny, systematic training, financial support, psychological encouragement, and corrective discipline. As George Steiner remarked in a study of the 1972 Fischer-Spassky match, in Reykjavik, "no society, no political system, had ever invested comparable energies in the perfection of a pastime." But KAISSA failed to hold its own at the second world championship, and soon disappeared from the international tournament scene. Apparently, lagging Soviet proficiency in the field of computer technology made it impossible for KAISSA to compete against machines of a rapidly advancing sophistication.

The most technologically sophisticated entrant in Cologne is undoubtedly HITECH, a machine that may represent the first of a new generation of chess computers. HITECH is the offspring of a team of computer scientists led by Hans Berliner, a professor at Carnegie-Mellon University. Berliner brings to the task of designing chess computers a perhaps unmatchable range of assets. To begin with, he is a surpassingly fine chess player who was once world correspondence champion. (A genius for playing chess by mail, in which complicated problems can be cracked by a kind of leisurely tenacity, would seem valuable to the chess programmer.) Although chess expertise is not an essential skill—even a middling player can, in time, program a computer to play excellent chess—it is extremely helpful. The middling player is apt to find that his task grows increasingly knotty as his machine advances; usually, the difficulty of "advising" a computer about situations that the programmer himself only dimly understands becomes insuperable at some point, and a chess expert is called in. This solution is far from ideal, however. It often results in an unbridgeable schism, in which the chess expert fails to understand the programmer's needs and the programmer misses the subtleties the expert brings to the task. In Hans Berliner, the programmer and the chess expert are one. In addition, his position at Carnegie-Mellon provides him with access both to a pool of graduate students eager to work on such a project and to some of the most advanced computer systems in the world. Under the circumstances, one is hardly surprised that HITECH is the overwhelming favorite in the tournament.

In a field of complex machinery, HITECH is an outstandingly complicated device. It runs on a relatively modest Sun computer, which has been outfitted with some special-purpose hardware that Berliner calls "the searcher." The searcher comprises a microprocessor and a number of modules dedicated to tasks such as move generation, move evaluation, and so forth. The move generator is equipped with sixty-four custom-designed microchips, one for each square of the chessboard. Each chip is responsible for following all the moves that can be made to its assigned square within the deepening play of an ongoing analysis. HITECH's most revolutionary aspect is the way in which its parts work separately as well as cooperatively; it represents a breakthrough in what is called parallel processing. The network of commands and comparisons by which millions and millions of calculations are eventually distilled into a single move is, of course, incredibly complex, yet manageably so—as HITECH's meteoric career has demonstrated.

Midway through the championship, I talk with Berliner about his work and his machine. A short, compact man in his late fifties, whose pause-strewn speech sounds at once tentative and assured, Berliner is clearly exhilarated. His machine has won its first three games handily, and the second of these victories—against the No. 8 seed, SCHACH 2.7—was a stunner. HITECH discovered a path to victory that none of the experts in the audience had spotted. "This was a game that will go around the world," he tells me. "I know enough about chess—know enough about what the chess public wants—to say that it will go around the world. If the world champion had played this game—the human world champion—everyone would ooh and ahh. But a *computer* did it, and that's going to get people's attention."

I ask him whether he thinks of his machine as a he, a she, or an it. "An it," he replies, "but it's very near and dear to me, obviously. I think of it sort of as a super-intelligent dog. I have a pretty clever dog at home, and this machine is clever, too, in its own way. When you have clever programs around, you form a kind of close relationship. Over a period of time, you gradually realize that the machine does certain things better than you do, and your definition of what those things are gets sharper and sharper. Two weeks ago, we played in a tournament, and HITECH lost a game to a human—the first time it had ever lost a game to a player rated below it. And it played terribly. Something was wrong, and the only way you could tell that something was wrong was that it seemed to be playing worse than it used to. Well, there were five of us who had worked on it, and we all examined what we had done, and we changed a number of things, and now it seems to be playing fine, but there are some things it did that we still can't explain. So you've got a situation where these machines assume a character of their own, and you're really just a helper. We can no longer say of its thinking, 'This is good, this is bad.' That can happen only when something considerably smarter looks at something considerably dumber. Its thinking begins to become a matter of style, instead of goodness and badness. A long time ago I worked on a selective-search program, and we have some plans actually to go back to selective search, but I'm certainly no longer driven by the thought of emulating human intelligence. I now believe I see intelligence out there all by itself, independent of what humans can do."

Having attained both the upper reaches of chess mastery and a comprehensive understanding of chess computers, Hans Berliner belongs to a very small international fraternity. Its members alone would seem to possess a perfect vantage for simultaneously observing the two irreconcilable sides of the game—its apparently infinite mystery and its ultimate mathematical limitations. For most chess players, whether novices or experts, the game's mystery is continually manifest, and yet its limitations are all but impossible to imagine. How can one see limitations when the possibilities are so numerous that they might as well be infinite? At the start of any game, both players know that within a few moves—sometimes fewer than ten—they are likely to encounter a position that neither has seen before, and, quite plausibly, one that *nobody* has seen before. That a game of such narrow strictures—thirty-two pieces, sixty-four squares—can generate such freshness, so many novelties at every turn, seems to bespeak an innate inexhaustibility, akin to William Blake's "world in a grain of sand."

The game's mathematical limitations are further concealed by the anthropomorphization of the pieces. Chess has always been a simulation of warfare; the modern rook, knight, bishop, and pawn were originally a chariot, horse, elephant, and foot soldier—the four wings of the ancient Indian army—and these wooden, puppetlike figures still hint at personalities extending well beyond the arithmetic of their simple duties. When assembled on the board, theirs becomes a world as rich as any fairy tale's: horses leaping beside castellated towers; zigzagging bishops; dwarfish, interchangeable pawns; gaunt, commanding queens; and vulnerable, reclusive kings. The mathematical limitations can be obscured even further by the fluctuations of expert analysis. To the student of chess, the game's history, and especially that of opening play, evolves in cycles: first a potentially powerful line of play is discovered, then refinements are added over the years by trial and error, and at length a crushing refutation is uncovered, perhaps rendering the entire line useless—until it is reborn, often more robust than ever, when some refutation of the refutation is arrived at. While this process should rightly be seen as a series of small steps toward the impossible ideal of a full understanding of the game, it can easily induce a sense that there is something loose and fugitive at the core of chess. One may begin to feel that the game offers no durable solutions—only an infinity of responses within responses, a regressive chain of refutations.

And yet the game remains finite. Although that estimate of possible games, 25×10^{115}, is so large as to be ungraspable by the mind even by means of metaphor, it does establish an upper bound no less real for its unimaginableness. To the mathematician specializing in game theory, chess is known as a finite "tree game." And when reduced by the game theorist to its diagrammatic essence, chess is shown to share the structure—in vastly more complicated form—of simple tree games like tic-tac-toe. In any finite tree game, all possible lines of play can be charted in a logical fashion, from opening moves to culmination. This charting is usually depicted as a branching tree, rooted, by convention, at the top rather than at the bottom of the page. A sketch of the tree for even a very elementary game like tic-tac-toe will soon outgrow the borders of any page. Nine nodes would be needed to represent the first move (one for each space on the board in which an "X" could be placed), and from each of these nodes eight branches would descend (corresponding to the eight squares left open to an "O"). The completed tree would catalogue more than three hundred and sixty thousand progressions and outcomes, and one begins to perceive that a chess game tree would soon grow astronomically large—like Ygg-drasil, the tree in Norse mythology whose fruit was the stars.

The immensity of the game tree for tic-tac-toe would seem to indicate that it is a complicated game—one congenial to devious subtleties. It is no such thing, of course, and this suggests that with a little scrutiny that enormous number of nodes could be drastically reduced. The game tree, after all, charts every possible way, in every possible ordering, in which the nine squares of a tic-tac-toe board could be filled with "X"s and "O"s. But it will often happen that one player will achieve an early victory, which renders all subsequent moves—each of them scrupulously included in the game tree—irrelevant. The tree also contains thousands of positional repetitions—cases where the board reaches identical configurations of "X"s and "O"s through moves taken in different orderings. And by turning the board on its side or flipping it upside down (something that the board's vertical and horizontal symmetry permits; there is no meaningful "top" or "bottom" to a tic-tac-toe board) thousands of additional repetitions are revealed. For the pragmatic player, those three hundred and sixty thousand possible lines of play reduce to a few simple guidelines. With "proper play" on both sides—play that seizes on all opportunities for victory while offering the opponent no unnecessary advantages—the game inevitably ends in a draw. And, because the outcome is never in question, tic-tac-toe soon holds no attraction for anyone except children so young that they cannot grasp its humdrum dynamics.

As a tree game, chess is ultimately subject to the same limitations that make tic-tac-toe so dully predictable. If two players could only know what proper play on the chessboard consisted of, their games would reach the same outcome every time. Either White would always win, the players would always draw, or Black would always win. (The last seems unlikely, given the evidence, amassed over hundreds of years and millions of games, that Black suffers a sizable disadvantage by granting White the first move.) So vast is the number of possible lines of play in chess—or, put another way, so extensive is our human ignorance—that we are unable not only to identify what proper play would consist of but also to determine which of the three outcomes it would unfailingly produce. While the nature of proper play on the chessboard remains a riddle that no human being has yet begun to solve, it is a riddle with a definite answer. Hence, when two grandmasters match wits over a chessboard, their confrontation is analogous to that of two children battling at tic-tac-toe; the activity is pleasurable and challenging only because the players lack the vision to discern the game's limitations.

A little-remarked-upon reason for much of the appeal of chess may be its enchanting blend of simplicity and complexity. An intelligent person can learn in an hour the rules and some of the basic "tricks"— the pin, the discovered check, the knight fork—but the search for mastery over these maneuvers can easily consume a lifetime. For the novice, there is something deeply pleasurable in watching world champions employ the same offensive tricks one learns at the very outset. This rigorous mathematical game offers a heartening sense of comprehensibility—more welcome every year, as other mathematical disciplines become increasingly impenetrable. In Isaac Newton's time, an educated person with only a limited talent for numbers could nonetheless understand all known mathematics, and as late as the beginning of this century it was possible for the specialist to have a grasp of the entire range of mathematical exploration. Since then, discoveries have come at a dizzying rate. In the late nineteen forties, the mathematician John von Neumann, who is often called the father of the modern computer, estimated that a skilled mathematician might understand ten percent of what was available. Today, even the most incandescent mind can perceive only a small fraction of that fraction.

In our time, the science of mathematics yearly grows more splendidly imposing and more icily remote. How satisfying, by contrast, is the clement mathematics of chess, where the weekend player can feel that the logic underlying even the most exquisitely subtle match is accessible with some effort! Admittedly, this sense of understanding may be illusory. The weekend player cannot begin to hold in his head all the multiplicities of potential movement, the thoroughly explored and ultimately dismissed cul-de-sacs, the delicate probings and burgeoning contingencies that have occupied a grandmaster during a game, and are as much a part of it as the skeletal record of his actual moves. But at least our weekend player never feels that the very vocabulary has become lost to him. Just as their finest games seem human artifacts, the greatest grandmasters remain human figures—a reassuring humanity, brought home when, as occasionally happens under time pressure, one of them blunders into a trap that even a novice might have spotted. For the weekend player, what pleasure can be more delectable than reading that Paul Morphy (1837–84), thought by many experts to be the greatest chess genius who has ever lived, once lost a game in twelve moves?

The surpassing ferocity of chess, its range of aggressive satisfactions, can almost obscure all sorts of quiet pleasures that would appear to disport themselves in a different sector of the mind entirely. While this side of the game—its joyfully tranquil reflectiveness, its celebratory playfulness—is never wholly lost in the clangor of competition, it perhaps comes to the fore only in that extraordinarily rich subworld of study focussed on the chess problem. Often dazzlingly ingenious, these problems usually take the form of a search for a winning sequence of moves ("White to mate in two"), although they can also be geared retrospectively, asking the solver to work backward from a given configuration to identify a previous move. For some brilliant minds, the composing or solving of these problems—a discipline whose history goes back at least a millennium—provides the supreme felicity of chess. Vladimir Nabokov was a problem-composer of great finesse, and in the introduction to *Poems and Problems* he portrayed the piquant joys of the problemist:

> Chess problems demand from the composer the same virtues that characterize all worthwhile art: originality, invention, conciseness, harmony, complexity, and splendid insincerity. The composing of those ivory-and-ebony riddles is a comparatively rare gift and an extravagantly sterile occupation; but then all art is inutile, and divinely so, if compared to a number of more popular human endeavors. Problems are the poetry of chess.

Yet the problemist's accomplishments extend even beyond what Nabokov suggests. Chess problems help to correct and balance our notions of what the game consists of. Just as the problem's remoteness from combat underscores the game's dispassionate beauties, its genius for concealing solutions in implausible places enlarges our conceptions of the board's potentialities. While many grandmasters delight in chess problems, a surprisingly large number view them with indifference, or even with active dislike. Because they are often composed around positions that would never arise in actual games, chess problems are of little use to those bent solely on improving their game skills. José

Capablanca (1888–1942), one of the game's greatest champions, once remarked that he was uninterested in positions that did not arise in "real play," and one senses that the oxymoron was unrecognized by him; for Capablanca, chess was play of a sort not to be approached with levity. Like many grandmasters, he did not—or could not afford to—allow the idle, aesthetic side of the game to engross him; chess was a battle first and foremost—albeit a graceful battle, since Capablanca was a player of unparalleled nimbleness. There have been champions who felt otherwise. Wilhelm Steinitz, the world champion from 1866 to 1894, observed, "A win by an unsound combination, however showy, fills me with artistic horror." But Steinitz went briefly mad after an unsuccessful attempt to regain his title; and for most great players the need for a victory, however ragged, has always been paramount. This blinkered hunger for victory helps to explain why the literature of chess, especially that written by its greatest practitioners, proves narrow and unreflecting. When one considers how many hours of brilliant, impacted cerebration have gone into the making of the various world champions and near-champions, one can only be astonished at the barrenness of the literature they have left to the outside, non-chess-playing world. Many of the best players seem to share Bobby Fischer's view that "chess is life"—in which case there is no "outside world" one need worry about. (Ironically, the Soviet defector Viktor Korchnoi and his despised nemesis, Anatoly Karpov, who twice defeated him in the finals of the world championship, have both written books entitled *Chess Is My Life*.)

Chess players resent the common portrayal of their champions as men of fervently straitened intellects, but the stereotype grows increasingly valid with every decade. Gone are the days when a world champion could devote little time to chess study and expect to retain his title. One finds, in the nineteenth century, figures like Howard Staunton, who was not only unofficial world champion but also a leading Shakespeare scholar, and in the early years of this century there was Emanuel Lasker, who devoted most of his energies to philosophy, mathematics, and social reform while remaining one of the world's strongest players for nearly fifty years. But in recent decades, as the study of chess has grown into a systematized discipline—has become a science—the contender who devotes less than full time to keeping up with its latest developments is proceeding under a severe handicap.

One suspects that an occluded vision of the world has become a prerequisite for top-flight chess. Today's ambitious young players have little time for outside interests. Most of them echo another of Bobby Fischer's celebrated monomaniacal sentiments: "All I want to do, ever, is play chess."

While any cultured person must recoil at such complacent tunnel vision, in fairness one should nevertheless examine the vast range of expression that the chessboard permits. The initiated speak of the existence in chess not only of power and grace but of bluster, trickery, irony, humor. The board even admits of paradox—circumstances in which a greater number of pieces does not aid a player but actually undoes him (when, for example, a player reduced to king and pawn can conceivably be checkmated by an opponent left with king and knight, but checkmate is impossible if the first player has only a king on the board). The board offers sequences that can be spoken of in terms of cowardice and courage, of punishment and justice, and an almost Platonic quest for an ideal—invulnerability—that may or may not exist. (We shall not know until, if ever, the game is solved.) This is a microcosm so capacious that there hardly seems to be anything "micro" about it. When chess is glimpsed from within—its beckoning challenges, its manifold riches all on display—any dry attempt to explain the game's hold on the imagination can look either off the point or self-evidently obtuse.

Anthony Scherzer meets an unwelcome surprise on the morning of the third round of the Fifth World Computer Chess Championship. Things have gone smoothly for him so far—BE-BE has triumphed with encouraging ease in the first two rounds—but now Scherzer discovers that he has been paired against CRAY BLITZ. And, worse still, BE-BE will be playing Black. According to Scherzer's figuring, BE-BE was not due to face truly stiff competition until the fourth round, and this unexpected turn clearly dismays him.

Actually, Scherzer has ample cause for optimism. The last time the two machines met—at the 1985 North American championship—BE-BE, playing Black on that occasion as well, gave CRAY BLITZ a drubbing; moreover, CRAY BLITZ has played unconvincingly in Cologne, amazing everyone by losing to BOBBY, the No. 9 seed, in the second round.

Scherzer can take heart, too, at the way his machine begins the game against CRAY BLITZ. BE-BE plays the Dragon Variation of the Sicilian Defense, a line she has employed often in the past, and, according to her own numerical evaluation of the game's progress, she quickly succeeds in overcoming the disadvantage of playing Black. BE-BE's appraisal is echoed by Michael Valvo, who calls the game's opening position "roughly even." He speculates, though, that the defensive structure around BE-BE's king may be unsound.

On the twenty-third move, with CRAY BLITZ holding the slightly better position, Scherzer has an abrupt inkling of disaster. He discovers that he has forgotten to punch his time clock after completing a move, and, as a result, BE-BE has less time remaining than her own internal, unofficial clock would suggest. To minimize the effects of errors of this sort, BE-BE has been programmed to ask periodically for a "time check," which she does again at move twenty-five. Scherzer, tapping at his keyboard, informs his machine of the error, and BE-BE, which has been programmed to adjust to such discrepancies as rapidly as possible, allows herself only a few seconds of calculation time on the next couple of moves. Rather than her usual seven-ply search, BE-BE undertakes a search only to three ply—which, according to Scherzer, is "almost like moving at random." CRAY BLITZ quickly seizes a commanding edge, and although, as Valvo remarks, "there is still some kicking left," the outcome is clear. Scherzer resigns for his machine on the forty-sixth move.

The nature of BE-BE's loss to CRAY BLITZ illuminates some of the difficulties lurking in Valvo's injunction that "machines should not be responsible for human error." On the one hand, it seems unfair to penalize BE-BE for Scherzer's oversight. On the other, BE-BE's method of making up lost time reveals a grave shortcoming in her play. In a better program, as Scherzer ruefully acknowledges, lost minutes would be made up gradually, by reducing slightly the time reserved for the next ten or fifteen or twenty moves. In any case, Scherzer does not present Valvo with an immediate appeal for some saving adjudication, and the loss must stand.

BE-BE's loss also highlights some of the problems found in the distinction—crucial to orthodox chess analysis—between tactics and strategy. Though the two terms tend to overlap, they are in conception cleanly separable. Tactics are defined as short-term plans, usually turning upon perceived opportunities for material advantage. The tactician naturally thrives in complex positions where his opponent may overlook a potential fork or skewer or pin; the strategist focusses on the game's long-term flow, often with an eye toward the uncluttered dynamics of the endgame. Tactical proficiency requires extraordinary meticulousness, an ability to envision in panoptic detail the branchings of all proposed moves and countermoves; strategy incorporates a degree of imprecision and uncertainty, and it is here that experts will most likely speak of a "feel for the game." BE-BE's unfortunate defensive structure was not so much a tactical error—although material loss finally resulted—as a strategic one: a failure to discern the game's eventual evolution and demands.

Chess machines are by nature tactical players. In Valvo's words, "chess machines don't make plans, they make moves." What they lack in perception or in the ability to formulate long-term strategies they can often compensate for through an astounding ability to sift through short-term complexities. Tactical opportunities usually stem from an oversight—something that chess machines, with their exhaustive analyses, are extremely good at uncovering in an opponent's play and avoiding in their own. Even grandmasters will at times miss obvious threats or opportunities, but except when there is some elementary bug in the system (which in the best machines occurs very rarely) a BE-BE or a CRAY BLITZ or a HITECH is immune to short-term oversights.

Chess machines have become such skillful tacticians that they are forcing a reevaluation of the intertwined natures and the relative importance of tactics and strategy. When a machine opens a game, it has, strictly speaking, no strategic vision whatever. Its analysis is restricted to the depth of search that time constraints permit—usually a depth of seven ply, in the early and middle stages of the game. Of the potential moves that lie beyond this depth it sees nothing; and, indeed, it has no concept—in any sense of that term—of the game's existence beyond the limits of its search. This blindness, which is known as the "horizon effect," can often produce risibly bad play. When, for example, a piece must inevitably fall but its loss can be delayed beyond the number of moves that there is time to evaluate, some machines will behave with an ostrichlike sense of security. Proceeding under the normally sound assumption that positional disadvantages are less calamitous than material losses, a machine may begin to interpose a variety of structurally disastrous delaying moves, failing to perceive not only that the loss of the piece is inevitable but also that such moves, when coupled with material loss, can prove ruinous. A human player in this situation can "outsee" his computer opponent. He has the discernment—lacking in the nongeneralizing, nonjudgmental machine—to recognize delaying moves for what they are and to penetrate to the essence of a position. Through a wide range of ingenious ad-hoc techniques, chess programmers have alleviated many of the problems associated with the horizon effect, but they have not yet begun to meet the larger challenges involved in teaching machines to think strategically.

The computer's inability to recognize patterns or to make long-range plans was once commonly seen as an insurmountable shortcoming: surely a machine incapable of strategy could never play top-level chess. Tactics have traditionally been regarded as the more pedestrian half of chess mastery, the game's true flights of genius being reserved for that cloudy zone where strategy's intuitions drift and assemble. BE-BE, HITECH, and other "tactical monsters" have shaken this notion. That machines incapable of strategy could be ranked with some of the best players in the country forces us to reappraise the limits of tactical play. Evidently, machines and human beings may follow widely divergent roads to chess mastery. Some programmers have begun to speculate that only minimal improvements in strategic abilities will be necessary to enable the computers of the future to compete successfully with the best players in the world—provided that tactical skills continue to improve through increases in computing speed. Robert Hyatt, the leader of the CRAY BLITZ team, is even more optimistic, believing that strategy may be wholly unnecessary. "We could stop working on CRAY BLITZ, and the program could still beat a human world champion one day, just because of technology," he says. "I mean, it plays well. And technology is coming along that will let it run faster. Now we're promised by the year 2000 another factor of a thousand in computing speed. That's another four ply, at least. We're talking about doing a twelve-ply exhaustive search. I think that's good enough to become world champion plus." On the other hand, the Englishman David Levy, who is an international master and the author of several books about computer chess, insists that without great improvements in strategic capabilities machines will still need well over a century to reach the top. Speed is not enough. Levy says of Hyatt's prediction, "I would happily bet him a million dollars right now that he's wrong." He notes that Hyatt's theory could be tested without waiting for an increase in computing speed, simply by permitting CRAY BLITZ to take an average of three thousand minutes per move, rather than the three minutes normally allowed. According to Levy, CRAY BLITZ would still be "wiped out" by any human world champion.

Levy emphasizes that the only way to understand the progress chess machines have made in recent years is to look beyond their tournament records and their improved ratings. Chess players throughout the world are given a point rating based on their tournament performances. For example, the mean rating of tournament players in America is approximately 1500. Gary Kasparov, the world champion, has a rating of 2735. The best computers now perform at about the 2300 level. Purely in terms of numbers, HITECH is closer to the world champion than to the average tournament player. But many chess programmers believe that that closeness is illusory. According to this view, it's not just a matter of machines climbing another five hundred points; rather, some sort of quantum leap is necessary. Computers cannot yet match the flexibility that a human being brings to the chessboard, or human powers of strategy, analogical reasoning, and pattern recognition—although, being impervious to fatigue, emotional problems, and lapses of concentration, computers can play unmatchably consistent chess.

Perhaps the greatest potential strength of chess machines lies in their ability (which even grandmasters must regard with longing) to view the pieces on the board not as individuals but as one organic whole. Actually, this is an advantage that the programmer creates by necessity. This enviably unified vision derives from the machine's need to reduce all the combinations of pieces to mathematical sums. Each potential configuration must be translatable into the one language the machine understands—a precise, binary language—before its "evaluation function" can select the best move from the multitudes available. Thus, each of the millions of positions that a machine will weigh before moving is, in the last analysis, nothing more than that position's assigned score. The computer has a promising advantage, too, in what might be termed its open-mindedness. A skilled human player approaches the game armed with various injunctions (e.g., "Do not tamper with your king-side pawns"), and these, while they are useful in most instances, may unconsciously cramp his thinking. Such rules of thumb—or heuristics, to use the chess programmers' term—have been programmed into computers, too. But in recent years programmers have moved toward more flexible play. Ideally, a good machine will often choose the same move that a heuristic would have suggested but will do so "thoughtfully" rather than mechanically. In the next decade or so, as chess programs continue to venture beyond set guidelines and conceptions, we can expect to see machines producing increasingly original, fertile lines of play, whose unfamiliarity will vex human opponents.

Finally, the computer is not subject to fits of egotistical stubbornness—the fear of looking indecisive or foolish. While a human player may be unwilling to return a piece to its former square lest this seem an acknowledgment that the previous advance was ill-conceived, a computer will retreat readily. It is not imprisoned by its previous analyses. Indeed, the computer, to an extent that a human being can scarcely imagine, approaches each move freshly, taking into consideration only the board as it currently stands. With each new move, the machine confronts an original mathematical problem, and there is no compelling link between one move and the next. Hence, when a chess machine encounters a particular position it will come up with a move unaffected by whether *it* brought the game to this state or someone else did (as when Ken Thompson offered BELLE a chance to commit anew Fischer's queen sacrifice in the "game of the century").

A chess machine needs all these advantages if it is to compensate for its inability to recognize what programmers call "garbage moves." HI-TECH sounds unbeatable when one first learns that it can analyze a hundred and seventy-five thousand positions per second, but all except a tiny fraction of these represent lines of play so ludicrously inept that not even a novice would bother with them for a moment. Garbage moves are so overwhelmingly predominant in any chess game tree that for some time many experts believed that no full-width machine could ever advance above a middling level of play; it was assumed that a machine that could not immediately dismiss such moves would never have time to probe plausible, promising lines of play to a sufficient depth. The surprising success of the full-width machines in the last two decades springs from two technical breakthroughs. The first is sheer speed; the emergence in the nineteen sixties of the silicon chip as a replacement for the transistor made it theoretically possible for full-width machines to sift with the necessary speed through the millions

of garbage moves inevitably encountered in any search running seven-
or eight-ply deep. The second breakthrough—or chain of breakthroughs—has been the evolution of remarkably efficient methods of
searching a game tree.

The most important of these, known as the alpha-beta search
method, descends from the game theory analysis of John von Neumann and Oskar Morgenstern in the nineteen forties—especially their
model of a "minimax" procedure, which assumes that each player
of a game is continually seeking to compel play along lines that will
minimize his opponent's strengths while maximizing his own. This
procedure employs a somewhat unrealistic but eminently useful
assumption—that one's opponent will make the best move available to
him, the "best move" being, in computer chess, the strongest according to the machine's evaluation function. Of course, the machine's
opponent may overlook the best possible move, or may discover what
might fancifully be termed a "better best possible move"—one based
on an evaluation more sophisticated than the machine's. Nonetheless,
by assuming that the best possible move will be made, the machine
generally ensures that if it misjudges its opponent it does so prudently,
deeming him more formidable than he is. The alpha-beta search
method allows a great many branches of a game tree to be preliminarily
dismissed—or "pruned," in programmer vernacular.

The best way to illustrate how an inanimate object narrows its own
field of analysis, thereby effectively simulating the human brain's invaluable talent for selectivity, is by means of a very simple game tree.
Let us assume that we have a chess machine named BLAKE, which
searches to a depth of only two ply. If BLAKE has four possible moves
(A, B, C, D), to each of which its opponent has four possible replies
(A^1, A^2, A^3, and A^4 corresponding to move A; B^1, B^2, B^3, and B^4 to
move B; etc.), then we have a game tree of sixteen (four times four)
terminal nodes. Assume, further, that BLAKE has evaluated the four positions resulting from the replies to move A and has assigned to them
scores of $+2.0$, $+1.5$, $+3.0$, and $+3.25$, when $+1.0$ would indicate an
advantage to BLAKE equal to one pawn. Then if BLAKE makes move A
and its opponent replies with move A^4, according to BLAKE's evaluation
the resulting position gives BLAKE an advantage equivalent to three and
a quarter pawns. The minimax procedure presupposes, however, that
the opponent would reply with A^2, thereby minimizing BLAKE's advan-

tage to one and a half pawns. Having evaluated all replies to move A, BLAKE would store these values and investigate move B. Now, if an evaluation of the position resulting from reply B^1 were to result in a score of only +.01, BLAKE could halt its analysis of *all* replies to B. It need not evaluate moves B^2, B^3, and B^4. Even if each of these moves would result in an enormous advantage to BLAKE, move B would still be deemed undesirable, because of the assumption that the opponent would choose the best possible option for himself—avoiding these three moves in favor of B^1, which effectively evens the game. By making move A instead of move B, BLAKE ensures that its opponent can do no better than minimize BLAKE's advantage to a score of +1.5. Upon "realizing" that it has analyzed move B sufficiently, BLAKE prunes the three other moves (B^2, B^3, and B^4) and begins its analysis of move C.

By itself, the alpha–beta method could not reduce a chess game tree to a manageable size. Additional streamlining was needed. In the last few years, programmers have found a partial solution in the fact that pruning tends to be far more efficient if an opponent's strongest moves are considered at the outset. If an opponent has even one strong response in a hypothesized line of play, then, according to the best-possible-move assumption, that line is vitiated; and the earlier this strong response is discovered, the sooner the entire line can be pruned. Various programming techniques have been devised to increase the likelihood that the opponent's best moves will be considered first. Once these are tentatively established, the order in which the computer is scheduled to search the game tree can be shifted accordingly. In a complex machine like BELLE or CRAY BLITZ, the ordering of the search is shifted constantly, even within the analysis of a single move. When depicted on paper, a game tree has a static appearance, much like a tree in nature, but the tree that lies encoded inside the machine is something else entirely. If one seeks to envision this thing that Ken Thompson calls a "weird space" (and without some image for the bewildered mind to fix on, the computer's tree search is all but incomprehensible), one is left with a picture of a tree whose branches are forever being lopped from one section of the trunk and grafted to another, all at lightning speeds.

A task at once monumental and unavoidable, the pruning of the game tree has provided programmers with an opportunity to display their keenest ingenuity. In many cases, they have reduced their tree searches by well over ninety-nine percent. This has, in effect, made their machines well over a hundred times faster. They have further speeded up their machines by programming them to think on the opponent's time. While its human adversary sits weighing his options, a computer may have already predicted his most likely move and begun the search for a powerful rebuttal. Of course, it often happens that this prediction is incorrect (though less often than one might suppose; against expert opponents, CRAY BLITZ can perform such "mind reading" with forty percent accuracy), and in that case all the machine's analyses are wasted. Nonetheless, the "wasted" efforts of an indefatigable machine are not analogous to those of a human being, who must conserve his mental powers. The computer has nothing to lose, and much to gain, by carrying on an unceasing analysis.

When laymen ask chess programmers about their work, the most frequent question is: Will computers eventually defeat the greatest human players? Over the years, embarrassingly rash predictions have been made. In 1957, Herbert Simon, a colleague of Hans Berliner's at Carnegie-Mellon and a pioneer in the field of artificial intelligence, predicted that "within ten years a digital computer will be the world's chess champion, unless the rules bar it from competition." In fact, the chess machines of 1967, notwithstanding astonishing increases in computing speed, were still playing at a level well below that of a good club player. Still, developments were coming quickly, and there were a number of programs already on the scene which were capable of solid, well-balanced play that incorporated the basic principles of opening, middle game, and endgame. It looked as though the only things lacking were elementary refinements and a mere increase in speed. So it seemed, anyway, to a group of computer scientists in 1968, who wagered David Levy, in a series of bets that ultimately totalled about twenty-five hundred dollars, that a machine would be able to defeat him within ten years. In 1977, a two-game match was arranged between Levy and a machine called CHESS 4.5, and Levy triumphed easily. A year later, with the evolution of an improved program named CHESS 4.7, Levy faced a stiffer challenge. Exercising extreme caution and slow, solid development—a "do-nothing-but-do-it-well strategy," according to Levy—he convincingly routed CHESS 4.7 by the score of

3–1–1. Levy's one loss resulted from a somewhat cocky attempt to overcome the computer by means of the sort of risky tactical play that it excelled at refuting. Nonetheless, he hesitated to make a similar bet on a match to be held in 1988, admitting that he was "not quite confident of my own ability."

Ken Thompson says that only after years of working with chess machines has he begun to appreciate the heights of human chess achievement. The apparent accessibility of grandmaster chess can work to obscure its magnificent and remote genius. Even the novice can perceive some of the dizzying height of human achievement on the chessboard if it takes the form of a flashy demonstration—as when the Hungarian international master Janos Flesch played blindfolded against fifty-two opponents simultaneously and won thirty-one of the games, drawing eighteen, and losing only three. But the celestial brilliance that illuminates the very summits of chess—the unbelievably complex analysis of hypothetical positions that lie ten and twenty and thirty moves off—burns at such an elevated altitude that it can hardly be glimpsed or imagined by the average player. Thompson's experience suggests that one result of better machines may be an appreciation, rather than a devaluation, of human achievement in chess—though at present it is very difficult to say exactly how computers will finally affect our view of the game. Expert opinion in both fields—chess and computer science—is divided.

David Levy, who for a time made a scanty living as a chess writer and professional (he is now the chairman of Intelligent Chess Software, Ltd., in London), offers reassurance to those wary of the machine. A remarkably articulate man who has given the matter a good deal of thought, Levy believes that chess machines will benefit almost everyone in the chess world. "The development of the motorcar did nothing to impede our interest in the footrace, did it?" he asks. He feels that, instead of siphoning away prize money, chess machines—through their manufacturers—will contribute to it, and points out that companies in the computer business are already sponsoring various master tournaments. Levy envisions human and mechanical players working together in fruitful and exciting combinations. "You could invent a tournament rule that said that each human being will have his own computer, and perhaps three times during the game the human being could get the computer to make a move for him," he explained in a recent conversation. "The human could choose on which three occasions to use the computer, but once he had used up his three occasions he'd be on his own." Levy views the chess machine as potentially the greatest single tool of instruction in the history of chess, believing that it will free the game from the urban centers where, traditionally, young players have found the dense variety of competition they need in order to grow. He foresees new generations of grandmasters emerging from rural areas, and from countries that have never had a strong chess heritage. What the radio did for music, carrying its richnesses and challenges into the hinterland, the computer will do for chess. "The game," Levy concludes, "is about to undergo a wonderful revolution."

It is a wonderful revolution that all sorts of players, and not merely budding professionals concerned about their careers, are dreading. Among weekend players, the prospect is generally viewed with undiluted anxiety—an anxiety often linked to a pervasive concern over the increasing presence of computers in our lives. Even among chess programmers, who naturally would like to see a machine become the world champion, one sometimes senses what might be called an anticipatory nostalgia for the days when human beings reigned over the board. For the public at large, a confrontation as stark as that of man versus machine on the chessboard could easily take on powerful significance. Man's threatened overthrow on the board might seem emblematic of a more minatory defeat. And one can easily see how psychologically lacerating the encounter might be if it took place between a monomaniac of the "chess is life" variety and a machine that was able to defeat all human opponents. How could such a player escape the conclusion that life is most ably enacted by the lifeless? At the very least, the ascendancy of the chess machine would force us to concede that a field traditionally regarded as artistic and intuitive can be mastered by means of a methodical and "unimaginative" mathematics. As soon as an indefinable "feel for the game" is no longer a prerequisite for a world champion, chess must undoubtedly undergo a demystification—one with implications ranging far beyond the chessboard. The triumph of the chess machine would be strong evidence that mastery of a variety of aesthetic, "humanistic" activities might be open to the computer.

The chessboard's accessibility to the computer's inorganic brain should perhaps be viewed as an extension of its hospitality to the peculiar mind of the child prodigy. In its narrow profundity, the prodigy's intellect suggests, after all, a kind of proto-computer. Even before the advent of chess machines, no one doubted that, for an "art form," the game calls upon an unusually restricted range in the psyche. Chess is one of the few mental disciplines in which the contributions of children have proved not only noteworthy but inseparable in kind from what the best adult minds have accomplished. Steiner wrote that "in only three human pursuits—mathematics, music, chess—have creative results been achieved before puberty." The three fields share obvious affinities. A number of grandmasters have been fine mathematicians (including the former world champions Dr. Max Euwe and Emanuel Lasker, both of whom taught at the university level) or musicians (most impressively, the eighteenth-century Frenchman François-André Danican Philidor, who was not only the most influential chess writer of all time but also a composer of lasting interest). Chess players and musicians alike resist the notion that their creativity may be reducible to "mere numbers," but both fields can reasonably be viewed as branches of mathematics. While it may well be that all creative activities will ultimately prove to have a codifiable, quantifiable basis, music and chess have a mathematical grounding that never lies very far below the surface, and the three disciplines present a range of similar demands and appeals: each requires little emotional maturity or knowledge of the world for its mastery; each employs patterns of a sufficient logical rigor to permit missing terms or sequences to be supplied through deduction; and each seems to exist in a hermetic zone whose independence of the larger world offers the promise of transcendental release.

Hermetic and logical, impersonal and transcendent—music, of all the fine arts, might appear to be the most accessible to the internal maneuverings of the computer. At the previous world championship, in New York, I discussed this question with Benjamin Mittman and Monty Newborn, the two co-chairmen of the tournament. Newborn is a professor of computer science at McGill University and the inventor of OSTRICH, one of the competitors. He is also one of only two people in the world who have competed in all five world championships. Mittman, a professor at Northwestern University's Graduate School of Management, was the president of the International Computer Chess Association from its founding, in 1977, until 1983. Their long-standing friendship seems to thrive on a pointed disagreement about the future of computer science; Newborn believes the computer capable of just about anything, whereas Mittman sees it as a wonderful but inherently restricted tool. In our talk, Mittman, in particular, appeared skeptical about a computer's ability ever to compose music that would be anything more than a novelty or a curiosity, while Newborn—with a glint in his eye suggesting that he enjoyed being provocative, but with patent conviction as well—said, "I wouldn't be surprised if computers turned out to be far better composers than human beings ever were." He foresaw a time, not so many years hence, when people would go to the concert hall to hear computer symphonies that "will bring tears to the eyes." He seemed to enjoy Mittman's hoot of disbelief. "There has always been hostility to things that change man's perspective of the universe," he said. "It's perfectly natural. It's consistent with everything else we've done. That's why computer chess is so interesting—because it's the first place where this relationship is being tested to the limit; it's the testing block for how much intelligence computers can have. The computer is reshaping man's position in the universe. Man started with the universe revolving around him, and then it wasn't revolving around him. He began as a special animal, and now he really isn't such a special animal. But then he figured his brain was special. Well, his brain ain't so special."

Just how "special" our brains are—which is to say, to what degree they are not duplicable by machines—has emerged as the central issue in the field of artificial intelligence. There is as yet no way of knowing whether any inherent boundaries exist to a machine's capacity for replicating human thought—or how, if such boundaries exist, they might be categorized or defined. Meanwhile, researchers in artificial intelligence tend to feel both vexed and amused at the way the public seems unthinkingly to shift its definition of creativity to exclude machines. In her book *Machines Who Think*, Pamela McCorduck observes, "There is superstition about creativity, and for that matter, about thinking in every sense, and it's part of the history of the field of artificial intelligence that every time somebody figured out how to make a computer do something—play good checkers, solve simple but relatively informal problems—there was a chorus of critics to say, but that's not *thinking*." In the next few decades, our society will certainly see machines dramatically extend their range of activities, and "creativity" will doubtless have to submit to a good deal of redefinition. Whether we will be able to keep the term at all—at least in its present guise as a process both mysteriously and uniquely human—is a question that encompasses deep neurological and philosophical issues.

Where an answer to the riddle of creativity might be found remains problematic. It may be encoded in the currently arcane chemical processes of the cortical network—or, indeed, it may lie in some disembodied quintessence that exists in the spirit, outside the laws of chemistry altogether. But if creativity is quantitatively encoded in the human brain, it could in time prove wholly comprehensible. Many in the artificial-intelligence community believe that research will eventually illustrate that there is no irreducible mystery to the mind. Its content will prove not only comprehensible but duplicable by machines. This view denies any fundamental difference between inorganic and organic processes, and also between man's thought and that of the lower animals. Its proponents often make much of the structural similarities between machine and human intelligence: both brain and computer work by on-off switches—neurons and bits, respectively—that fire other on-off switches in elaborate, looping communication networks. These are not people who speak dismissively of the brain's capabilities. Everyone who works in artificial intelligence is daily compelled to marvel at how much more the mind can do than any machine, a superiority all the more remarkable given the severe handicap the brain labors under as a communication system: it works slowly. A single neuron can be "switched" on and off only some hundred times per second, many thousands of times slower than the speed attained by a computer bit. And, of course, machines are getting much faster, year by year, while the brain's speed is neurologically fixed. The genius of the brain as an information-processor system resides in its hardware—that Gordian knot of neural loops and windings, so unbelievably complex that present-day computer scientists cannot begin to see how some apparatus composed of silicon and metal might ever be constructed to match its range and flexibility. Given the present impossibility of understanding the mind's chemical operations, computer scientists interested in exploring the overlap of artificial and human intelligences have naturally focussed not on parallels of internal structure but on external results. The game of chess engages the computer scientist because it provides a zone in which satisfyingly complicated results can be achieved by divergent structures. Man and machine, flesh and metal, here compete as equals.

The ghost of the great British mathematician Alan Turing lingers over this emphasis on duplicating external results rather than internal structures. An enigmatic and often beleaguered figure, whose life ended in apparent suicide in 1954, Turing was a wide-ranging theorist whose fanciful notions had a way of infiltrating and shaping the domain of the practical and workaday. In the thirties, he hypothesized the existence of a forerunner of the modern computer which he called an abstract universal computing machine, and showed how it could be built. His machine could, in principle, duplicate the functions of any far more sophisticated computer. While a specialized machine might be designed to perform one task with formidable efficiency—as has in fact come to pass in the special-purpose hardware of BE-BE and BELLE— Turing's machine could be programmed to match its every operation, provided the storage tape was long enough. In reality, this tape would have to be of stupefying length even for relatively simple operations. Turing's hypothetical apparatus, however, suggests that all modern computers are fundamentally alike. They are universal machines, and each one can, in principle, be reprogrammed to duplicate the operations of every other. Turing's accomplishment encouraged the belief that differences between machines and men might likewise prove superficial. His machine may have been even more universal than he originally conjectured: it could conceivably provide a model for the duplication of the human brain.

In 1950, attempting in characteristically workmanlike fashion to come to grips with the horrific complexities of defining "thought" or "thinking," Turing published a paper entitled "Computing Machinery and Intelligence," in which he began with the simple question "Can machines think?" and proposed an equally simple experiment. A man is to be placed in an isolated room, from which he will conduct two interrogations through a teleprinter—one with another human being, and the other with a computer programmed to feign (by outright lying, if necessary) that it, too, is human. If the isolated interrogator is unable after a sufficient length of time (Turing believed that five minutes might be fair) to distinguish the human being from the machine, then it would be "the solipsist point of view" not to concede that the machine could think. Turing's reasoning was the more persuasive for its commonsensical tone. Surely the existence of thought in others can be determined only through external evidence. While one's own thinking is perceptible directly, through the constant inner tumult of consciousness, that of others is detectable only through their behavior, and chiefly through what they say. So if a machine could produce the very same evidence of thought that we require of human beings, it would be unfair to deny that it has the ability to think. Turing compiled a list of possible refutations to the concept of machine thought, beginning with what he called the Theological Objection ("Thinking is a function of man's immortal soul"), which he dismissed with a predictably terse impatience. (Ironically, this man who in so many ways disdained the vaporous and spiritual believed in extrasensory perception, and considered it the one mental activity that might forever lie outside the abilities of machines.) Turing is perhaps to be criticized for his narrow philosophical materialism, but, having pitched his experiment from the outset in terms of empirical behavior, he is in fairness entitled to be countered on that level.

What Turing sought was learned, scientific opposition—of the sort that has lately come from Joseph Weizenbaum, a professor of computer science at M.I.T., whose book *Computer Power and Human Reason* is a leading text on the possible restrictions, both physical and moral, on computer development. Weizenbaum contends that modern society has gradually been duped into viewing thought as a narrowly rational activity rather than as a range of processes infrangibly linked to a physical anatomy and a social upbringing—to the interactions of an organic body with other such bodies. For Weizenbaum, the concept of thought independent of corporeality is both illogical and, in its distortion of human nature, menacing:

A theory is, of course, itself a conceptual framework. And so it determines what is and what is not to count as fact. The theories—or, perhaps better said, the root metaphors—that have hypnotized the artificial intelligentsia, and large segments of the general public as well, have long ago determined that life is what is computable and only that. . . .

But, and this is the saving grace of which an insolent and arrogant scientism attempts to rob us, we come to know and understand not only by way of the mechanisms of the conscious. We are capable of listening with the third ear, of sensing living truth that is truth beyond any standards of provability. It is *that* kind of understanding, and the kind of intelligence that is derived from it, which I claim is beyond the abilities of computers to simulate.

Alan Turing expected to see a machine pass his test by the year 2000—a prediction that most experts now regard as grossly unrealistic. It seems, then, that at least in the next few decades we will not need to confront all the issues raised by the Turing test. Yet the questions it poses are profoundly troublesome, and a debate has begun to take shape. The arguments made by both sides—those who, with Turing, perceive no insuperable physical or ethical limitations on the creation of thinking machines, and those who, with Weizenbaum, believe that such machines are inherently limited, and dangerous insofar as the limitations are not recognized—will doubtless undergo considerable refinement as it becomes clearer what computers are capable of. But we may already have before us the core issues of contention. In the next century, this debate could well become the central controversy of philosophers throughout the world; and how our children and grandchildren regard the machine—or how, perhaps, the machine compels them to regard themselves—may well define what it is to be a person in the twenty-first century.

The potential complexity of the debate and some of the bizarre issues it could generate are adumbrated in Geoff Simons' book *Are Computers Alive?* Simons, of the National Computing Centre, in Manchester, England, envisions no limits to what thinking machines will do. He paints a future in which the thought processes of computers will be so complex that we will feel ethically compelled to accord them protection: "Sophisticated computers and robots will be capable of suffering, and if we are concerned with justice we will have to address ourselves to this question." He goes on, "People will have duties to feeling robots, as people have to each other; and robots will have duties not only to other people . . . but also to other robots." One should note, if this seems to smack of comic-book fantasy, that even the conservative Weizenbaum considers it possible to develop robots so advanced in their thinking that we would have to consider them an "organism," a "kind of animal." As such, they would doubtless be entitled to "animal rights" of their own.

Whether computers will ever be regarded as thinking beings, to say nothing of beings entitled to rights, may finally depend on whether programmers can instill into a machine a sense of self-consciousness. This is a daunting task. Merely to formulate a satisfactory definition of self-consciousness is difficult, to say nothing of creating one artificially. How does one go about defining that intangible, essential *something* inside a person which frequently alters and at times seems to disappear altogether—that thing which is subject to comas, psychoses, fugue states, sleep, and daydreams, as well as the myriad modifications imposed by daily existence over the course of a lifetime? Perhaps the most useful definition I've met, charming for its brevity, comes from the philosopher Daniel C. Dennett, of Tufts University: in *The Mind's I,* a book he co-edited with Douglas R. Hofstadter, he describes creatures with consciousness as "beings it is like something to be." He writes, "It is not like anything at all to be a brick or a pocket calculator or an apple. These things have insides, but not the right sort of insides—no *inner life,* no point of view. It is certainly like something to be me (something *I* know 'from the inside') and almost certainly like something to be you (for you have told me, most convincingly, that it is the same with you), and probably like something to be a dog or a dolphin (if only they could tell us!), and maybe even like something to be a spider." But it would not be "like something" to be today's world computer-chess champion—even if its games might rightfully be called creative.

Is it possible, then, to be a kind of "artist" and yet lack the power of self-consciousness? Chess represents the first significant creative field in which even an expert often cannot distinguish human from mechanical activity. In the chess world, anyway, machines have already passed the Turing test. One must conclude from this either that chess players over hundreds of years have been wrong and the game is not inherently creative or that computers have already demonstrated a talent for an aesthetic, "human" discipline. Those tempted toward the former conclusion should be warned of the substantial possibility that they will soon confront increasingly knotty questions; for instance, when computers write jokes that make us laugh, or compose string quartets that leave us weeping, will it be possible to say that neither humor nor music is a creative activity? If time proves that many of the creative arts are accessible to computers, then quite likely Donald Michie's judgment that research into chess machines is "the most important scientific study that is going on in the world at present" will be wholly vindicated. And if, as Turing believed, nearly all human mental activity can be replicated, then the overall effect of thinking machines on society and on the individual psyche will surely prove so sweeping that Michie's judgment will in the end seem conservative.

Even if all human thought should ultimately prove accessible to the computer's precise, thorough, systematic binary operations, this would not disprove the existence of some mysterious, noncomputable quiddity afloat in the universe. But it might rule out the possibility of our ever coming to perceive or understand that mystery—which by definition would exist outside the bounds of the computerlike processes that regiment our own thinking. And if our minds blind us to whatever rare truths and beauties are hovering around us, we would have to expect that our machines—created in our own image, mirroring our own thought processes—would prove similarly delimited. We could hardly count on our machines to introduce us to some state of widened enlightenment. Whether best described as "organisms" or "mechanical brains," they—poor things—would be circumscribed by (to borrow another phrase from William Blake, that prophet who detested science) "mind-forg'd manacles": the very manacles that imprison their makers. It may be, then, that the ultimate limit on machine creativity and intelligence is the human one.

On the last day of the Fifth World Computer Chess Championship, BE-BE (3–1) is matched up against REBEL (3–1), and CRAY BLITZ (3–1) against HITECH (4–0). REBEL, the creation of a Dutchman, Ed Schröder, is a lightweight machine capable of evaluating a mere five hundred moves per second—only one percent of what BE-BE can do. Drastically limited by its lack of speed, REBEL has been programmed to carry out a full-width search to only three ply, after which it must rely on the always chancy probings of a selective search. Although REBEL, the No. 16 seed, has performed creditably so far, having defeated the No. 5, the No. 7, and the No. 9 seeds, it would seem no match for a machine of BE-BE's power and experience. Even the ever-anxious Anthony Scherzer admits this morning to feeling somewhat optimistic.

Scherzer also feels confident that HITECH will defeat CRAY BLITZ, which has just come off a somewhat shaky victory over SCHACH 2.7.

Because of time limitations, the game between CRAY BLITZ and SCHACH 2.7 could not be completed, and Michael Valvo was asked to adjudicate. The final position was so evenly balanced, however, that Valvo felt hesitant about making a determination himself. He called in for consultation Vlastimil Hort and Helmut Pfleger, two of the finest chess players in West Germany, and together they concluded that victory should be granted to CRAY BLITZ on the basis of its winning chances—although Valvo continues to feel skeptical that CRAY BLITZ could have capitalized on them. If the fifth round turns out as Scherzer envisions—and his expectations are shared by almost everyone at the tournament—HITECH will win the world championship outright. Standings in this tournament are ultimately determined by a point system—with one point being given for a victory, a half-point for a draw, and nothing for a loss. If HITECH finishes as predicted, it will wind up with a perfect 5–0 record, and five points. BE-BE, with a 4–1 finish, will have four points and a tie for second place—another second!

But mischief—the upsetting of all expectations—is in the air this morning. REBEL puts up unexpectedly stiff resistance against BE-BE's assaults. On the twenty-first move, BE-BE causes a stir in the audience by daringly advancing her king's rook pawn. This move is difficult to evaluate at once. Although it looks premature, it may turn out to be the leading edge of a potent attack and the beginning of the end for REBEL. On the other hand, if the attack should fail, BE-BE's king will stand unprotected. "No one could ever accuse BE-BE of being a coward" is Valvo's response; "I wish she wouldn't do things like that" is Scherzer's.

By the thirty-fifth move, BE-BE's attack has stalled, and by the fortieth she looks headed for trouble. REBEL, that little David in a field of Goliaths, seems on the road to another upset victory. By the fiftieth move, BE-BE—under attack and behind in material—has arrived at what the experts agree is a hopeless position. Gradually, the eyes of the audience drift elsewhere.

Most of them focus upon the battle between HITECH and CRAY BLITZ, where a complex position prevails well into the middle game. For a time, expert opinion divides as to who stands better. But as the shape of the endgame gradually emerges it grows clear that HITECH's twenty-ninth move, in which a knight was exchanged for a bishop, was a mistake. CRAY BLITZ has come off with a pawn advantage. What remains to be seen is whether it has the vision, and the precision, to convert this small edge into a victory against the fastest machine in the world.

Meanwhile, having attained its "won position," REBEL displays a curious lassitude. Rather than forcing a few exchanges of pieces that would leave it with a routine and inexorable victory, REBEL devotes a series of crucial moves to retreating its king into a corner—a doubly unwise decision, since this concern about the king's safety is groundless and the corner itself poorly chosen. BE-BE is being granted a reprieve, and although her situation remains desperate, she plays as she must, advancing her central pawns as quickly as possible. After a few more moves, REBEL unexpectedly and wholly avoidably finds itself placed on the defensive. BE-BE may be able to squeeze out a draw—or even, given REBEL's abrupt ineptitude, a victory. An extraordinarily happy outcome for Scherzer floats into view. Steadily, but with tantalizing slowness, BE-BE's position continues to improve. Not a man to keep tension bottled up within, Scherzer at one point can be seen simultaneously tapping his foot, smoking a cigarette, and rapping a pencil on the tabletop. "I've never been so nervous," he confesses. "Except maybe when I got married. And maybe in my first auto race." And yet with each of BE-BE's moves, as this unlikely racing driver must finally admit, he has less and less to worry about. BE-BE has clearly found her game at last. Having gained a solid purchase on the board's center, she is not about to relinquish control until victory has been achieved—any more than CRAY BLITZ, a few tables away, is going to let up against HITECH. In both games, the end is in sight. Berliner resigns for HITECH on the sixtieth move, and Shröder for REBEL on the seventieth. BE-BE has apparently won a share of what Scherzer at the outset of the tournament called "almost too much to dream about": first place.

Four machines—HITECH, CRAY BLITZ, BE-BE, and SUN PHOENIX— end up with four points and identical 4–1 records. According to the tournament rules, deadlocks of this sort are to be resolved by a further numerical comparison: "The order of finish of the participants will be determined by the total number of points earned. If two teams have an equal number of points, the sum of opponents' points will be used as a second factor." Although everyone concedes that a fairer and less arbitrary means of breaking ties would be a series of play-off games, there is no time for additional rounds. Instead, the prescribed comparisons are made, and it turns out that CRAY BLITZ is the actual winner, followed by HITECH, then BE-BE, and then SUN PHOENIX. So, depending on how Scherzer chooses to look at it, BE-BE has placed either first or third—but, in any case, not second.

At least so far as the programmers are concerned, the four-way tie for first place has left the field of computer chess in a happy muddle. At the moment, no single program or methodology is indisputably preeminent. Each programmer can return home with the hope intact that he alone is on the track to what will eventually prove the soundest method of achieving machine mastery over the chessboard. Perhaps the only clear "winner" of the tournament is REBEL, that little machine whose selective searchings carried it so much farther than anyone foresaw. Subsequent calculations reveal that had REBEL beaten BE-BE to finish with four points—as it came so near to doing—the tie-breaking system would have awarded it first place. That a machine of such limited speed could almost win the world championship suggests that there may be a brighter future than supposed for those "human machines" that do a selective search.

Given the pace of technological advance, one is not surprised that the future of computer chess remains unclear. This is a point that Scherzer likes to illustrate with an example drawn from his hometown. "When I was a kid growing up in Chicago," he says, "I liked to go to the Museum of Science and Industry. I remember especially a machine that played tic-tac-toe. It had been designed by Bell Labs, probably in the early fifties. You dialled in your moves on a regular telephone dial. Well, I've heard people say, 'Why don't they put in a microprocessor?' Of course, they were missing the point. This is a museum. As far as I'm concerned, the point is that the machine actually took *time* to make its moves. At tic-tac-toe!" Scherzer shakes his head in wonder. "Back in the early fifties, things like integrated circuits weren't even dreamt about. That machine was a creature of its time—its level of play was what you could expect from a machine when I was a kid. And now it's a dinosaur."

(1987)

A PECULIARLY DARK UTOPIAN

H. G. Wells

ʚ

"Discoveries and Conclusions of a Very Ordinary Brain" was the sub-title H. G. Wells gave to his voluminous *Experiment in Autobiography,* and having got off to an unbeatably modest start, he went on to confess that much of his literary output had been "slovenly, haggard and irritated," as well as "hurried and inadequately revised." Of the "gray matter of that organized mass of phosphorized fat and connective tissue" which he identified as the "hero" of his autobiography, he noted that its thinking was "slack" and "easily fatigued." By way of summary, he hypothesized that "If there were brain-shows, as there are cat and dog shows, I doubt if it would get even a third class prize."

If modesty is a rare trait among world-famous authors, rarer still is the ability—which Wells possessed in abundance—to analyze perceptively one's own literary shortcomings. The critic who sorts through Wells's prodigious oeuvre (he had published more than one hundred books before his death in 1946 at the age of seventy-nine) must be struck by how often Wells identified, and hence partially disarmed, whatever objections might be made against him. His fiction, he warned us, depended on "conventional types and symbols"; his "psychologically unsubtle" novels could be "artless self-revelatory stuff"; and as a stylist he "did not worry much about finish."

Protestations of this sort seemed excessive or insincere to a number of critics when *Experiment in Autobiography* was published in 1934, but Wells clung stoutly to his assertions of mediocrity. In a manuscript entitled "Postscript to an Experiment in Autobiography"—published, along with other personal addenda, as *H. G. Wells in Love*—he accused those who would find him guilty of an "inverted arrogance" of treating him with undue cynicism. "I meant exactly what I said; it was a very typical common brain," Wells reiterated, but added that it had one great strength, a "disposition to straightforwardness."

Straightforward he certainly could be—often scandalously so. He outraged English society, and suffered the loss of many friendships, as a result of his open and incessant sexual promiscuity. Both in conversation and in print he was a tireless proponent of free love, although one whose urgings had a curiously businesslike tone seemingly tinged by the Protestant work ethic: "A man or woman ought to have sexual intercourse. Few people are mentally, or morally, or physically in health without it. For everyone there is a minimum and maximum below which lies complete efficiency. Find out your equation, say I, and then keep efficient."

Today, Wells's reputation as a libertine seems to have overshadowed the spanning range of his iconoclasm, and one is apt to forget that he waged war against his country's legal system, military system, and educational system, its class prejudices and social customs and religious traditions—against most of what made England England. He railed, in fact, against anything he deemed an obstruction to the emergence of a "planned world-state," a cause that Wells in middle age came to adopt as his "personal religion." Although Wells was an atheist for most of his adult life, his fervent belief in the redemptive powers of rationalism characteristically partook of religious trappings and rhetoric. "The idea of creative service to the World-State towards which the modern mind is gravitating," he wrote at the end of *Experiment in Autobiography,* "differs widely in its explicitness, its ordered content and its practical urgency, from the All of Being, the Inner Life, the Ultimate Truth . . . and all those other resorts of the older religions, but its releasing and enveloping relation to the individual *persona* is, in spite of all that difference of substance, almost precisely the same." The emergence of the world-state was "inevitable," Wells repeatedly insisted, and yet he bridled with frustration at anything that seemed to hinder its progress.

For all the confidence of his predictions, our globe's various nation-states have not disappeared—but neither have the books of this "slovenly" artist. His novels continue to attract a readership whose diversity is almost unparalleled in our century. What other modern writer could boast of having won the loyalties of children, science fiction buffs, and exacting literary aristocrats like Borges and Nabokov? His books are accommodatingly multitiered, permitting child and sophisticate alike to feel that he speaks to them on their own level. With his roundabout locutions and his quaint vocabulary ("contraposed," "ostended," "incontinently"), Wells seems on occasion a solidly Victorian writer; at other moments, especially in his best science fiction, he can seem a contemporary figure or even (given that so few contemporary authors display much interest in the scientific and technological revolution that daily transmogrifies the world they live in) a writer slightly ahead of our time. Manifest in nearly everything he wrote was prodigious intellectual energy—the strong sense of a mind probing continuously as it goes. His investigations displayed an impressive scientific impartiality; he analyzed himself with the same cool rigor he trained upon the external world. And surely one source of Wells's potent literary appeal resides in that paradox whereby, in book after book, this most straightforward and analytical of authors remains an oddly elusive figure.

As such, he presents an irresistible quarry for biographers. Wells was not merely extraordinarily prolific, he was also peripatetic on a grand scale, and David C. Smith, in his *Desperately Mortal,* has been commendably dogged in sorting out and re-creating Wells's journeys through Italy, Russia, India, Australia, and America. Smith has dug through mountains of manuscript material, and the student of Wells must be grateful for many fresh quotations and anecdotes. And yet, despite the book's bulk, Wells remains curiously inert in its pages. It would appear that Smith has been too respectful—even cowed—in his approach. Certainly, Smith too often takes Wells, with all his rationalistic claims, at his word. What is frequently missing is the complement to Wells's optimistic rationalism—that side to the man which could be despondent and cold and resentful and childishly selfish.

Readers in search of a more vibrant portrait might better begin with Anthony West's biography, *H. G. Wells: Aspects of a Life,* even if, as its title suggests, it makes no attempt to be exhaustive. According to West, Wells remains elusive partly because he was sometimes misleading or dishonest when writing about himself. West ought to know. As the illegitimate son of Wells and Rebecca West, he approaches his subject from a unique vantage, singularly intimate and distanced. The scandalous love affair between the very young, very driven Rebecca and the middle-aged, hugely successful, but also very driven Wells, which began in 1913 and produced Anthony the following year, was tempestuous even in its happiest times, and left after its final dissolution in 1923 a great residue of resentment on both sides. Anthony, the sole child of the affair, was raised by his mother, and therefore must for many years have perceived his father through the filter of hostile eyes. But most of the biography's venom—of which there is a great store—is reserved for Rebecca, whom her son portrays as a scheming woman whose accounts of her love affair with Wells are self-pitying and self-serving. Anthony West regards his father with affection and forgiveness, even when airing his dishonesties and obliquities, which were considerable; for all of Wells's advocacy of sexual candor, he was, according to his son, a man compelled to seek out situations that would require double-dealing. Wells was also less than candid—though perhaps understandably so—when writing about his troubled childhood. His autobiography gives a touched-up portrait of his father, the failed proprietor of a china shop, who was, in addition to other shortcomings, an extraordinarily immature man, and of his mother, a former lady's maid, who bitterly resented her husband for removing her from the elevated society she had, however collaterally, once inhabited.

Yet the chief source of Wells's elusiveness is probably located in something more unusual. He was a literary pioneer in so many ways that even now, four decades after his death, his work resists categorization. He is, for example, often regarded as the "father of science fiction," but this was a genre not yet identified when Wells, beginning with *The Time Machine* in 1895, embarked upon that remarkable collection of books which he called "scientific romances" and which are likely to prove his most durable achievement. It was not until the twenties that the term "science fiction" achieved wide currency through Hugo Gernsback, the founder of *Amazing Stories* magazine, and probably not until the thirties or forties that the reading public had assembled some common notions about the powers and limitations of this fledgling genre. Wells found himself, then, in an exhilarating and perplexing position: a writer of a type of genre fiction that had not yet become a genre. As far as Wells and his readers knew, his scientific romances were not so much progenitors as descendants—the heirs to books like Samuel Butler's *Erewhon*, Swift's *Gulliver's Travels,* and even Lucian's *A True Story*. One can understand why Joseph Conrad appeared so happily nonplussed when writing to Wells of *The Invisible Man:* "Impressed is the word, O Realist of the Fantastic." It must have been a liberating advantage for Wells not to know he was working in what critics would later determine was a limited and ancillary literary form; on the other hand, he felt at times unhappily confused about where he stood as an artist, and he spent much of his life trying, with only fair success, to define his theory of the novel and to map the sources of his own originality.

Wells's earliest articles and stories were published a hundred years ago, and surely by now we ought to have some solid grasp on his literary strengths and weaknesses, and on the relationship between "mainstream" fiction and its heady young offspring, science fiction. And yet, as Frank McConnell argues in *The Science Fiction of H. G. Wells,* we may have misunderstood Wells by "understanding" him too easily, and thereby arranged to misinterpret the character of science fiction as well. According to McConnell, "Wells may not have been the first man to acknowledge the importance of Darwinian theory for the future of civilization and the business of fiction, but he was certainly the first to acknowledge and assimilate that theory, in all its corrosive effect upon ideas of what fiction was for and about" and "not until *The Time Machine* did the real power, and the real terror, of evolutionary theory find adequate expression in fiction." Wells came by his understanding of Darwin through an unrivaled source: T. H. Huxley, with whom he studied at the Normal School of Science in South Kensington during the 1884–85 school year. Wells quickly perceived that although Darwin's *Origin of Species* had been hugely controversial since its publication in 1859, its import had not been fully assimilated by the public at large. Wells himself was constantly aware of the temptations and dangers in misreading Darwin. He chided George Bernard Shaw for shying away from "the heartless impartiality of natural causation" and "endowing it with an ultimately benevolent Life Force," and he ridiculed Catholic theologians for discovering that "the Church had always known all about Evolution and the place of man in Nature, just as it had always known all about the place of the solar system in space."

McConnell calls *The Time Machine* a "masterpiece" and a "great first book"—claims powerfully at odds with any notion that ultimate justice is at work in the distribution of literary classics: surely no masterpiece ought to be put together so quickly and haphazardly. Wells had manifestly little sense of where he was going in this brief novel. The story's genesis lay in an impossibly arch, deservedly abandoned short story, "The Chronic Argonauts," in which the main character bears the name of Dr. Nebo Gipfel. This tale was then recast for possible publication in W. E. Henley's magazine *The National Observer* as a series of reflective articles about time travel. The series fell so far short of editorial expectations that it was canceled before completion—and might have been forever abandoned had not Henley, now installed as the editor of the *New Review,* requested that it be reworked in a shape closer to the book we know today. In any case, the novel shows signs of laxness and haste throughout. What is intended as its one tragic scene—the death of Weena, the little woman of the future who befriends the Time Traveller—teeters on the rim of bathos. And the book's most haunting passage, in which the Time Traveller takes his machine forward into the future, further and further, until he winds up on a dying shore under a dead exploded sun, did not originate with Wells himself; it was a postscript appended at Henley's suggestion.

Clumsy, uncertain, bathetic it may at times be, and yet *The Time Machine* brims with an unmatched wonder and sweep and originality that render McConnell's claims plausible after all. (So much for ultimate literary justice . . .) Wells helped to bring a new strength to the English novel: an awareness of something beguiling, even voluptuous, in the cool—and, for some, godless—splendors of modern science. What other novelist of his time (or, for that matter, of ours) could have peered at a "mere rock" under a microscope and beheld there what Wells did? "One saw the jumbled crystals thrust against each other, distorted by unknown pressures, clouded and stained by obscure infiltrations. . . . It was not simply an astounding loveliness, it was, one felt, a profoundly significant loveliness that these sections revealed. They were telling in this bright clear and glowing fashion, of tensions, solutions, releases, the steady creeping of molecule past molecule, age after age. And in their interpretation lay the history and understanding of the Earth as a whole." Wells found in evolutionary theory not merely a challenge to traditional religious notions but a demand for a new morality: "Soon, for very many, as now for only a few, the pursuit of Science will become a part of the Moral Law. It will be felt as an imperative that, in order to do that which is right, man must know that which is true."

The Time Machine is unmistakably the work of a man who perceived in our slow-evolving planet, in its stones no less than in its life forms, a scientific and yet magical process—one all the more magical for being deducible. And it's a magic evident from the first page of this, his first book. Already Wells had found that marvelously matter-of-fact tone, seemingly so collected and direct, by which he would over the years propel his readers again and again into the realm of the fantastic: "The Time Traveller (for so it will be convenient to speak of him) was expounding a recondite matter to us. His grey eyes shone and twinkled, and his usually pale face was flushed and animated." (The opening of *The War of the Worlds* similarly smuggles in enchantment under a rational dress: "No one would have believed, in the last years of the nineteenth century, that human affairs were being watched keenly and closely by intelligences greater than man's and yet as mortal as his own. . . ." That slippery reference, or near-reference, to God—the greater but immortal intelligence in which people *would* have believed—is a brilliant, off-putting stroke.) And the streamlined *Time Machine*, unlike many of his later novels, with their wooden dialogue and weighty didacticism, never relinquishes its magical hold.

The story opens with a dinner party at the home of the Time Traveller. The party includes a doctor, a psychologist, a mayor, and the book's "I," who is notable chiefly for the open-mindedness with which he, unlike the other guests, listens to his host. After a leisurely meal, the Time Traveller begins to speculate about the emerging, still unfamiliar, notion of Time as a fourth dimension, and raises the possibility of directed travel through the ages. In fact, he reveals to his guests, he has been engaged in a little experimentation, and would like now to provide a modest display. He leads them out to his laboratory and a small, puzzling device, "scarcely larger than a small clock, and very delicately made." When, at the Time Traveller's bidding, the psychologist turns one of its tiny levers, the device swings around, fades, and disappears— possibly to race for all of eternity into eternity. The guests ask to be let in on the "trick." But the Time Traveller insists that what they have witnessed is not magic but science. He arranges to have them return in a week, for what he hopes will be some more convincing demonstration.

When the guests arrive a week later, their host is nowhere to be found. They decide to dine without him, in the expectation that he will soon appear—which he does in thunderous fashion, staggering into the party in a ragged and semi-delirious state. His clothes are bloodstained and his hair appears to have whitened. He reports that he has just returned from a sojourn of eight days in the world of the year A.D. 802,701.

The future the Time Traveller paints for his skeptical guests is a horror. The class divisions of industrialized nineteenth-century England have led to a genetic bifurcation: mankind has split into two species. The Eloi are pretty, feckless creatures whose "too-perfect security" has apparently led to a "general dwindling of size, strength, and intelligence." Theirs is a garden world in which they spend their childish days eating fruit, picking flowers, playing games. The wan, disgusting Morlocks inhabit a network of deep tunnels in the earth, where they toil amid clanking machinery. They are the end product of those pent-up colliers and factory workers, who, sunless as ghosts, haunted the humanitarian conscience of Victorian England. To the Time Traveller, the world initially appears to belong to the Eloi—but their imparadised days conceal a life of nocturnal terror, of dark raids by the Morlocks, who cannibalize them. (The Eloi will inevitably evoke for the contemporary reader the "flower children" of the Hippies' mellow heyday, and to see them eventually eaten up by the representatives of industry lends the novel a painful black humor.)

The book has some wonderfully spooky moments, particularly the Time Traveller's discovery, at the end of an idyllic day, that his machine has disappeared. To contemplate being trapped forever in the year A.D. 802,701 is to perceive Robinson Crusoe as a man who had merely gone off for a weekend at the seashore; the book widens our definitions of what exile can be. Later in the novel, the Time Traveller's fumbling struggle with a match, while the clambering Morlocks attempt to overpower him in the darkness, is gruesomely claustrophobic. And, even if the idea did originate with Henley, that final journey to the world's end is a haunting triumph. Like the poet in the Keats sonnet, the Time Traveller stands on "the shore of the wide world," confronting an image of death before which "love and fame to nothingness do sink." Indeed, this sonnet may have been in Wells's mind—he steeped himself in Romantic poetry—during the composition of the book's last pages.

And yet the final desolating vision of *The Time Machine* was one that the Romantics, writing in the first half of the nineteenth century, could never have conceived. Wells wanted us to see that death itself had been transformed in the century's intervening decades. Darwin's work had altered forever the condition of *Homo sapiens*—had rendered man a changing, transitional animal, to be understood only when viewed across those monumental geological epochs that our Time Traveller had traversed in order to beach up on his dying shore. What Wells had absorbed—so profoundly that it reconstructed his soul—was the notion, apparently simple but finally revolutionary, that many of humankind's most significant certainties are to be found millions of years away. We cannot begin to say what will happen in Europe next month, but we might speak assuredly about the fate of the earth: the sun will burn out, life as we know it will disappear.

And for Wells, unlike the Romantics, life could be fully accounted for without recourse to the notion of God. Natural selection provided a means of explaining not only the birth of mankind but also its probable lines of development. Darwinism encouraged extrapolation. "I flung myself into futurity," the Time Traveller at one point announces to his startled guests—and the same could be said of Wells's adult imagination. "We overrate the darkness of the future," he wrote in his autobiography—and so he pluckily set forth, hoping in his novels and essays to reveal truths about the near future (divined through the study of politics and sociology) and the distant future (to be discerned through biology, astronomy, and physics).

Truths of this latter sort are often regarded as hidden in the "mists of time," veiled by numbers so vast they smother the intellect, but it was Wells's particular virtue to discern determinate shapes in these mists (he prided himself on having a "brain good for outlines"). It seemed possible to Wells that he might identify the directions in which evolution was impelling not only the human body but the human brain and its thinking. What good fortune! To have reached adulthood at a time when all sorts of discoveries—biological, paleontological, astronomical—were razing some of the walls by which mankind's conception of itself had always been bound! Unlike so many of his contemporaries, who seemed to find these new vistas numbing or threatening, Wells peered into the freshly opened expanses and found them exhilarating. He made this point quite memorably in 1902, in one of his earliest public lectures: "All this world is heavy with the promise of greater things, and a day will come—one day in the unending succession of days—when beings, beings who are now latent in our thoughts and hidden in our loins, will stand upon this earth as one stands upon a footstool, and laugh, and reach out their hands amidst the stars."

Wells's grasp of the principle of evolution was in itself a source of great literary verve and originality; but it became something more—became perhaps the distinctive genius of his imagination—when combined with a second historical insight. Far more lucidly than most of his contemporaries, Wells perceived that modern science had recently launched the entire world toward a revolution. He seemed to understand intuitively how far-reaching and irreversible were the transformations that technology was effecting across the globe. While his contemporaries were apt to regard the Wright brothers' airplane as a delightful curiosity, Wells saw in its brief ascent a confirmation of his suspicions that humanity might eventually master the air—and the airless vacuums of space. Early in his career, he recognized technology's fundamental force as a "change in the scale of human relationships and human enterprises brought about by increased facilities of communication"—an insight equally applicable to the "information age" of our ongoing computer revolution.

This vision of a rapidly evolving, technology-dominated future enriched and balanced Wells's other, grander vision of a world millennially shaped by the promptings of evolutionary trial and error. If his Darwinism encouraged in Wells a sense of weary fatalism, the promise of technology kindled urgency and hope; what originated in man presumably might be steered by him, and Wells vowed to do everything possible to see that the new technological age turned out as it should. He became an incurable utopian, who converted to the "religion" of the scientific world-state even while recognizing technology's potential dangers. He was, in short, a peculiarly dark utopian—one whose visions, both short-term and long-term, were colored by glimpses of disaster. The apocalyptic held a murky appeal for Wells, who sometimes impatiently sensed that his awaited heaven-on-earth might be expedited by vaguely fascistic intellectual strong men or the purging of a "war that will end war"—a phrase, incidentally, of Wells's own coinage, and one that came back to haunt him in the early months of the

First World War, as it became deadeningly apparent that carnage would usher in neither wisdom nor unselfishness.

Wells's celebrated literary dispute with Henry James, which brewed for a number of years before coming to a head in 1913, is perhaps best understood in relation to his "dark" utopianism. James had seen much to admire in Wells's early work, particularly the social comedies in which Wells was, in his own words, seeking to create along "Dickens-Thackeray lines." James had called *Kipps,* published in 1905, a work of "genius" and of "TRUE truth." But James had found later books disappointing, and in September of 1913 wrote rather imposingly to Wells to say so. James lamented the shallowness of Wells's characterizations in *The Passionate Friends,* a complaint that struck Wells at a doubly vulnerable point: it forced him to confront not only this particular book's shortcomings but also his larger inability to define his aesthetic ends. Wells had no clear rebuttal to James's consciously noble belief in the primacy of the artist. ("It is art that makes life, makes interest, makes importance," James wrote to Wells.) He had by way of answer only a vague sense that his books were devoted to something larger than art, to the cause of human progress in a confused and imperiled age.

The two men aired their differences chiefly by letter. James is generally perceived as the clear winner of this exchange, so much so that Wells's replies may be treated with condescension. In retrospect, the debate does look hopelessly lopsided, given that James was an exacting, deliberative genius and Wells at best a haphazard, intuitive one. And Wells's unwillingness to put the debate behind him, to resolve it and let it go, has all the earmarks of the smarting loser; it is a little depressing to see him in his autobiography, two decades later, still carrying on a one-sided debate with James's formidable ghost.

And yet, as the Time Traveller himself discovered, determinations about who is the victor and who the vanquished can prove tricky; it may well be that in the end Wells comes off respectably. Certainly with each passing decade one must grow more forgiving of the inarticulateness of his literary theorizing; it becomes increasingly apparent to us, as so much of the technology Wells foresaw pervades our lives, that he was attempting to open his fiction to processes and objects that demand entrance into our literature.

As an artist, he seems to have felt both pride and loneliness about his passion for science. He worked hard to convert others to his point of view. He served for a time as a driving force in a group called The Committee on the Neglect of Science, which sought, among other things, to increase the time that students in state-supported institutions spent in scientific study. Wells turned with eagerness to the young partly because he felt that his own generation, even its intellectuals and artists, was in this matter almost beyond redemption. At one point in his autobiography, Wells lumped together some of his most prepossessing literary contemporaries—Conrad, James, Crane, Shaw—and called them "uneducated." Shaw, in particular, had "no sustained and constructive mental thinking" and was a "philanderer with facts." All these men lacked, according to Wells, a "central philosophy," and hence they "lapsed—though retaining their distinctive scale and quality—towards the inner arbitrariness and unreality of the untrained common man." He felt, and the years bear him out, that in failing to come to grips with the transformative powers of modern science, they were failing to see things whole.

Wells's perception of himself as a man with an urgent, and for the most part unappreciated, insight into the impact of technology led him naturally into didacticism; whether presenting himself as essayist or novelist, he remained a man with a message. Ours is not an age that feels comfortable with didactic fiction (especially with all of those Soviet attempts to render art "useful" still fresh in the memory), but if we are to be fair to Wells, we must seek to approach anew the notion of instructive art. It *is* true that much of his work was an attempt to educate and prepare readers for an "inevitable" social revolution—and yet how lightly the best of his books, especially the scientific romances, wear their purposeful designs! *The War of the Worlds,* for example, is in part an attack on British colonialism (the heartlessness with which the Martians slaughter mankind is repeatedly analogized to British indifference about "primitive" peoples), but the book never seems a mere political tract. In forgoing character study and the subtleties of emotional interchange in his novels—in forgoing, that is, the complex of personal dealings that most of his contemporaries regarded as fiction's proper province—Wells restricted himself far less than one might have supposed. Anthony West describes his father as a "visualizer," but it seems appropriate instead to invoke that grander and much overused term, a "visionary."

For Wells had an extraordinary eye, both in its venturesomeness (eager to wander off into the future, or out to another planet, or down to the bottom of the sea) and in the keen particularity with which it would abruptly fix upon some singular, telling detail. *The Time Machine* is probably Wells's finest visionary achievement, but all the scientific romances have their moments of glorious sightedness, images apt to linger in the mind long after the characters' names and professions and foibles and difficulties have vanished. What reader could soon forget the picture of an unpeopled London tropically overrun by scarlet Martian plants at the close of *The War of the Worlds*? Or the night journey by rowboat in *The Island of Dr. Moreau*, during which a crewman's eye glints greenly, the reader's first unignorable hint of someone not quite human? These are images that momentarily require us to revise our world—much as Swift (a writer Wells loved and emulated) made us look anew at the nature of time when he gave us Lilliputians of such finely calibrated eyesight they could discern the continuous, minuscule creeping of a clock's hour hand.

As Wells moved into an august middle age, his sense of himself as a messenger and teacher eclipsed what had been most purely artful in his novels, until he reached the point of claiming he'd never been an artist at all, but merely a "journalist." In retrospect, this remark looks like a defensive attempt to exempt himself altogether from the sort of stinging criticisms James had once directed at him. Wells alternately argued, more persuasively, that his work represented efforts to expand the novel, to make it a congenial place for, among other things, the "philosophical dialogue"—and if this pursuit required his characters to "indulge in impossibly explicit monologues and duologues," then he would just have to let the demands of naturalism suffer. Valiant and expansive as his intentions may have been, however, posterity has not regarded the later Wells generously. Nearly everything it has chosen to preserve—the scientific romances, and the "Dickens-Thackeray" comedies like *Tono-Bungay* and *Mr. Polly*—was written early in his career, before his literary falling-out with James, before the arrival of the Great War, and before (perhaps most discouraging of all for this impatient utopian) peace at last returned, bringing with it a widespread, unthinking conviction that business could again go on as usual.

However harshly one views Wells's later work, there is something bracing in the picture of this vigorous old man who was forever dashing off a new manuscript to his publishers. To have written more than a hundred books and still feel, as Wells did at the age of seventy-five, "intolerable impatience lest some unforeseen obstacle should hold up this most urgent and conclusive work," bespeaks an unmatchable capacity for hopefulness. Probably no other author of our century has been so breathtakingly ambitious while managing to make his goals sound rational and perhaps even reachable. When, in 1920, Wells published *The Outline of History* (a book whose astonishing sweep—it begins with our Paleolithic origins and concludes with projections about our future—was arguably grander than that of any volume the world had ever seen), he claimed to have provided "just that general review of reality of which we stood in such manifest need if any permanent political unity was to be sustained in the world." If this talk sounds bold, Wells certainly had justification for it in the book's success: *The Outline of History* was the third greatest seller of its age, surpassed by only the Bible and the Koran. And when it was supplemented in 1930 by *The Science of Life* (in which Wells attempted to set out "everything that an educated man—to be an educated man—ought to know about biological science") and in 1931 by *The Work, Wealth and Happiness of Mankind* (an attempt "to fuse and recast" social, political, and economic science "into one intelligible review of Man upon his planet"), Wells had arguably accomplished one of the most remarkable feats in the history of education. Wells himself, anyway, made an even grander claim: "these three works taken together do, I believe, still give a clearer, fuller and compacter summary of what the normal citizen of the modern state should know, than any other group of books in existence."

And yet the process by which that modern world-state might actually emerge remained nebulous. Wells watched the years go by with gathering alarm. Neither the rigors of the Great Depression nor the widening ravagement of the Second World War appeared to foster among nations any recognition of their common aims and needs. Toward the very end of his life, Wells painfully renounced his seemingly unshakeable optimism. In *Mind at the End of Its Tether,* published the year before he died, he proposed that mankind had no future at all.

Despair had been an intermittent and yet insistent presence in his work all along, but only with the emergence of *H. G. Wells in Love* could the reader clearly see the degree to which Wells could be privately afflicted by darkness while publicly professing optimism. Liberated by the knowledge that this Postscript would appear only posthumously, he gave in to doubts banished from the autobiography; when he speaks of his cherished world-state, he sounds oddly wistful. The Postscript concludes with a chapter called "Shadow of Age: the Suicidal Mood," which Wells inserted and removed from his manuscript numerous times as it sat unpublished over the years. This short chapter offers a touchingly simple portrayal of a man weighted with difficulties he cannot outwardly admit and with a somewhat surprising capacity for self-dislike: "The most conclusive argument for suicide I find in my mind is the conviction of my own unworthiness. . . . Sometimes I realize something in myself so silly, fitful and entirely inadequate to opportunity, that I feel even by my own standards I am not fit to live." Wells ultimately decided to delete this chapter, a decision posthumously overturned by his son G. P. Wells, the editor of *H. G. Wells in Love,* who thought it "too interesting, and too relevant" to conceal forever.

H. G. Wells in Love takes its epigraph from a passing observation in *Experiment in Autobiography:* "This particular brain . . . has arrived at the establishment of the Socialist World-State as its directive purpose and has made that its religion and end. Other systems of feeling and motive run across or with or against the main theme. . . . I suspect the sexual system should be at least the second theme, when it is not the first, in every autobiography, honestly and fully told." The Postscript would redress that imbalance through a candid, serial account of sexual triumphs. The result is a colorful, lively, sometimes shocking, often humorous—and in the end pretty depressing—account. Wells prefaces his chronicle with some characteristically modest doubts. Although never "able to discover whether my interest in sex is more than normal," he is "inclined to think that I have been less obsessed by these desires and imaginations than the average man"—and then plunges into a numbingly long catalogue of sexual conquests. Wells's account of his dealings with women purports to be not merely one man's "particular story" but a "tale of a world of dislocated sexual relations and failure to adjust." It is subtitled "On Loves and the Lover-Shadow," and opens with some scattered and not very original reflections about the essence of desire. Unfortunately, Wells wrote much less movingly about his yearnings for love than about his yearnings for death. (His literary treatment of sex and romance had always been notoriously clumsy, earlier earning him some merciless ribbing from, among others, Rebecca West.) It is remarkable how little, really, the sexual chronicles of this reflective man rise above the personal to regard passion dispassionately. One comes away with a deep sense of muddle, and because Wells proves so unsuccessful in his attempt to go beyond the self's "particular story," he inevitably sounds smug and exhibitionistic—which returns us to the question of Wells's "inverted arrogance."

What is one to make, in the end, of Wells's eagerly modest pronouncements? Can we take them at face value? Would it be unfair to see in the boundless ambition of his books, and in the wayward and gargantuan passions of his life, an underlying arrogance? On the one hand, Wells possessed a largeness of vision, a view of innate human frailty in the face of the universe, which seems to have served as a constant check on his egotism; all human beings in the twentieth century are, he wrote in his autobiography, "like early amphibians . . . struggling out of the waters that have hitherto covered our kind." On the other hand, he obtained a different self-image when he examined himself in relation to his countrymen. He commonly moved among the most successful people of his age, and to find that their perspectives were "narrow"— these "uneducated" authors and "blind" political leaders—touched him with gloating pride.

Wells had good reason to feel proud of his vision. His prophetic powers were often astonishing. When he trained his eye on warfare, he predicted the coming of the armored tank, the revolutionary effects of armed aircraft, and, in 1914, a device of "continuous explosives" that he named the "atom bomb." When he turned his imagination to a world in peace, he foresaw space travel, the supplanting of the book by devices analogous to videocassettes, moving sidewalks, and totalitarian censorship of the news through what he called "Babble Machines." And when one discovers that Wells in 1924 was writing about the need to preserve the whale, one hardly knows whether to applaud his prescience or to despair at how his wisdom has been ignored.

Yet for all his foresight, and insight, that "inevitable" world-state at the core of his vision seemed to grow more unlikely with time—and seems today still more unlikely, as governments continue to fragment and the number of nations to multiply. Wells's faith in the power of rationalism looks more naïve each year. His utopianism was grounded in a conviction that there was not only one single, irreducible Truth in regard to the issues people have always argued most passionately about—religion, ethics, history, sex, property—but that it could in time be discerned by everyone. This grandly didactic man appears unwittingly to have presented us with a life that might serve as a cautionary tale. If even Wells, with all his visionary power, could end up so wrong about the future, what chance do we have today of comprehending where we are headed? Although Wells could not resist occasional boasting, the books he left behind ironically convey another sort of message: they would ask us to be humble.

(1986)

SEARCH FOR THE HUMBLING
Science Biographies

Whoever would write the biography of a scientist shares many obstacles with a poet's biographer. In either case, the life under examination is apt to be largely reflective and sedentary. Like the poet, the scientist will usually move in a narrow circle of fellow obsessives. And both sorts of biography will probably wind up leaving readers with a feeling of incompleteness. When we pick up, instead, a book about a man of action—a military figure, a sports hero—a clear recounting of "what happened" may strike us as sufficient. It is another matter with the scientist, the poet, the artist, the philosopher. Their stories invite a sense of a tale left unfinished, since their central subject—the life of the mind—resists exhaustive treatment.

The science biographer often faces a difficulty, though, that the literary biographer is spared. If he chooses to write for the layman, in all likelihood the accomplishments on which his subject's renown depends will be unavailable to his audience, most of whom will be unable to grasp the complexities involved. Readers must take greatness on faith. It is as though the literary biographer were asked to portray a writer of genius whose works had not yet been published. Three recent science biographies highlight some of the challenges of the genre: Robert Kanigel's *The Man Who Knew Infinity: A Life of the Genius Ramanujan,* Abraham Pais's *Niels Bohr's Times, in Physics, Philosophy, and Polity,* and David C. Cassidy's *Uncertainty: The Life and Science of Werner Heisenberg.*

As it happens, each of these biographers enjoys the benefit of a subject whose life boasts exceptional extrascientific color and event. In the annals of mathematics, where many a curious life-story resides, Srinivasa Ramanujan remains something of a nonpareil. He was born in Erode, India, a county seat some two hundred and fifty miles southwest of Madras, in 1887, to a family of impoverished Brahmins. A college dropout, he was in essence an autodidact. When he was fifteen, a copy of George Shoobridge Carr's *A Synopsis of Elementary Results in Pure and Applied Mathematics* fell into his hands, a skeletal compendium consisting of some five thousand theorems; proofs and commentary were sparsely supplied. Over the next decade, mostly on his own, Ramanujan fleshed out Carr's theorems—analyzing, proving, embellishing—in a series of legendary notebooks which, eight decades later, are still pored over by experts, for both their mathematical insights and their illuminations into the cognitive evolution of the advanced mathematical mind. So penniless that he sometimes could not afford paper for his calculations and was compelled to work on an erasable slate, Ramanujan nonetheless managed to scale heights of such elevation that nobody in India stood qualified to judge the features of his genius—a task all the more problematic because, lacking formal training and a circle of colleagues, Ramanujan fabricated his own idiosyncratic notations and methods. Fortunately, genius did eventually "out," when one of the leading mathematicians of the day, G. H. Hardy of Trinity College, Cambridge, discerned the buried genius in an unconventional manuscript Ramanujan had sent him. The young Indian—Ramanujan was then in his mid-twenties—was invited to England, where in a few years he became the first Indian inducted into the Royal Society and made a Fellow at Trinity. He returned to India in 1919, ailing with tuberculosis, and died a year later, age thirty-three. "The most romantic figure in the recent history of mathematics," according to Hardy, he was someone who "defies almost all the canons by which we are accustomed to judge one another."

Niels Bohr, one of the century's greatest physicists, was born in Copenhagen, in 1885. In 1913 he proposed the first model of the atom which incorporated quantum theory, a breakthrough that Einstein called "an enormous achievement" and that pointed the way to the discovery of quantum mechanics a decade later. In 1921, the University of Copenhagen created for him an Institute of Theoretical Physics, which allowed him to blend successfully the roles of administrator, mentor, and researcher. He was a blend, too, in terms of ancestry. His father, an eminent scientist descended from one of the most distinguished families in Denmark, was Lutheran. His mother, who came from a wealthy, likewise distinguished family of bankers and politicians, was Jewish—a fact that would loom ever larger in her son's life as Europe drifted into the Second World War. Bohr escaped Nazi-occupied

Denmark in 1943, fleeing by night on a fishing boat to Sweden. The following year he was out at Los Alamos, working on the atomic bomb. Increasing misgivings about the threat of nuclear weaponry led him, after the war, to take an active role in advocating the peaceful uses of atomic energy. Over time, he became more and more of a public figure, and merely to glance through the photographs in the Pais volume (Bohr with Einstein, with Churchill, with Nehru, with Buber, with Louis Armstrong, with Queen Elizabeth) is to partake of a life rich in plenty and acclaim.

Werner Heisenberg became in his early twenties a disciple of Bohr's in Copenhagen. He was born in Wurzburg, Germany, in 1901, the son of a classics professor. Shy, athletic, literary, physically brave, musically gifted, he seems to have been widely and loyally liked—no small accomplishment for someone whose precocity (he received the Nobel Prize, for his work on quantum mechanics, at the age of thirty-two) must have everywhere stirred envy. Although Lutheran, he was initially distrusted by the Nazis, in part because his preference for theoretical over experimental physics allied him with Einstein, but they eventually embraced him as someone who might further "deutsche physics" over "Jewish physics." Throughout the war, Heisenberg continued to revere Bohr, whom he visited in Nazi-occupied Copenhagen in 1941. He was, simultaneously, working hard to ensure the extermination of Bohr and his brethren, for by then he'd been put in charge of Germany's atomic research, which included, as early as 1939, when Heisenberg submitted a secret report to the German army, the vision of a bomb whose power "exceeds that of the strongest available explosives by several powers of ten." Had the research proved fruitful, Heisenberg would have gone down in history as the father of the Nazi atomic bomb.

Each of these books has its considerable shortcomings. When dealing with Ramanujan's upbringing, and Eastern spirituality generally, Kanigel—who spent a little over a month in southern India on research—displays the free-summarizing glibness of the recently initiated; if he knew more, he would certainly volunteer less. Pais, who was a close friend of Bohr's, seems to presuppose on the reader's part an intimate acquaintance with his subject; he sounds at times like a speaker at a memorial tribute, pitching his words to Bohr's colleagues and friends. And Cassidy never fully quickens his subject. In particular,

Heisenberg's last decades (which, by rights, ought to be riveting: an amiable genius tardily confronting his deadly collaboration with monsters) are presented as a sketchy and arid affair.

Whatever its deficiencies, each book has its share of wonderful vignettes. Poignancy abounds in the account of Ramanujan's arranged marriage, at the age of twenty-one, to an uneducated girl who was about nine years old; a soul ever in isolation, he was fated to be, by nature of age and education, as far removed from his spouse as, by nature of temperament and upbringing, he was from his English colleagues. Pais's account of Bohr's haunted, affectionate, at times exasperated relationship with Einstein (who could never accept the element of chance and uncertainty in Bohr's conceptualizations; Einstein had Bohr in mind when he issued his famous pronouncement that God "doesn't throw dice") has an Olympian majesty; like the friendly struggles between Apollo and Hermes, this is a rivalry between gods. And Cassidy's account of the English internment camp where Heisenberg, along with other German nuclear physicists, was confined after the Allied victory presents an unforgettably harrowing image: on being informed of the bombing of Hiroshima, the Germans were thunderstruck, devastated—not by sorrow at the carnage, nor by fear of its apocalyptic implications, but by competitive dismay at seeing the Americans succeed where they themselves had failed.

Of course, most scientists do not lead such surpassingly interesting lives as did Ramanujan, Bohr, and Heisenberg, so the appeal of the standard science biography can hardly be laid to its characteristic wealth of anecdote or adventure. Why is it, then, that some of us are drawn to the life-stories of men and women whose supremacy we cannot understand? For readers whose formal scientific education ended, like mine, early in college, I suspect that the genre provides vicarious adventure of a sort akin to that of spectator sports. Just as the armchair athlete glories in the feats of physical bodies whose hurtling poise— muscles drilled to the point where the miraculous finally becomes the instinctual—he can only dimly imagine, so will some readers thrill to accounts of mental gymnastics enacted on a plane that is itself scarcely conceivable.

A tennis-playing friend of mine who had a very successful varsity career and idly considered turning pro offers an instructive anecdote. Later on, when he was in his mid-twenties, he was given some excellent tickets to the U.S. Open. For four years he had competed against some of the best college players in the country, and for much of his life he had, of course, studied world-class players on television. But watching, up close, the absolute monarchs of the game, he discovered a virtuosity he'd never dreamed of. It was not merely that they were enormously better than he'd ever been; they played tennis as he'd never envisioned it could be played. It was for him a salutary, if sobering, moment—one in which the world's potentialities expanded—and I suppose the layman embarks on a science biography in a search for similarly humbling revelations. Some years ago I read a biography of the British mathematician Alan Turing by Andrew Hodges, a book flush with compelling details. (Turing lived a life of heartbreaking heroism: after being assigned by the British government to help crack Nazi intelligence codes, a task whose ultimate success, much of it attributable to Turing, was instrumental in the Allied victory, he was prosecuted by that same government for Gross Indecency—homosexuality—and was eventually subjected to the barbarous "organo-therapy" of hormone injections. He died a suicide.) But what made the most lasting impression on me was a footnote in which the work of another mathematician, S. Skewes, was discussed. Skewes had shown that if the Riemann Hypothesis (which concerns the correlation between the location of immense prime numbers and a "zeta factor") were valid, a change in predicted behavior would occur before $10^{10^{10^{34}}}$. The footnote began: "10^{34} is 10,000,000,000,000,000,000,000,000,000,000,000—a number comparable with the number of elementary particles in the observable universe. But $10^{10^{34}}$ is far bigger; as 1 followed by 10^{34} zeroes it would require all the matter in the universe even to write it out in decimal notation. It could be thought of as the number of all possible universes. Skewes's number was much bigger again, as 1 followed by $10^{10^{34}}$ zeroes!" The notion that on the planet *someone's* life had a place for $10^{10^{10^{34}}}$—found it as handy and practical in his daily work as a mechanic might find a monkey wrench—was, like my friend's experience at the Open, both vertiginous and clarifying. For a moment, the breadth of the world, the full unslakable outflung reach of human exploration and mastery, seemed to stand clear.

．　．　．

The schism between the scientist and the layman is often discussed with reference to the "two cultures"—C. P. Snow's phrase for the disjunction between the scientific and humanistic visions in modern life. Actually, Snow has a particular relevance to one of the books at hand, for his essay was greatly inspired by his intimate ties to Hardy ("intellectually the most valuable friendship of my life," Snow wrote after Hardy's death). Snow's essay laments the "gulf of mutual incomprehension" between the two fields: "The intellectual life of the whole of western society is increasingly being split into two polar groups." But probably of greater significance to the modern reader, who is apt to take this gulf for granted, is the blinding pace of scientific progress since Snow wrote. His essay is relatively recent—it alludes to Sputnik—but in the three decades since its appearance we've seen the emergence of technology of a sort that would have boggled not only Snow but Hardy as well.

In truth, those of us who are not scientists, who come to the science biography with an outsider's curiosity and awe, sometimes may feel that the cultures are not quite as "two" as we'd like. Uneasiness may arise not so much from the two cultures' separation as from the one-sidedness of their commerce; more and more, science impinges on what was thought to be the artist's domain. The computer generates the images in the animated films our children watch; machines supply the percussion to the music on our radios; metal boxes compose chess solutions whose elegance confounds the grandmaster. One would like to suppose that influence moves both ways, but technology seems to roll forward in juggernaut fashion, almost independent of social and artistic trends, philosophical qualms and queries. There is something alluring to power so encompassing, needless to say, and the quasi-scientific dress of so much recent literary criticism (for Snow, the "literary intellectual" was the very epitome of humanistic thought) hints at a grudging admiration and envy of the hard sciences. (Interestingly, even at its most opaque, much current literary theory tacitly embraces the notion of progress in criticism—the belief that "advances" are being made that render earlier interpretations obsolete. If there is no progress in art, as Hazlitt suggested, there is a pervasive faith in the progress of art criticism.)

A stunning example of the unexpected spread and penetration of scientific discovery is to be seen in the recountings of the development of quantum mechanics in the Bohr and Heisenberg biographies. If the building blocks of the theory—the Zeeman effect in spectroscopy, anharmonic oscillators, matrix mechanics—lie well beyond the layman's grasp, the theory's long-reaching implications are made powerfully apparent. Bohr and Heisenberg became convinced that the combination of Heisenberg's famous "uncertainty" article of 1927 and Bohr's "complementarity" theory evolved later that same year must alter every thinking person's vision of reality. They believed that the indeterminacy at the core of their theories—specifically, the ultimate unknowability of certain aspects of electron behavior—undermined orthodox assumptions about causality. The links that bound *any* event to its successor would have to be refigured. In particular, they felt that they had dislodged a cornerstone in Kant's philosophy, which had taken causality as one of its a priori principles.

That an investigator of subatomic particles might upend Kantian philosophy is a heady thought. But more dizzying still is the notion that a giant philosopher might be tumbled by somebody whose mind was not fixed on philosophy. Whether or not Bohr's grander speculations were sound, he offers us the prospect of a world in which answers to timeless philosophical questions arrive as mere by-products of a scientist's "real" work.

If Bohr and Heisenberg embody the limitless incursions of science, Ramanujan evokes a contrary, somewhat comforting sense of its possible boundaries. There can be no doubting that mathematics was the cardinal passion of his life. In its pursuit he forsook his native India and his wife and family in order to study in a country whose food he abominated, whose social hierarchy and racial prejudices continually balked him, and whose damp and dark and chilly weather oppressed him. (The heat of southern India had left him so unprepared for English weather that, months after his arrival, he still had no idea what blankets were for; wrapped in an overcoat, shivering fiercely, he'd been sleeping upon rather than under them.) Yet even as he sacrificed his social life and in many ways his happiness to the furtherance of mathematical thought, Ramanujan—who dabbled in palmistry, astrology, and psychic phenomena—harbored intimations of something still more magnificent behind it, of which numbers were but a pallid offshoot: he once said that an equation has no meaning unless "it expresses a thought of God."

Brilliance alone is hardly enough to ensure a mathematician's fame among laymen, a point memorably made by the mathematician Alfred Adler two decades ago:

> For example, it would be astonishing if the reader could identify more than two of the following names: Gauss, Cauchy, Euler, Hilbert, Riemann. It would be equally astonishing if he should be unfamiliar with the names of Mann, Stravinsky, de Kooning, Pasteur, John Dewey. The point is not that the first five are the mathematical equivalents of the second five. They are not. They are the mathematical equivalents of Tolstoy, Beethoven, Rembrandt, Darwin, Freud. . . . All professions reward accomplishment in part with admiration by peers, but mathematics can reward it with admiration of no other kind.

Those mathematicians who do manage to reach a wider public are likely to do so because their achievements easily lend themselves to some accessible, useful metaphor. A reader of novels is hardly surprised when Lawrence Durrell, in a note to his *Alexandria Quartet,* cites Einstein as a guiding inspiration; whether or not Durrell had mastered relativity theory, he shared with the public at large an Einstein who symbolized the impossibility of the artist's establishing any reliable, sure point of vantage—the lack of (in the words of the poet May Swenson) any "hitching post" in the universe. Similarly, Heisenberg's uncertainty principle, which proposed that the would-be observer of electron behavior inevitably skews the world he would observe, operates as a cautionary metaphor for the journalist, the psychiatrist, the anthropologist, the poll-taker, the documentary filmmaker—all of whom must worry that their attempts to probe at the truth unavoidably alter the truth. Of course, for every Einstein or Heisenberg there will be legions of others whose titanic feats of intellection do not happen to lend themselves to simple analogy or explanation. They and their triumphs must forever dwell apart from the rest of us.

This point was strikingly illustrated ten years ago, when Gerd Faltings, a West German mathematician at Wuppertal University, proved a conjecture that had bedeviled mathematicians around the world for

six decades. Working on his own, he made a discovery of such commanding brilliance that articles about him appeared in the New York
Times, the Los Angeles *Times, Newsweek*—in papers and periodicals
around the world, no doubt. But the forty-page proof (he verified what
is known as the Mordell conjecture, which asserts that most polynomial
equations higher than the third degree have only a finite number of
rational solutions) was of so specialized a nature that—so the bedazzled
layman was informed—it was difficult even for other mathematicians
to follow, save those thoroughly versed in algebraic geometry. A subtle
appreciation of what he had accomplished was restricted to a minuscule subset of a minuscule subset—those professional mathematicians
whose area of expertise overlapped Faltings'.

The distance which the layman feels from the scientist—especially
the mathematician—is occasionally enhanced by pronouncements that
make plain that words are, in comparison to mathematical symbols, a
substandard mode of discourse. Late in his career, Ramanujan's friend
Hardy composed a brief, deft volume, *Apology of a Mathematician,*
which is sometimes spoken of as a classic. It's an appealing meditation,
which acknowledges gratefully but with a sense of their subservience
the role that friendship and family have held for a man who has given
his all to mathematics. In the light of his priorities, the production of
even so charming a book must be treated as an admission of failure:

> It is a melancholy experience for a professional mathematician to find
> himself writing about mathematics. The function of a mathematician is
> to do something, to prove new theorems, to add to mathematics, and
> not to talk about what he or other mathematicians have done. . . . Expo-
> sition, criticism, appreciation, is work for second-rate minds.

He has turned to a general audience only because "like any other mathematician who has passed sixty, I have no longer the freshness of mind,
the energy, or the patience to carry on effectively with my proper job."
Needless to say, there is something both beguiling and disconcerting in
the dolor of a man who finds, his powers dimming, that he must live
and speak with the rest of us.

Having first dismissed himself as not "competent" to evaluate such
matters, Hardy modestly addresses the question of "mathematical real-

ity"—whether it is "mental" or "outside and independent of us." He comes down in the latter camp: "Pure mathematics, on the other hand, seems to me a rock on which all idealism founders: 317 is a prime, not because we think so, or because our minds are shaped in one way rather than another, but *because it is so*." Yet he acknowledges that his devotion to the field is unconnected to such philosophical issues. It is passion—a keen aesthetic ardor—that has always driven him on. "Beauty is the first test: there is no permanent place in the world for ugly mathematics."

If mathematics has no extrahuman existence, one must yet marvel at the boundary-crossing universality of its appeal. Bohr and Heisenberg recognized between themselves a core brotherhood, though when the war came down they ended up effectively working for the other's annihilation. And what could have been a more unlikely alliance than that between Hardy and Ramanujan—the urbane don, born for Trinity High Table and the cricket pavilion, and the pudgy impoverished Indian who, adhering faithfully to his Brahmin dietary proscriptions, could be found night after night cooking his lentils over a gas burner? Theirs was a friendship that seems rarely, if ever, to have broached any serious discussions of religion, sexuality (the evidence suggests that Hardy was, in the words of a close colleague, a "non-practicing homosexual"), or even upbringing. Why grant time to such ephemera? Didn't the two of them share a proficiency with modular equations, infinite series, partitions and congruences, highly composite numbers? And if phenomena such as these were not in some ulterior sense "real," they served nonetheless as an illusion of breathtaking fecundity—one capable of infusing the spirit with wonderment, beauty, entertainment, sustenance.

(1992)

NO LOYALTY TO DNA
Hans Moravec's *Mind Children*

Queer happenings are afoot in the tree of life. That's the message one gets, in any case, from Hans Moravec's *Mind Children: The Future of Robot and Human Intelligence.* At a time when many science books for the layman document the steady pruning of life's tree—the dwindling of plant and animal species through environmental spoliation—Moravec focusses on a prospective branching out: the emergence of new life-forms that soon will, he feels quite certain, "mature into entities as complex as ourselves." He is asking us, in effect, to transform our taxonomy at the roots. No longer would the complementary kingdoms of plants and animals represent the primary division; he foresees a still more fundamental bifurcation—that between what might be called the empire of organic life and the empire of inorganic life. We are about to enter a "postbiological" world. Imminently—perhaps within the lifetimes of our children—robots of such advanced capabilities will emerge that "our DNA will find itself out of a job, having lost the evolutionary race to a new kind of competition."

As a genre, the popular science book boasts a number of distinctive traits, several of which are present in *Mind Children.* Books about rapidly developing technology can often seem undeservedly cheerful, and at various points Moravec might be faulted for scanting the darker psychological and moral implications of the vision he conjures up. He brings to his subject both the natural optimism of the technician whose field is mushrooming before his eyes and the belief—which seems to keep creeping in, despite his express disavowals of it—that technology will necessarily save us from technology. *Mind Children* also illustrates, as books of the genre commonly do, that the modern proliferation of research effectively makes each of us—scientist and nonscientist alike—a layman; as knowledge expands breathtakingly, in every direction, even the scientist must greet most discoveries with head-shaking incomprehension. Although one's primary reason for picking up a book like *Mind Children* may be to get a grip on a burgeoning new field, one is probably also hoping to throw off some of the dazzled numbness that comes of living in a technologically explosive age. Doubtless many readers who turn regularly to the best science popularizers—to authors like Loren Eiseley and Stephen Jay Gould and Paul Colinvaux and Douglas Hofstadter—do so to combat this numbness; the reader seeks the haphazard saving moment when an impossibly distant object or an unthinkably complex equation comes alive.

Another characteristic of the genre is that the guilt one feels toward unread books diminishes on a steady, almost graphable basis. The reader who buys but fails to open, say, *The Tale of Genji* or *Njal's Saga* or Hobbes's *Leviathan* or Boswell's *Life of Johnson* introduces into his home a durable source of guilt; such books are classics, and they reproach us unremittingly as long as they remain unread. But the reader who buys the latest volume on artificial intelligence or quantum theory or paleontology or black holes knows that with each passing month its urgency will fade; within a few years, it will make no claim whatsoever, since by then it can safely be deemed out of date. One would be making a mistake, though, to let *Mind Children* recede unopened into a guiltless oblivion. It's a tonic book, thought-provoking on every page. And it reminds us that, in our accelerating, headlong era, the future presses so close upon us that those who ignore it inhabit not the present but the past.

Hans Moravec, who is the director of the Mobile Robot Laboratory of Carnegie-Mellon University, possesses a lucid, reassuringly commonsensical style and a flair for analogical simplification which together make the recondite seem approachable and the revolutionary plausible. Ever since completing his graduate training at the Stanford Artificial Intelligence Laboratory almost a decade ago, he has concentrated on robot locomotion and vision, and he devotes part of the initial chapter of *Mind Children* to a detailing of the difficulties inherent in any attempt to endow a robot with sight. The theoretically simple business of "hooking up" a computer to television equipment proves fiendishly complex in practice. The field of robotics is, in fact, full of unexpected reversals. Tasks that look elementary often prove formidable. In general, scientists have had a much easier time teaching a robot to perform the "higher" functions that formerly belonged solely to human beings (reading, proving theorems, diagnosing diseases) than the "lower" functions that animals have mastered (hearing, seeing, grasping objects). Improbably enough, a robot is more easily taught to play expert chess than to move the pieces.

As Moravec points out, there are evolutionary reasons for the higher being more accessible than the lower: "Encoded in the large, highly evolved sensory and motor portions of the human brain is a billion years of experience about the nature of the world and how to survive in it. The deliberate process we call reasoning is, I believe, the thinnest veneer of human thought, effective only because it is supported by this much older and much more powerful, though usually unconscious, sensorimotor knowledge." Given the irregularities and uncertainties of terrain outside the laboratory, freewheeling movement is not merely tricky but often hazardous for a robot. The monumentality of the programmer's task becomes evident when one considers that a truly flexible and autonomous robot would have to have enough of what researchers call "world knowledge" to translate all relevant physical conditions—every shifting object, every stray obstacle—into the strings of binary numbers which are its language of operation.

So thoroughgoing and convincing is Moravec on the subject of the complexities of robot movement that one comes away from his early pages feeling that the goal of autonomy is almost insurmountable— and also feeling that in the face of such a sober-minded assessment one must treat even the most outlandish of his subsequent predictions with respect. In its less than two hundred pages of text, the book undertakes quite a journey. By its close, the reader has met robots that can go on risky vacations for vicariously adventurous human beings, "protein robots" so minuscule that they can assemble machinery molecule by molecule, even robots that can construct other robots in factories out in the asteroid belt.

Near the start, while discussing some of the ways in which a mechanical object could be programmed to behave like a human being, Moravec takes an intellectual sidestep. "The conditioning software I have in mind would receive two kinds of messages from anywhere within the robot, one telling of success, the other of trouble," he begins. "I'm going to call the success messages 'pleasure' and the danger messages 'pain.' Pain would tend to interrupt the activity in progress, while pleasure would increase its probability of continuing." But once he has dropped the quotation marks around "pleasure" and "pain" he treats the terms as though each was genuinely synonymous in its robotic and its human applications. He acknowledges no potential confusion when describing machines in emotive language: "Modules that recognize other conditions and send pain or pleasure messages of appropriate strength would endow a robot with a unique character. A large, dangerous robot with a human-presence detector sending a pain signal would become shy of human beings and thus be less likely to cause injury." In short, he appears to accept as a given the hypothesis that the mind is merely a kind of machine—one whose meditations and commands are ultimately duplicable by other, inorganic machinery—and thereby finesses a question that lies at the core of current debate in the field of artificial intelligence: is there any area of human activity which is obdurately, permanently inaccessible to machines? Moravec, who once remarked that he has "no loyalty to DNA," may be sound in assuming an underlying identicalness between the human mind and the machine (most experts in the field would probably agree with him), but he was unwise in choosing to pass over so fertile and significant a controversy. Readers who look elsewhere for discussion of the subject—perhaps to the contentious essays assembled in *The Artificial Intelligence Debate,* a collection edited by Stephen R. Graubard—will likely encounter a tangle of human emotions, including skepticism, anger, foreboding, and indignation, that are all but missing in Moravec's expansive, self-assured projections.

But readers who are willing to go along with him, at least temporarily, on the issue of duplicability—something which the patent joy he derives from speculation invites one to do—will find that his arguments proceed with a sureness that verges on the inexorable. Attempting to place the modern computer in historical perspective, he ventures back a hundred years to examine Herman Hollerith's punch-card tabulator (a device that eventually became a sort of founding father of IBM), and he concludes that since the beginning of the century "there has been a *trillionfold* increase in the amount of computation a dollar will buy." He estimates that in terms of computational power the largest of the present-day supercomputers "are a match for the 1-gram brain of a mouse," but that in time we may be able to build machines that operate at a million million million million million (10^{30}) times the power of a human mind. What can one say in response to such a number? If duplicability is possible, is it not inevitable? And even if we assume that it is *not* possible, how can we deny that machines of such unreckonable energies would not be capable of a rich and ranging inner life of their own?

Isn't it only a matter of time, Moravec asks, before we can transfer, or "download," our minds into computers? Copies could then be made of copies and stored in separate, secure places, not all of them on the earth—a procedure that would virtually ensure our immortality. He foresees a number of ways in which downloading might take place. A person could wear each day a miniaturized observational device whose data, compiled over years and years, would serve as the memory bank of a new intellect. Or you might enter a hospital for brain surgery to be performed by a robot whose hands are microscopically precise and whose command of speech allows the two of you to proceed collaboratively. Since the brain registers no pain when it is subjected to an incision, you could be fully conscious during the entire operation. Equipped with an encyclopedic understanding of human neural architecture, and proceeding millimeter by millimeter, the robot surgeon would develop a program that would model the behavior of a discrete layer of brain tissue. This program would produce signals equivalent to those flashing among the neurons in the area under scrutiny, and a series of cables would allow the robot to create "simulations," in which the program is substituted for the layer of brain tissue. The simulation process would be analogous to what's now available in sophisticated audio shops, where a customer can test and compare components at the push of a button and without breaking the flow of the music:

> To further assure you of the simulation's correctness, you are given a pushbutton that allows you to momentarily "test drive" the simulation, to compare it with the functioning of the original tissue. When you press it, arrays of electrodes in the surgeon's hand are activated. By precise injections of current and electromagnetic pulses, the electrodes can override the normal signalling activity of nearby neurons. . . . As long as you press the button, a small part of your nervous system is being replaced by a computer simulation of itself. You press the button, release it, and press it again. You should experience no difference. As soon as you are satisfied, the simulation connection is established permanently.

The brain tissue is now impotent—it receives inputs and reacts as before but its output is ignored. Microscopic manipulators on the hand's surface excise the cells in this superfluous tissue and pass them to an aspirator, where they are drawn away. . . . Eventually your skull is empty, and the surgeon's hand rests deep in your brainstem. Though you have not lost consciousness, or even your train of thought, your mind has been removed from the brain and transferred to a machine.

A slower and seemingly less traumatic transfer might be achieved by installing in the corpus callosum—the main cable that unites the brain hemispheres—a microscopic monitor linked to a computer that would "eavesdrop" in order to make a model of your mental activities:

> After a while it begins to insert its own messages into the flow, gradually insinuating itself into your thinking, endowing you with new knowledge and new skills. In time, as your original brain faded away with age, the computer would smoothly assume the lost functions. Ultimately your brain would die, and your mind would find itself entirely in the computer.

Any such event would compel a further modification in our taxonomy. The distinction between organic and inorganic life—and, indeed, all the subdistinctions by which a species is fitted into a unique biological niche—would dissolve. Although Moravec has disappointingly little to say about religion, his ultimate vision incarnates widespread theological convictions about the "oneness" of all life:

> Mind transferral need not be limited to human beings. Earth has other species with large brains, from dolphins, whose nervous systems are as large and complex as our own, to elephants . . . and perhaps giant squid, whose brains may range up to twenty times as big as ours. Just what kind of minds and cultures these animals possess is still a matter of controversy, but their evolutionary history is as long as ours, and there is surely much unique and hard-won information encoded genetically in their brain structures and their memories.
>
> Our speculation ends in a supercivilization, the synthesis of all solar-system life, constantly improving and extending itself, spreading outward from the sun, converting nonlife into mind.

Actually, Moravec might plausibly contend that conventional theological debate is hardly germane to his argument. If he is mistaken about human duplicability, most of his projections at once reveal themselves as pipe dreams that connect only remotely and hypothetically with religious issues. And if, on the other hand, he is correct in supposing that human minds will be transferred into or otherwise fused with machines, it seems likely that traditional religious questions—and even the traditional religions themselves—will either melt away or suffer wholesale metamorphosis. Debates about Heaven and Hell—to take but one example—would hold little relevance for an immortal creature. One wishes, however, that he had accorded greater space to psychological considerations. Many people experience an instinctive unease at the incursions of the mechanical—a feeling concisely summed up by Emerson a century ago: "Machinery is aggressive." And although such people might reconcile themselves in time to the notion of a man/machine cohabitation—most of us, in the course of modern life, have already grown used to hearing computers speak to us—the conviction that there is something innately "special" about human beings would surely die hard, and at great cost.

The modern scientist and his offspring are often likened to Mary Shelley's Victor Frankenstein and his monster, but the nineteenth-century novel that Moravec most vividly evokes is Stevenson's *Dr. Jekyll and Mr. Hyde*. In a document found at his death, Dr. Henry Jekyll explained how, troubled by the "polar twins" that dwelt in his "agonised womb of consciousness," he conceived the prospect of a sweet divorce: "If each, I told myself, could be housed in separate identities, life would be relieved of all that was unbearable." These words are echoed in Moravec's prologue: "In the present condition we are uncomfortable halfbreeds, part biology, part culture, with many of our biological traits out of step with the invention of our minds. . . . It is easy to imagine human thought freed from bondage to a mortal body." *Mind Children* makes light of the possibility that a deathless human being is not a human being at all—that the condition of mortality so informs our lives as to render them unrecognizable without it. It may be (to pose a paradox of a sort that Moravec himself might relish) that on the day when man makes himself immortal he makes himself extinct. The future that Moravec sees is certainly one in which "timeless" truths—the eternal verities of the poet—are set on their ear. Algernon Swinburne observed that "All men born are mortal but not man." Moravec everts this dictum: in his world, the individual would become deathless, but man in the aggregate—that species whose hopes and expectations have been framed in the phrase "threescore years and ten"—would vanish.

One has to wonder how the art that we have safeguarded throughout the centuries would survive the transformation. Whether one is listening to Hamlet speculate on the bourn from which none return or contemplating a ukiyo-e print of rice harvesters or reading *Gilgamesh,* the appreciation of any work of art generally requires us to cross a gulf—both geographical and temporal—on the bridge of our kindred uncertainty and helplessness in the face of death. Any art that might be fabricated in Moravec's new world would be composed, in effect, in a new language. Without question, it would be extraordinary. But surely much of what we now revere would suffer in translation.

Readers who are curious about Hans Moravec, and long for greater personal detail than is provided in *Mind Children,* will find him in fine form, witty and engaging and professorially eccentric (a favorite snack is Cheerios topped with bananas and chocolate milk), in Grant Fjermedal's *The Tomorrow Makers,* whose subtitle is *A Brave New World of Living-Brain Machines.* In pursuit of his book, Fjermedal spent a number of clearly quite exhilarating months in this country and Japan, drifting from one artificial-intelligence center to another and meeting a wide range of individuals who, for all their singularities, seem to share a penchant for working all night and sleeping catch as catch can on the morrow. And who share, as well, a daily, ingrained perception that the intertwined evolution of man and machine—of which downloading might be regarded as the apotheosis—is steadily speeding us toward an alien world.

Even readers who view the prospect of downloading with confident disbelief or squeamish distaste will appreciate the poignance that at present suffuses the field. A number of researchers have come to believe that they were born just a little too early—that the immortality toward which their collective efforts are reaching will not be attained soon enough. For them, death is an ailment that will not be cured in their lifetimes. Fjermedal quotes one researcher as saying, "Everyone would like to be immortal. I don't think the time is quite right. But it's close. It isn't very long from now. I'm afraid, unfortunately, that I'm the last generation to die."

According to Moravec, however, such pronouncements are unduly pessimistic and final. He speculates that by dint of a gathering mastery of a range of disciplines, including history, genetics, anthropology, and computer simulation, much that has disappeared may prove retrievable. Having effaced so many familiar categories, the future will eventually soften even the distinction between itself and the past. Time will turn ductile:

> Now, imagine an immense simulator (I imagine it made out of a super-dense neutron star) that can model the whole surface of the earth on an atomic scale and can run time forward and back and produce different plausible outcomes by making different random choices at key points in its calculation. Because of the great detail, this simulator models living things, including humans, in their full complexity. . . . Such simulated people would be as real as you or me, though imprisoned in the simulator.
>
> We could "download" our minds directly into a body in the simulation and "upload" back into the real world when our mission is accomplished. Alternatively, we could bring people out of the simulation by reversing the process—linking their minds to an outside robot body, or uploading them directly into it. In all cases we would have the opportunity to re-create the past and to interact with it in a real and direct fashion.

When that day comes, we will have a choice about which pasts we want to consign to the past and which we will summon to accompany us into the future. In the meantime, though, the reader is left to wonder what the human cost would be of never losing anything.

(1989)

PROSE PROSODIST
Italo Calvino's *Mr. Palomar*

In the courtroom of the literary journal, book reviewers should rarely
be permitted to plead the ineffable. As a general rule of advocacy, paragraphs that begin *It is impossible to describe the pleasures of* . . . or *No mere
summation can* . . . should be strictly debarred. And yet what *is* a re-
viewer to do with a writer like Italo Calvino, whose books with such
fine, lawless abandon seem to leap free of all critical regimentation,
eluding equally any easy condensation or categorization?

How, for example, is one to do justice to a book like *Cosmicomics*
(1965), that endlessly inventive re-creation of our myths of Creation,
whose main character, one Qfwfq by name, remembers the passing of
the dinosaurs? One might matter-of-factly call it the sort of book that
contains a sparklingly comic domestic argument taking place moments
before the solar system is born and an affecting account of the first
queasy stirrings of love in a Carboniferous protoreptile. But this is only
a covert variation on the ineffability plea.

Of course, to be tongue-tied can itself prove a pleasure, particularly
in regard to an author who wrote at such eloquent length about the
meanings and richnesses of silence. Those same complexities that make
his work so difficult to describe are often what make it so rewarding
to read. And a state of quiet gratitude might seem especially appropriate
now, so soon after his death, which came on September 19, 1985, at
the age of sixty-one—the result of a stroke that had left him in a coma
for a week. But while his passing should be cause for universal mourn-
ing, his many books—now that he has slipped into a silence that does
indeed look eloquent—call anew for celebration.

The special difficulties that a critic encounters with Calvino are only
enhanced in the case of *Mr. Palomar,* the last of his novels, published in

America in the month of his death. Whenever an author dies prematurely and unexpectedly, his last work is often lent a wholly extrinsic and yet all-but-ineradicable sense of fatefulness. We're likely to detect everywhere in its pages premonitions of mortality and attempts at a final summing up. And yet even while a conscientious reader will resist such temptations, *Mr. Palomar*'s hints of a ghostly prescience are not easily dismissed. Its last chapter is entitled "Learning to Be Dead." The book has an autumnal, conclusive feel arising from more than the mere timing of its appearance. Although Calvino during the last years of his life remained both an unflaggingly vigorous writer and a man apparently blessed with sound physical health, the book echoes with the tolling tones of a last will and testament.

The Mr. (first name unknown) Palomar of *Mr. Palomar* provides a puzzling hero to a puzzling book. We learn nothing about his origins, and of his last name only that "perhaps because he bears the same name as a famous observatory, [he] can boast some friendships among astronomers." Little else about him can be confidently stated. One can say with certainty that he is thoughtful, quiet, and inquisitive (especially about the natural world), and with near-certainty that he is regarded as kindly and absentminded by those around him. One learns in the book's 126 pages almost nothing about Palomar's marriage or his past, the aims behind his travels (he seems to spend most of his time in Rome, but is also found in Paris and Barcelona and Kyoto), or the means by which he pays the bills. The book consists of a series of short reflections that might be called essays. At times, especially when Palomar as a physical presence retreats to the periphery (in the chapter entitled "Moon in the Afternoon," a lovely meditation on what our dream-haunted moon undergoes when exposed to the rational light of day, he appears only in the last sentence), we might almost have stepped into a fine collection of popular scientific essays. We are not far from the work of Stephen Jay Gould or Loren Eiseley.

In the first of the book's short chapters, Mr. Palomar stands on a beach contemplating the flow of the sea. He himself would deny that his activity is anything so grand as contemplation, which for Palomar requires the "right temperament, the right mood, and the right combination of exterior circumstances." No, he is merely "looking." (To that brief list of adjectives which describe Palomar, one might add "modest" and "circumspect.") His goal, as he peers at the sea, would appear simple enough. He wishes merely to isolate one wave from the rest and to follow its progress until it collapses on the shore. This goal proves troublesome, however, for Mr. Palomar finds it difficult to separate one wave from another. The sea presents no clear boundaries. What Mr. Palomar seems to be reflecting upon is the age-old, and still unresolved, question of whether time is continuous or discrete—whether time proceeds as an indivisible continuum or, like film projected onto a screen, in a series of imperceptibly short frames. Toward the end of the chapter, the correspondence between oceanic and chronological motions is made explicit:

> In addition, the reflux of every wave also has a power of its own that hinders the oncoming waves. And if you concentrate your attention on these backward thrusts, it seems that the true movement is the one that begins from the shore and goes out to sea.
>
> Is this perhaps the real result that Mr. Palomar is about to achieve? To make the waves run in the opposite direction, to overturn time, to perceive the true substance of the world beyond sensory and mental habits? No, he feels a slight dizziness, but it goes no further than that.

This tinge of vertigo is characteristic of Palomar, a man whose psyche trembles at the edge of what may be either illumination or dissolution—one cannot say for certain. Meditation seems to be a hazardous undertaking in, as Palomar defines our age, "the era of great numbers." Whether he seeks to isolate a single wave, or to comprehend the essence of a plot of grass, his hunt for a narrow and secure base from which to observe the larger universe—a search for "the key to mastering the world's complexity by reducing it to its simplest mechanism"—inevitably founders. He never finds anything solid and simple enough to serve as his observational base. It is Palomar's blessing and hardship to perceive always the underlying intricacy that any apparent simplicity masks, to move through life with a preternaturally, almost microscopically, sharp eye that is forever turning up tiny, subtle individualities.

Calvino chose well in opening his final novel at the seashore, for the flow of Palomar's mind might also be described as wavelike. Again and again in the book's succeeding chapters, the reader witnesses a gathering of cerebral energies, a push and fling at some resistant object, a dispersion and a regathering; to Mr. Palomar, a man whose mental energy seems boundless, a retreat is merely the preparation for another advance. As the currents of Palomar's thinking begin in time to grow familiar, the reader no longer regrets knowing so little about his marriage or his past. For all of Palomar's sketchiness as a fictional character, one begins to recognize how his mind works—and given the supernal regions in which Palomar spends so much of his time, this is actually to feel one knows him rather well.

He is a man whose search for self-knowledge begins outside himself. He instinctively looks to the natural world for illumination of his own interior. The little chapter entitled "The Gecko's Belly," for example, presents a lizard in such detailed, anatomical precision that the reader never feels the gecko has been chosen as a mere symbol; the creature is clearly regarded as a marvel in itself. Yet the chapter is equally an attempt to come to terms with the cold-blooded reptile in oneself.

Although a reader can scarcely be expected to detect it on a first reading, the book's far-flung reflections are in fact fitted around an extraordinarily intricate, architectonic scheme—as Calvino reveals in a curiously curt note at the close of the volume. *Mr. Palomar* is composed on a system of triads within triads. Each of its three main sections ("Mr. Palomar's Vacation," "Mr. Palomar in the City," and "The Silences of Mr. Palomar") contains three subsections, which themselves are each composed of three subsections. The first element within any particular triad focusses upon some visual experience; the second, upon some cultural or linguistic phenomenon; and the third, upon "more speculative experience, concerning the cosmos, time, infinity, the relationship between the self and the world, the dimensions of the mind." In its tiered intricacy, and in its prominent and thematic use of numbers, *Mr. Palomar* may remind readers of the marvellous *Invisible Cities* (1972), the seventh of Calvino's books to be translated into English, but the first to win him a solid reputation in America.

The complicated patterns of so many of Calvino's fictions resist description largely because the art of prose fiction, unlike that of poetry, supplies the critic with so few fixed forms that might serve for either an analogy or a departure point. Where are the prose forms that would correspond to the sonnet, the villanelle, the rondeau, the pantoum, to blank verse and ottava rima and the Rubáiyát stanza? Certainly the language of versification, despite its egregious clumsiness (the result of its ancestry in classical poetry systems that have little in common with ours), provides a range of analytical methods and expectations subtler than anything found in the lexicon of fiction criticism. Italo Calvino's career, particularly in its last years, might well be viewed as an ongoing attempt to create a compendium of useful new prose forms. One might call him a prose prosodist. The peculiar structure of *Invisible Cities,* for example (with its identical stanzalike blocks or sections, its strict pattern of predictable repetitions, and a newness emerging each time from within the block), might be seen as a kind of hybrid prose counterpart to poetry's sestina and terza rima—both Italian inventions, happily enough.

Yet the formal intricacies of *Mr. Palomar* somehow enrich the book less than one would hope. The beauty of its overarching symmetries does not quite manage to perfuse the lowest level of the text, where one sentence follows another. Structurally, the book remains something of a cool tour de force. This failure is only in part a result of a scheme of organization so unobtrusive that the reader may not initially perceive it. Even on a rereading, *Mr. Palomar* lacks the reciprocal magic (present in earlier volumes like *If on a winter's night a traveler,* or *Cosmicomics,* or *Invisible Cities)* by which, somehow, rich complexities of form create complex richnesses of content. On the other hand, *Mr. Palomar* is clearly not intended, as those earlier books were, to boast any such strict interconnectedness. Much of the book's considerable charm lies in its air of freedom, which allows Calvino to drift a bit, to sail on the waves of Palomar's thinking.

Freedom of this sort naturally carries artistic risks. Because each of the book's little meditations stands in some isolation, there is always a danger that *Mr. Palomar* will abruptly go slack. And in truth a few of the meditations are disappointing: here and there, Calvino slides into predictability, and reflections that were obviously intended to be delicate look merely thin. But the best of Palomar's observations are haunting, and in ways not apt to be found in either a good natural history essayist (who almost certainly will lack Calvino's poetic and imaginational powers) or a good fiction writer (who is unlikely to match Calvino's openness to the animal and the mineral world). It is a rare and admirable sensibility that could envision an iguana in this way:

Then there are other spiky crests under the chin; on the neck there are two round white plates like a hearing aid; a number of accessories and sundries, trimmings, and defensive garnishings, a sample case of forms available in the animal kingdom and perhaps also in other kingdoms— too much stuff for one animal to bear. What's the use of it? Does it serve to disguise someone watching us from in there?

But it is a still rarer mind that, beginning with these acute, good-tempered observations, could proceed by means of a powerful induction to a lovely judgment on the meaning of life itself:

> Life in the reptile house appears a squandering of forms without style and without plan, where all is possible, and animals and plants and rocks exchange scales, quills, concretions. But among the infinite possible combinations, only some—perhaps actually the most incredible—become fixed, resist the flux that undoes them and mixes and reshapes; and immediately each of these forms becomes the center of a world separated forever from the others, as here in the row of glass case-cages of the zoo; and in this finite number of ways of being, each identified in a monstrosity of its own, and a necessity and beauty of its own, lies order, the sole order recognizable in the world.

The ultimate subject of Italo Calvino's final novel is the universe— which, as Mr. Palomar himself might point out, can make quite an interesting subject.

In "On Italo Calvino," Gore Vidal took issue with *Time* magazine's characterization of Calvino as a "surrealist." Calvino "was, of course, a true realist," Vidal argued, and quoted from a television interview Calvino gave in the last months of his life:

> Only a certain prosaic solidity can give birth to creativity: fantasy is like jam; you have to spread it on a solid slice of bread. If not, it remains a shapeless thing, like jam, out of which you can't make anything.

There's something to Mr. Vidal's contention, although to speak of a writer as a realist in whose pages Marco Polo laments the impersonality of airports and sailors in ships equipped with tall ladders harvest "lunar cheese" may seem to twist realism out of recognition. I would add, then, that this fussing over literary categories—usually the most sterile and logomachous of academic exercises—serves a worthy purpose in

Calvino's case. His work is most fully appreciated when examined beside our notions of what realistic fiction consists of.

For many of us, literary realism is inseparably bound up with portrayals of poverty. In many ways, this is doubtless a good thing—in a world in which people starve for lack of a few dollars, we need constant reminders of the hardships some encounter in their search for a raw livelihood. If the notion that the poor are "realer" than the rich is an illusion, it's one we abandon only at our ethical peril. On the other hand, this is a conception of realism that ultimately restricts our vision.

Italo Calvino, that fabulist whose final hero, Mr. Palomar, seems to live in a detached and privileged world in which money and the constrictions of indigence hardly exist, earlier in his career wrote hauntingly about the poor. Many of his first stories, composed in the late forties and early fifties and collected in English as *Difficult Loves* and *Adam, One Afternoon,* offer wrenching visions of need and scarcity. Even more harrowing in many ways is *Marcovaldo,* which paints a ferociously claustrophobic portrait of the life of an unskilled Italian factory worker.

Yet this is a claustrophobia continually eased by an author whose antic imagination delights in undoing realism's tight conventions. When a rooftop avalanche of melting snow so thoroughly buries Marcovaldo that he is taken for a snowman by a group of passing children, the story teeters on burlesque. And when one of the children inserts into the head of this snowman a carrot, which our beleaguered and ravenous hero begins to nibble on, thereby frightening the children away, we have entered a land of unpredictable comic metamorphoses, of disaster distanced and softened by magic: the realm of the fairy tale. (Calvino's love of the fairy tale glimmers in nearly everything he wrote, realistic or fantastic, and the anthology he assembled in the sixties, *Italian Folktales,* already holds a claim as a classic of world literature.)

If Calvino subverts the conventions of literary realism on one end by his attraction to the fairy tale, he undermines them on the other through his deep fascination with science. Calvino was rare among fiction writers in responding so strongly, with both wonder and skepticism, to scientific discovery. His work displays a venturesome eagerness to incorporate even the most awesome revelations (as in *Cosmicomics,* that paean to the expanded universe uncovered by the "big bang" theorists) and a clairvoyant discernment of its dangers (as in "Smog," which, though written in the fifties, seems to foresee an Italy in which the corrosive exhausts of the automobile—that technological marvel of our age—would begin to cannibalize those "timeless" monuments that were themselves the technological feats of an earlier civilization). Calvino seemed to absorb not just rationally, but viscerally, with heart and soul, the notion that as the forces of technology transform the world right before our eyes, a realism that does not change with it is no longer realistic.

This notion certainly sounds unexceptionable enough. But if one looks at "mainstream" American fiction since the Second World War—since Calvino embarked on his literary career—one comes away astonished at how little science impinged on just those naturalistic writers whose work might reasonably be expected to chart technology's effects on everyday life. It is a little hard to believe that, say, John Steinbeck or John O'Hara was still writing books in the space age; their reality belongs to an earlier age entirely.

This is not to suggest that Calvino was always as broad a writer as one might have wished. We might have seen more about family life in his work, and certainly a larger infusion of romantic passion, more courtships and longings, would have been welcome. It was at once Calvino's great strength and weakness that, although witty and playful and tender, his books reveal the coolness, the preference for the cerebral over the physical, that one associates with the mathematical temperament.

One might turn to the history of mathematics itself for a useful comparison. As Michael Guillen so lucidly sets out in his wonderful little book for the mathematical layman, *Bridges to Infinity,* the evolution of mathematics can be viewed as an endless exclusionary struggle, in which the people who erect some pure and satisfying mathematical system are inevitably set upon by a host of unruly, gate-crashing entities. The Pythagoreans were shocked by, and apparently tried to suppress, the discovery of irrational numbers like pi—which, however, could not finally be suppressed, for these "messy," nonrepeating fractions turned out to be indispensable for simple geometric calculations. The emergence in the sixteenth and seventeenth centuries of the imaginary numbers, whose very name suggests lingering doubt about their status and practicality, was met with derision—but in the twentieth century they proved essential for mapping the Einsteinian universe.

Analogously, the literary critic who would keep realism "pure" by excluding a fabulist like Calvino runs into difficulties. Calvino's wildest fantasies are usually grounded in the equally wild, equally fantastic advances of modern science, and they have an uncanny way of illuminating how it is, and where it is, that we actually live. To read *Cosmicomics* (probably his best book—a claim made all the more vociferously for my sense of being in a minority on this one) is to experience an exhilarating, altered view of what it means to share a universe with volcanoes and dinosaurs, with light years and black holes. Of course, to be a human being at all is—necessarily, organically—to live a drastically occluded existence. The limitations of our intellects and our senses, and the brevity of life itself, ensure that we can accept the immensities of scientific discovery only in a kind of numb, concessive paralysis. Yet one comes away from *Cosmicomics* feeling that one's aperture on life has been widened by some tenth of one degree—which is to say, given the extent of our benightedness, widened considerably.

In recent years, the mathematician and essayist Douglas Hofstadter has encouraged a reexamination of the ways in which literature that might seem dryly cerebral often clarifies the features of modern life. In *his* wonderful book for the mathematical layman, *Gödel, Escher, Bach,* he elucidates how the concerns of philosopher, mathematician, and cognitive scientist all overlap, and together themselves overlap with the work of the great literary "gamesmen" of our time—writers like Borges, Lem, Nabokov, and Calvino. These are writers for whom puzzle and paradox have limitless appeal, and whose fondness for ideas sometimes has led to accusations of sterility and disengagement. Yet the longer one lives beside their work, the clearer it becomes that theirs are often the ideas we live by, or need to live by. A patient, probing reader will come away broadened by Borges' reflections on variant worlds and the interrelationship of parts and wholes; by those concealed meditations on time and memory and consciousness that Nabokov was forever weaving into his multilayered fictions; by the speculations on free will and theology that Lem injects into his tales about artificial beings.

No modern writer was more adept than Calvino in that delicate gardener's art of transplantation by which ideas are inserted, live and fruitful, into a work of fiction. To his long list of successes, one now must add *Mr. Palomar*, a book that might be viewed as an extended meditation on the unavoidable frustrations of solipsism. Like the rest of us, Palomar is trapped for life within the obstruction of a single body, but unlike most of us he feels this limitation as an immediate and continual anguish. He yearns for some escape from the self, for even a momentary glimpse of how the universe is apprehended by a gecko lizard, or by a starling settling onto a sycamore at the close of a glorious autumn afternoon in Rome, or by the world's only great albino ape from its cage in the Barcelona zoo.

He is obsessed by what is surely one of the central peculiarities of modern life—the way in which continual refinements in our prosthetic devices steadily pull us farther away from the reality presented by our naked five senses. Our microscopes and telescopes, our tape recorders and atomic clocks, our laboratories full of gadgetry designed to venture where our senses are too insensitive to go, all increasingly show us that our eyes and ears and fingertips are deceivers. What a position this puts us in! The mind—that lonely and immobile monarch, immured in the throne room of the skull—begins to realize that all of its messengers are liars. Here is Palomar taking a swim at dusk:

> Can this be nature? But nothing of what he sees exists in nature: the sun does not set, the sea does not have this color, the shapes are not those that the light casts on his retina. With unnatural movements of his limbs, he is floating among phantoms.

Palomar accepts fresh scientific advances with delight and wonder, but also with a boggled bewilderment at finding that the gulf between the realities of intellect and body continually widens.

A realist only in a most inclusive sense—the one that the term deserves—Calvino looked at the world steadily, doggedly, and amusedly. He was forever trying to figure out how the discoveries being revealed around him should change his sense of what it is to be a human being. He understood that whatever conclusions he drew would be partial and somewhat erroneous. He was pessimistic and good-humored. He was humble. To all of which one might add, realistically, that the world is diminished by his loss.

(1988)

VOICES IN THE CLOCK

Colin Martindale's *The Clockwork Muse*

ɞ

At first glance, Colin Martindale's *The Clockwork Muse* has the look of a titanic folly. The book comes stuffed with seemingly parodic graphs and tables, in which, for example, the "hedonic value" of an artistic stimulus is charted against its "arousal potential"; the "primordial content" of American song lyrics is matched up with national unemployment figures; and Edgar Allan Poe, Marianne Moore, and I. A. Baraka are incorporated into dots on a set of Cartesian axes that track something called the Composite Variability Index from Revolutionary War days to the present. The last time I encountered a critical study that created a first impression of such imposing absurdity was a couple of years ago, when I chanced upon a scholarly journal whose cover promised to "reinvent" the Marx Brothers. Lest the Wonderland magic of that promise dissolve on a closer inspection, and one of life's little joys be forever lost, I scrupulously left the journal unopened.

It would be a shame if prospective readers were likewise to give *The Clockwork Muse* a miss, for it is a book guaranteed, at the very least, to stir lively rethinking about the essence and the evolution of art. Martindale, a professor of psychology at the University of Maine, is also versed in statistics, and there is something tonic in his urgings on behalf of a criticism of greater lucidity and testability. His aim is nothing less than the unveiling of "universal laws of art history," discoverable only through a "scientific approach to literature and art." The questions he raises go well beyond the individual graphs and tables he offers. At issue, finally, is the role that quantification—the whole business of methodical measurement—can and will play in our evaluations of art. Who is that knocking at the door of the aesthete's salon? It is the scientist, hoping to get in.

By way of overcoming one's initial skepticism, it may be helpful to place Martindale in the long tradition of English-language critics who have sought to wed aesthetics to scientific methodology. One thinks of Ezra Pound declaring, sixty years ago, that "the proper METHOD for studying poetry and good letters is the method of contemporary biologists." Of Coleridge urging his countrymen, nearly two hundred years ago, to "let a communication be formed between any number of learned men in the various branches of science and literature." And of Dryden observing, more than three hundred years ago, that a person "should be learned in several sciences and should have a reasonable, philosophical, and in some measure a mathematical head, to be a complete and excellent poet." If Martindale's study boasts a technical density greater than any of theirs, if it seems the offspring of a "number cruncher" who has been granted unrestricted computer time—well, ours is a technological, number-crunching age. Martindale might plausibly argue that his recondite statistical techniques—his detrendings and multidimensional scalings and autoregressive equations—are high-precision tools of just the sort his predecessors yearned to employ.

Traditionally, most poets and artists haven't shared this faith in science's capacity for illuminating art; a hostile skepticism appears to have been the general rule. And yet, with each new decade's technological refinements, it has grown increasingly difficult, even in negotiating the mysteries of art, to support George Bernard Shaw's breezy maxim that "science is always wrong." One recalls how, in perhaps the most famous forgery hoax of this century—the string of Vermeers produced by Hans van Meegeren in the thirties and forties—a preeminent expert, Abraham Bredius, was so thoroughly taken in as to proclaim one of them "*the* masterpiece of Johannes Vermeer of Delft." He proceeded on what now seems a naïve assumption—that scientific corroboration in such cases is superfluous, since the heart knows best how to distinguish the genuine from the ersatz. Most critics would be warier today. They have seen time and again how even the broadest heart knowledge can collapse before a minuscule but stubborn technical irregularity— chemical traces of aluminum discovered in an Etruscan sculpture, say, or microscopic trailings indicating that a historic document was composed partly with a ballpoint pen.

Martindale addresses the issue of heart knowledge versus machine knowledge—the connoisseur versus the technician—with an engaging feistiness. He seeks to take the connoisseur down a peg or two. Most literary and art critics have operated "on the worst possible level of analysis," he says. "Far too particularistic and caught up in details, they can't see the forest for the trees." He clearly exults both in an awareness that within some critical circles he represents "bad" technology (things like the statistician's graphs and tables) rather than "good" technology (things like the word processor) and in the realization that it is the nature of technological advances to efface such distinctions and to impose themselves wherever they prove useful. Given the vast amounts of psychological research now being done into the nature of art and creativity, one might regard *The Clockwork Muse*—a book grounded in the conviction that five or six equations could probably "capture the rich complexity of six hundred fifty years of British poetry"—as an inevitability.

Martindale would doubtless extend this line a little further. He feels confident—justifiably, in my view—that his branch of criticism will redesign the face of literary and art criticism, particularly within the academy. When this might happen would be hard to say, owing to the uncertainties surrounding scientific progress and to the insular nature of much academic criticism (a conservatism often posing as its reverse). But it does seem likely that there will soon arrive a time—ten years? twenty?—when the illuminations emerging from the cognitive scientist's laboratory will throw too much light to let critics ignore them. Pathbreaking revelations will clarify for us how, physiologically, art works its effects on us. One can foresee a time when a new school of criticism, steeped in the intricacies of brain research, will complain, with some grounds, that previous schools adopted the commanding technical nomenclature of hard science while eschewing its rigor.

Whatever gripes one may have with Martindale, he's not to be faulted for any lack of rigor. From chapter to chapter he advances systematically and—as soon becomes apparent—indefatigably. Early on, he sets out his theory, which he calls a psychological theory of aesthetic evolution, and begins subjecting it to one complex statistical analysis after another. His book is not large—there are some three hundred and seventy pages of text—but it is built, like a coral atoll whose aggregate mass is all but submerged, upon a mountain of numbers.

The generating postulates of his theory, which he describes as "altogether analogous to Darwin's theory of biological evolution," are simple and reassuringly commonsensical. He proposes that the driving evolutionary force behind all art—from "high" forms, like paintings and poetry, to "low" forms, like pop songs and television commercials—is "habituation," which he defines as "the phenomenon whereby repetitions of a stimulus are accompanied by decreases in physiological reactivity to it." This is a "universal property of all nervous tissue": the laboratory jellyfish that registers diminishing responses to an electrical impulse is in a sense kin to the jaded art collector who thirsts for "fresh blood." Because of the effects of habituation, aspiring artists must do something original if they are to succeed like the artists of the past; this "need for novelty" is a historical constant, goading new generations of would-be creators across the millennia.

According to Martindale, novelty is usually achieved in one of two ways: artists forge a radically new style or, while working in an established style, pursue an ever-greater unpredictability ("increasing remoteness or strangeness of similes, metaphors, images, and so on"). This dichotomy is grounded in a Freudian continuum, one end of which is occupied by "primary-process cognition" (where the remote or strange similes, metaphors, images are apt to come from, for it is "free-associative, concrete, irrational and autistic") and the other by "secondary-process cognition" ("abstract, logical and reality-oriented"). In Martindale's scheme of things, secondary-process cognition, which he calls "conceptual thought," comes to the fore during periods of stylistic change; primary-process cognition, which he refers to as "primordial thought," serves as the wellhead of creative illogicality. Over time, artists working within an established style are pushed, by the novelty requirement, into deeper and deeper levels of primordial thought. The mounting effort and cost of these "regressions," in conjunction with the gathering threat of incoherence, eventually gives birth to a sweeping stylistic change, which, by its very newness, eases the need for unpredictability. Of course, the new style will, over time, exact its own deeper and deeper regressions, until it, too, yields to a sweeping stylistic change. The process is not only inevitable but, in the main, punctual—for ours is a clockwork muse.

This is a vision of art's numerous branches as relatively independent of society and of each other. Each genre contains the gentle curves of its own steady regressions, the steep slopes of its own abrupt stylistic revolutions. Martindale's experiments have convinced him that the best predictor of artistic evolution is art itself. Social conditions matter far less than we might suppose: "The empirical evidence suggests that art tends in fact to evolve in a social vacuum, and that non-evolutionary factors are comparatively negligible. . . . Furthermore, social forces are analogous to *friction,* in that they impede or slow down the progress of an artistic tradition. They do not cause change in art: they distort it."

His views offer interesting links—only sketchily traced, unfortunately—to the New Critics. The New Critical tenet that art can be meaningfully examined outside its historical and social milieu is almost universally discredited in contemporary academic circles, where it is typically regarded as a naïve and sentimental attempt to "purify" art of its coarse, workaday surroundings. But since there's no better way to counter charges of sentimentality than by recourse to the cold world of numbers, Martindale manages to place the debate on a new footing. Could it be that critical attempts to fix a work of art in its historical and social context are almost inherently distortional? And could it be that the truly naïve and sentimental are those who would, through a distaste for the exact sciences, "purify" art of its mathematical underpinnings?

The value of *The Clockwork Muse* hinges on a couple of points. One must first assume that the primordial/conceptual continuum is indeed central to all artistic creation. One must then accept the more troublesome proposition that the approximate place of an artwork on the continuum—the relative proportions of primordial and conceptual thought which went into its composition—can be ascertained by means of Martindale's experiments, many of which consist of questionnaires and surveys administered to "artistically naïve" undergraduates. (More worldly testees apparently bring to their evaluations prejudices that skew the data.) He wishes us to accept his statement that after asking his undergraduates to evaluate an art work in terms familiar to them—whether it is "dreamlike," "meaningless," "tense," "strong," and so forth—he can accurately translate their judgments into numerical placements on his continuum. What the book consists of, in bulk, is a succession of reports on experiments in which he or his colleagues have sought to measure, for a wide diversity of art forms, variations along the continuum over time. (These experiments, it must be said, are recounted with such punctilious regard for procedure that readers may sometimes feel they've stepped out of a literary text and into the world's longest footnote.) Having converted art into numerical data, Martindale can comfortably "cross over" from one medium to another—make comparisons, for instance, between trends toward greater dissonance in classical music and increased abstraction in painting. We are approaching the realization that art history is a "completely deterministic process," ultimately expressible in "mathematical equations embedded in an objective theory."

The Clockwork Muse would be an easy book to lambaste. It invites criticism deliberately, both in the grandiose sweep of genres it contemplates (English verse, French painting, pre-Columbian sculpture, Japanese ukiyo-e prints, even New England gravestones) and in its baldly dismissive pronouncements (with the help of "computerized-content analytic methods," he assures us, "one could study the history of a literary tradition without ever reading any of the literature"). And it invites criticism unwittingly, through the frequent crudeness of its aesthetic discriminations. One can envision indignant specialists taking it apart piece by piece. Although no specialist, I found that within the area of his survey dearest to me—the evolution of American verse—Martindale misses as much as he gets. He is one of those literary critics (a distressingly familiar breed) who feel an almost theological yearning for some First Cause, in which all uncertainties of influence can be put to rest. He traces virtually everything that has happened in the last hundred and fifty years directly to Emerson, and an unschooled reader might well leave *The Clockwork Muse* convinced that without Emerson's example poems about modern everyday objects—gas stations and movie houses and electric guitars—would never have emerged in this country. (The teachings of the Romantics, as crystallized in Wordsworth's declaration that poems should be "found in every subject which can interest the human mind," seem to occupy a point outside the plane on which American poetry is to be charted, and so does any awareness that modern poets around the world, for most of whom Emerson is as remote a figure as the anonymous author of *Gilgamesh,* have embraced such subject matter as their own.)

Yet particularized carping of this sort is probably off the mark. The gist of the book lies elsewhere—in the laws it seeks to divulge, and in the charts and graphs intended to illustrate and vindicate them. The book solicits, ideally, a tripartite analysis. There is first the issue of whether its statistical methods are, from a technical standpoint, sound and soundly pursued (a matter in which this reader has no expertise). There is then the question of whether what might be called Martindale's digitizations—his conversion of artworks into strings of numbers—make sense intuitively. Do his conclusions accord with our lives? Does he speak to what we experience when we stand before middling art and immortal art and everything in between? Even sympathetic readers will probably feel that Martindale's readings can be alarmingly nuance-free. One certainly wishes that he wouldn't so often seem to invest greater faith in his theories than in common sense, as when he concludes, after examining his data, that the neoclassical poets, like Pope and Dryden, show a greater "arousal potential" (defined largely in terms of "ambiguity, novelty, incongruity") than the Metaphysicals, like Donne and Vaughan and Marvell. Obviously, this is not posterity's judgment, and never has been; over succeeding centuries, it would have seemed absurd to Johnson, Browning, Eliot. In such instances, if Martindale seriously aspires to upend conventional wisdom, he will need far more compelling evidence than what he provides. In the meantime, he might keep in mind that when a physicist determines that bees cannot fly is no time for beekeepers to dismantle their apiaries; rather, it's time for the physicist to embark on new theories of aerodynamics.

Thirdly and finally, there is the question of how insightfully Martindale applies his findings to the wider world. How keenly does he perceive—in a book that rather too insistently stresses the need to see the forest rather than just the trees—the broader issues of his research? On this level, his book can be trying. One problem is that he only intermittently acknowledges that many modern artists are themselves familiar with the dichotomies he would investigate, and that this familiarity may imbue their art with complications not immediately apprehensible to his questionnaires. One wonders what his indexes would make of a poem like Auden's "A Lullaby," in which the elderly poet, in effect bifurcating himself into parent and infant, reconceives himself in a baby's body and sings himself to sleep:

> Now you have licence to lie,
> naked, curled like a shrimplet,

jacent in bed, and enjoy
its cosy micro-climate:
Sing, Big Baby, sing lullay.

In this queer, haunting poem we find many of the elements of a deep regression—images of dreaming, suckling, fetal curling, and so forth. But the poem is not a retreat into infantilism so much as an elaborate, stylized meditation, by a poet steeped in Freud, on the allurements of such a retreat. Any analysis of the poem, literary or scientific, that fails to note this distinction misses its target. "A Lullaby" might be said to be "about" the sensation of hovering above the very continuum that Martindale would calibrate. *The Clockwork Muse*—like so many critical studies—would profit by a fuller understanding that the artists it scrutinizes are, now and then, at least half as resourceful as their commentators.

"A Lullaby," in its self-consciousness, its deliberate manipulation of the critic's tools and symbols, highlights some of the obstacles that Martindale meets when he ponders the art of our time. His thesis requires that modernism in its various guises be viewed as just another oscillation, a stylistic "bump" along a sort of sine curve. He allows little room for the possibility of any artistic or social climacteric that would irreversibly alter the meaning of art; in his system, the players change but the rules of the game remain fixed. At the outset of his book, he postulates that "people are always and everywhere about the same." Now, this may well be a necessary axiom for a literary statistician (one that legitimates surveys in which undergraduates assess the art of the ages). It may even—who knows?—be true. But with this happy assumption Martindale sidesteps all sorts of challenging speculations about radical shifts of outlook—for example, Eliot's hypothesis that the elaborate poetic conceits of the Metaphysicals reveal that in the seventeenth century "a dissociation of sensibility set in, from which we have never recovered." It also ignores the injunctions of many contemporary scholars of non-Western art that any meaningful appreciation of, say, haiku or raga requires a fundamental reeducation. One would have welcomed, at the very least, some brief avowal by Martindale of what, with his adoption of such postulates, he may have forfeited from the start.

As "bumps" go, modernism surely offers some arresting irregularities. If it represents but one more swing of the pendulum, why is it so stubbornly resisted by the general populace? Wordsworth and the Romantics may well have been as revolutionary in their century as Eliot and the moderns have been in ours, but you would never know it from your local newspaper's Poet's Corner or a Hallmark greeting card. These would sound, if they only could, like Wordsworth in the "Lucy" poems, and not like Eliot or Pound or Moore, although these three are figures we've been acquainted with for three-quarters of a century. The moderns remain oddly undomesticated. Similarly, the average Sunday painter is closer to Monet and Renoir than to Picasso and Braque, and the average film score closer to Tchaikovsky and Dvořák than to Schoenberg and Webern. Martindale has little patience with any talk of the Zeitgeist, which he regards as an unprofitably nebulous term, but there is a striking collectivity, to say the least, in the public's longstanding rejection of so many facets of modernism. The resulting schism between artist and public strongly suggests that we may have entered a new terrain—one where the surveyor's usual tools are suddenly inappropriate.

Martindale's own data hint at this in places. One of the most impressive aspects of his book involves studies of "word replacement," where he has repeatedly and painstakingly calculated the percentage of vocabulary abandoned in the transition from one poetic period to another. For readers like me, who have lingering qualms about the applicability of many of his questionnaires, there is a pleasing firmness about this simple tabulation; one needn't worry here (as one must when queries about an art work's "dreamlike" or "meaningless" or "strong" characteristics are slotted into some primordial/conceptual continuum) about whether things "fit." Common sense tells us that great stylistic revolutions will produce high word-replacement indexes, and that is what Martindale's data in fact indicate. Common sense also tells us that since it isn't possible to replace more than every word in one's poetic lexicon, the index theoretically has a ceiling of a hundred percent, and that the natural self-preservation of language over time, which permits us to read Chaucer with no great effort, ensures that the theoretical ceiling will never be closely approached. At this juncture, however, common sense and the word-replacement index part ways. Martindale's data suggest that in the next century we will enter an era in which the index will rocket above a hundred percent. Evidently, modern poets have slipped so many new words into their verses, and scuttled so many old ones, that any extrapolations into the future catapult us into the realm of the nonsensical.

In theory, some comfort is to be had in Martindale's defining metaphor of the clock. Into an artistic realm that often feels overstretched—one that must encompass everything from the music of John Cage's "4′ 33″" (four minutes and thirty-three seconds of silence) to the paintings of Yves Klein (canvases produced by rolling naked, paint-smeared bodies over them)—he brings a vision of process and regimentation. He reassures us that the disruptions of our time were to be expected—indeed, that the precise degree of their extravagance might have been foreseen. (There is even a sort of cynical solace in the thought that our country's most television-stunted youth, those who are all but untouched by any heritage of great painting, music, and literature, may in a sense become cultural navigators by providing usefully unschooled evaluations in Martindale's experiments.) But such reassurances do not take us very far. I suspect that most readers will come away from *The Clockwork Muse* slightly depressed by the thought that Martindale—the truth or falsity of his constructions aside—would substitute one vision of confinement for another. His book stands in opposition to the ever-expanding shelf of academic criticism dedicated to the proposition that the Zeitgeist is inescapable, and that the artist's occasional sensation of "release" from the bounds of racial or sexual identity, from the era's enveloping political, social, religious, or sexual attitudes, is illusory. (Ironically, the same academies simultaneously issue volume after volume bent on censuring dead artists for succumbing to the benightedness of their age, as when Shakespeare is blasted for slighting women or Swift for believing in a natural social hierarchy.) But in Martindale's universe, too, an artist's progress and development are typically shaped by external rules that he or she is unaware of. Either way, whether subservient to the Zeitgeist or to a psychological theory of aesthetic evolution, the artist is a tethered individual, rarely ranging far from, respectively, the social or the statistical norm.

And what of those bleak, masterly novels, stories, poems, paintings of our age which erupt from an aggrieved sense of the artist's essential apartness? Are their cries, when attended to over a sufficient critical distance, revealed as nothing but the internal grindings of a clockwork mechanism? Perhaps—and yet, if so, one must expect the artists enclosed within it to greet this discovery only as cause for fiercer crying.

(1991)

KASPAROV BEATS DEEP THOUGHT

In a crowded auditorium, the champion hunches over a chessboard. He is surrounded by cameramen. Taking refuge in himself, he pillows his jaw in his hands. He is thinking hard in order to make himself think harder.

His opponent, also a champion, is some three hundred miles away, pondering the next move, engaged in calculations on a scale too colossal for anyone in the audience to grasp.

The first champion, Gary Kasparov, is considered by many aficionados the greatest genius the game has seen. He became world champion by defeating his Soviet countryman Anatoly Karpov in the fall of 1985. Twenty-two at the time, Kasparov was the youngest person ever to gain the title.

The second champion, DEEP THOUGHT, is a good deal younger: roughly two years old. DEEP THOUGHT is a computer. It usually plays its games by telephone hookup. In the spring of 1989, it defeated all comers at the Sixth World Computer Chess Championship, held in Edmonton, Alberta. DEEP THOUGHT is, far and away, the fastest chess machine yet devised.

The two-game match between the champions, which took place in New York City on October 22, 1989, was designed to illuminate just where, at the highest levels, human chess and computer chess intersect. The mere existence of the match is, in a sense, a victory for the computer. Before the advent of DEEP THOUGHT, no machine had been developed that might challenge a human world champion. In the rapidly evolving relationship between people and their machines, this match is an acknowledgment of a new, and inherently short-lived, state— one of essential parity on the board.

On the day when computers begin to dominate the greatest human players—an inevitability—they will do so forever. If, taking an overview of the game, we regard the set of all human chess players as a single, collective organism, we see that this is a "life-form" driven toward self-betterment: it ventures into new territory, tests and retests its hypotheses, pools its knowledge. But its rate of improvement simply cannot keep up with computers, whose progress is measured exponentially. In 1986, the fastest computer was looking at roughly one hundred and fifty thousand different chess positions per second. DEEP THOUGHT examines about one and a half million. Machines that evaluate ten million, even a hundred million positions per second may not be far off. Some computer scientists are now predicting that within another three to five years, machines will have ranged so far beyond our capabilities that a confrontation between human and computer world champions would be boringly one-sided.

On the day before the match, I go out for coffee with a group of chess devotees that includes Murray Campbell and Feng-hsiung Hsu, two of the chief architects of DEEP THOUGHT. Although physically a study in contrasts—Campbell is lanky and neat, Hsu compact and disheveled—the two scientists have a lot in common. Campbell, who grew up in Alberta, Canada, is thirty-two; Hsu, born in Taiwan, is thirty. Both earned doctorates in computer science at Carnegie-Mellon in Pittsburgh, where DEEP THOUGHT is located, and both have recently become researchers at IBM's Thomas J. Watson Research Center in Yorktown Heights, forty miles outside New York City. They are working exclusively at the moment on chess computers.

They also share, on the eve of the match, a no-lose situation. Because DEEP THOUGHT is a decided underdog, they needn't worry whether it will win or draw either game; two defeats, provided it plays solidly, would suit them just fine. Whatever happens, they are already looking ahead to a new machine, which they hope to develop within two or three years, and which Campbell predicts will represent a "significant leap forward." Their primary worry is that some bug in the program will spring up, in poltergeist fashion, to make them appear ridiculous.

But the question remains: is even one draw feasible? Campbell sets the odds at one in ten. Because DEEP THOUGHT never gets discouraged, it can play marvelously tenacious chess when in trouble, often sneaking

into an improbable draw—what Campbell calls its "weasel phenomenon." Unlike the other members of the DEEP THOUGHT team, Campbell
used to play competitive chess, which gives him a privileged insight
into DEEP THOUGHT's "behavior" and enables him, through the machine, to attack far stronger opponents than he could on his own.

The business of predicting chess outcomes is greatly facilitated by an
international rating scheme called the FIDE system, based upon performance in sanctioned tournaments. DEEP THOUGHT's rating would be
approximately 2450–2500, which places it among the top thirty players
in the country. Kasparov's rating, recently elevated to about 2800, is
the highest in the history of ratings—he has exceeded even Bobby
Fischer in his prime.

Uncertainties arise, however, when a machine rather than a person
is being evaluated. DEEP THOUGHT has achieved some signal victories,
including one over the Danish veteran Bent Larsen, once a contender
for world champion. But how much were these the product of intrinsic
prowess, and how much of human jitteriness before a radically unfamiliar opponent? Of course Kasparov is not immune to nerves, either.
There is nothing to say he won't find himself rattled by a machine
adversary and play far below strength—in which case DEEP THOUGHT
could finesse the odds and seize a victory. "I'll tell you one thing," says
a member of our party: "If DEEP THOUGHT wins the first game, there
won't *be* a second game. Gary will refuse to play."

The two-game match takes place at the New York Academy of Art,
an unexpectedly appropriate site for a chess contest. Much of the artwork on display in the academy's auditorium depicts fragments of the
human body: here are drawings and sculptures of a hand, a torso, a
head. The effect is a view of humanity as an assemblage of component
parts—just the perspective fostered by the match. For we can see this
encounter as a contest of mind versus mind, the two antagonists unbur-
dened of bodily limitations.

Chess has a physical side, naturally. At the championship level, mental demands are so exorbitant that only the fit of body are likely to
stand up under them. Kasparov is an avid sportsman who enjoys tennis,
soccer, and long-distance swimming. Yet the game's physical dimension is something chess players are always working to overcome. It is a
commonplace of chess literature that the advance toward mastery involves a process of neutralizing one's surroundings. The better the

player, the less aware he'll be of his environment—a freedom rendered dramatically manifest whenever experts play multiple or blindfold games. Even a middling chess player may catch inklings of a state of mind in which the corporeal is transcended.

Ironically, this exalted state resembles the "mind-set" from which a computer commences play. It "listens" only to its own mathematical language of evaluation. It has no idea that the game involves actual pieces. In fact, it has no idea that it is playing a game. In many ways, DEEP THOUGHT looks like chess apotheosized: a show of skill enacted on a plane purified of such distractions as lighting and noise, mood and personality, victory and defeat.

DEEP THOUGHT may be a long shot, but going into the first game it has three sizable advantages. Under the terms of the match, photographers and camera crews will be allowed free rein during the first eight minutes, which obviously cannot disturb DEEP THOUGHT but may rattle Kasparov; the machine has been assigned White in Game One and Black in Game Two, and so will have the first move to begin with; and each side will be allowed only ninety minutes in all. Since this is a fraction of the time allotted in an ordinary tournament game, Kasparov might find such an irregularity unsettling.

The game begins; Kasparov hunches under the popping lights. He is a darkly good-looking man, the only child of a Jewish father, who died when the boy was seven, and an Armenian mother. His is a face that was made for brooding. Within moments he is very deep in thought.

In sharp contrast, Hsu, who sits across from Kasparov, maintains a relaxed demeanor behind his computer keyboard. At this point, his job is largely secretarial: a matter of recording moves and serving as a liaison between Kasparov and DEEP THOUGHT.

Concentration for Kasparov is not to be equated with immobility, and as time wears on he ranges through an impressive variety of gestures. He shrugs his shoulders, pops his knuckles, drums his fingers, scratches his forehead, chews his nails, clenches his jaw; and yet, for all this activity, the game unfolds quietly. What becomes evident after eighteen or so moves to the best players—and there are a number of grandmasters present—can be seen by almost everyone a dozen moves later: Kasparov has wrested control of the game. DEEP THOUGHT—in the person of Hsu—resigns on the fifty-third move.

Before resting up for the second game, Kasparov briefly addresses the crowd upstairs. He is clearly in high spirits. His talk is exultant to the point of grandiosity. "I can't visualize living with the knowledge that a computer is stronger than the human mind," he says; to challenge the machine is to "protect the human race."

One might simply attribute such remarks to the monomania of champions in almost any field; but this would fail to explain the sympathetic hearing they receive. Perhaps the deepest impression left by the first game is of the audience's partisan fervor. DEEP THOUGHT is disliked. Upstairs, where talking is permitted, its play is treated to scorn and condescension from the start. And as Kasparov begins to crush the machine, the crowd's contempt turns into catcalls, laughter, hoots of incredulous contempt.

There is something both appealingly loyal and disturbingly delusive about this response. The simple truth is that DEEP THOUGHT could squelch all but a tiny handful of the chess fanatics assembled here. So why is the audience so worked up? In part, it's a matter of simple identification with a hero; people would feel many of the same tensions if Kasparov's opponent were a human being. But the match engages the spectator on another level as well, roping in even those few who (like some of the photographers) scarcely know how the pieces move. For everyone understands winning and losing.

Not that chess is like other games. Whoever wins at pinball or Asteroids or Nintendo has gained a qualified victory, one undermined by the certainty that it arises only through the machine's "mercy." No one doubts that a pinball machine or video game could be constructed against which the human hand and eye would flounder. Chess is different. At present, it may provide the only activity in the world in which an all-out struggle between man and machine is a fair fight. In chess, the best human beings and the best machines possess capabilities both similar enough to allow meaningful competition and diverse enough to ensure that the outcome is not a foregone conclusion. Their battle recalls Roman gladiatorial days, when a lively asymmetry was achieved by equipping one combatant with net and trident and the other with sword and shield.

The question the chessboard continually poses, for both man and machine, is a straightforward one: what is my strongest move? Yet if they pursue the same end, they go about it in radically divergent ways. Given the brain's relative slowness, a man can scrutinize no more than an infinitesimal fraction of the moves available at any juncture. In the typical case, his decision is bifurcated: he will first determine, by a somewhat mysterious process called intuition, a small number of plausible candidates for the optimal move—perhaps as few as two—and then study these possibilities at great depth, narrowing his choice from the few to the one. A machine like DEEP THOUGHT, conversely, will look at every possible move—however unlikely or even transparently inane many of these may be. This process of exhaustive investigation is called a "brute force" search, as opposed to an intuition-simulating "selective" search.

Partly because intuition has eluded machines, and partly because it represents an area of the psyche especially difficult to describe or categorize, many chess players have seen in it a final, impregnable defense against the incursions of the machine. Kasparov said as much a few years ago: "If a computer can beat the world champion, the computer can read the best books in the world, can write the best plays, and can know everything about history and literature and people. That's impossible."

About ten years ago, when even the best computers were fodder to a grandmaster, a study was carried out in which many top international players estimated the proficiency that computers might eventually achieve. Despite variations in expertise, a consistent pattern emerged: respondents tended to envision computers reaching a level of play about 50 points below their own. Such results no doubt reflect a characteristic need among highly competitive people to assert their superiority. But they probably also reflect a heartfelt conviction that chess, when carried out at the highest and most rigorous levels, is so shaped by inexplicable promptings—by creative or mystical or artistic impulses—that a mere machine could never master it.

In fact, computer ratings have continued to go up. Each time computers have crossed a new threshold, various chess experts have speculated that some sort of natural ceiling had been reached and that without human intuition they could not climb much higher. But computers have steadily shown that mere acceleration may be a satisfactory substitute. The human realm—a realm supposedly inaccessible to machines—turns out to be more vulnerable than we thought.

In years to come, the descendants of machines like DEEP THOUGHT will doubtless compel us to examine the nature and importance of human intuition. The rise of the chess computer conclusively demonstrates that at least for those tasks in which a narrowly defined objective is formulable (as in chess, where every goal is subordinate to checkmating your opponent), and in which all possible lines of behavior can be charted (every contingency in chess can be set out in a simple, if astronomically vast, diagram), intuition may be a useful but expendable tool. To be able to scan all possibilities on a chessboard, you don't need to be smart in the usual sense. You can be dumb, in fact, provided you're fast—blindingly, electronically fast. DEEP THOUGHT makes us ask, *What next?* Which areas in our lives, in our "history and literature, and people," might prove accessible to the brute force of a monster number-cruncher?

Playing White in the second and final game, Kasparov lashes out fiercely. He plays a Queen's Gambit, in which White offers its queen's bishop pawn in exchange for a firm position on the board's center; and when DEEP THOUGHT accepts the pawn, Kasparov advances his king's pawn two spaces—an aggressive line. By the tenth move, with the game still theoretically in its preliminary stages, Kasparov has managed to do something to DEEP THOUGHT that no one has ever done: make it look silly. His forces are powerfully posted; DEEP THOUGHT has just gotten started. The game is essentially over before it has begun.

Kasparov handles a microphone with much the same assurance he brings to his chess moves; in his brief victory speech, he notes that the computer still has "a lot to learn," including "how to resign." His closing lines are graceful and ingratiating: "When playing versus a human being there's energy going between us. Today I was puzzled because I felt no opponent, no energy—kind of like a black hole, into which my energy could disappear. But I discovered a new source of energy, from the audience to me, and I thank you very much for this enormous energy supply."

In the next day or two, most newspaper accounts of the match will present an upbeat report on DEEP THOUGHT's performance—acknowledging Kasparov's easy triumph but predicting that in a few years' time the outcome may be different. On the night of the match, though, feelings are a good deal less sanguine—at least among those closest to the machines. Summing up the match, Campbell explains to a circle of journalists: "This was a very clear demonstration of one of the weaknesses of the program. We'd seen glimpses of it before, but this was an exceptionally clear and well-conceived exhibit of DEEP THOUGHT's lack of long-range planning. It's a huge problem."

After the match I talk with Monty Newborn, a professor of computer science at McGill University, and Hans Berliner of Carnegie-Mellon. One reads so frequently that computer science is still a discipline in its infancy that it comes as something of an illumination to speak with men who measure their research not in terms of months and years but of decades. Newborn is fifty-one and has been active in the field for twenty years. Berliner is sixty. In addition to chess programming, he designed a backgammon-playing computer—which defeated the human world champion in 1979. These days, he is a designer of HITECH, after DEEP THOUGHT the world's strongest chess computer.

Berliner probably has no peer in the world when it comes to a dual grasp of chess theory and of the technicalities of computer-chess programming—and tonight he comes away disheartened. He has long been an optimist about chess computers. When I met him, in 1986, he foresaw equality in five years.

Things look different tonight. "I really expected to see DEEP THOUGHT get at least one draw," he admits, and adds that he certainly hadn't expected to see Kasparov win so effortlessly. Kasparov simply saw farther, "much, much farther," than the machine. And while Berliner says he would still bet that a serious machine challenger will appear in three or four years, he recognizes that the existing hardware is limited, and he allows the possibility that man will "still be master at the end of the century."

I meet Kasparov and his business manager, an Englishman named Andrew Page, for breakfast on the morning after the match. (Kasparov's business interests are large and, in the days of glasnost, growing. In addition to his substantial fees—the ten thousand dollars he received for battling DEEP THOUGHT is said to be typical—he has endorsed a chess computer and Schweppes tonic water.)

A first encounter with the world champion comes as something of a surprise. In view of the stereotype of the chess genius as an insular eccentric, he seems unexpectedly normal. One might even say disappointingly normal, since the notion dies hard that chess achievement of his magnitude is purchased only at the cost of a diminished aptitude for daily life. That a world chess champion could present himself as witty and engaging and intellectually broad—as Kasparov does—seems patently unfair.

"I am a man of many interests," he acknowledges. Last summer he gave an interview to *Playboy* in which he tossed out blistering condemnations of Soviet economic policy, social policy, the unreliability of the media, and preglasnost mores ("Intellectual life was frozen, and sexual life, too"). Clearly proud of his openness, Kasparov relishes the chance to speak out broadly, and confesses that a future in politics "may be inevitable." All the more curious, then, is his unwillingness to entertain hypothetical questions about his chess career. When I ask what he might have become if chess had never been invented, he counters with, "But it was." What would have happened if he'd lost a sixth game to Karpov in their first encounter? "But I didn't." And if the computer had defeated him yesterday? "Oh, it couldn't."

It seems peculiar that a man who makes his living by exploring unfollowed contingencies—roads not taken—should resist such hypotheticals, but Kasparov has strong feelings about Fate. "I was fated to be world champion," he explains, with an odd but characteristic mixture of forcefulness and merriment. "You ask would I eventually have become champion anyway, if I'd lost a sixth game to Karpov? But you see, I was fated not to lose a sixth game." The thought amuses him enormously.

Did the pressure ever get to him? Any trouble sleeping before a match? "Andrew should answer that one," he replies, and calls across the table, "Do I have trouble sleeping before a match?" "Oh, he has a problem sleeping all right," Andrew reports. "Put him on a sofa for five minutes, or in a taxi, or in an armchair, and he falls asleep. It's a terrible problem."

Both men laugh. They have every reason for feeling ebullient this morning. Yesterday's match has brought Kasparov more attention than any event since the last world championship. He's on the front page of every newspaper they've seen so far. He scans the articles with good-humored interest. One quotation, from Murray Campbell, particularly delights him: "DEEP THOUGHT didn't get a chance to show what it can do." Kasparov reads this aloud. "But that's exactly the point!" he exclaims. "I didn't let it. The highest art of the chess player lies in not allowing your opponent to show you what he can do."

At the moment, Kasparov reigns over the board as no one has for decades. Karpov, his predecessor as world champion, shared his crown with a ghost—that of the notoriously temperamental Bobby Fischer, from whom Karpov received it by default. None of the postwar champions who predated Fischer was ever more than first among equals. Looking back, one has to go a long way to find a suitable counterpart to Kasparov; looking forward, one may find none at all. At twenty-six, he could plausibly hold his title for ten or fifteen more years—by which point even conservative computer scientists expect to see machines surpass the best human players. He reigns without peer, human or mechanical—a privilege that none of his successors may ever know.

The arrival of an unbeatable machine will hardly be a death knell to human players. The game will go on as before; there will still be human tournaments, flush with all the anguish and exultation of old. But psychology at the uppermost echelons will be irreversibly altered. Not even the world champion will be allowed a sense of untrammeled superiority. Kasparov is perhaps the last of a kind.

The new machines will represent triumphs of human doggedness and ingenuity, and we owe it to ourselves to acclaim their makers. But we also owe it to ourselves to grasp that within the transitional terrain we have now entered, where machines rapidly close in upon the human world champion, something inspiring is passing away. If we have reached the last world champion to whose name no asterisk is attached—the one who was champion of all and everything—it is heartening that this should prove to be Gary Kasparov. For he is a man who has not only climbed Everest but stood on its summit as though he belonged there.

(1990)

Postscript—*1994*

My two computer chess articles are an attempt at journalistic calculus: they seek to fix the instantaneous rate of change on a steeply sloped curve. Chess machines continue to advance at a hurtling pace, and it is inevitable that computers will best human beings in the "art" of chess. With great reluctance, a torch is being passed in the richest, and one of the most ancient, competitions the world has ever seen. I've aimed to memorialize something of this passage before it vanishes.

On August 31, 1994, a computer, Pentium Genius, defeated Gary Kasparov in the first round of the Intel Grand Prix in London. It would be easy to make more of this than we should. The game, which was not played under true tournament time allowances or conditions, was something of a "throwaway." Nonetheless, one can imagine the turmoil it engendered in the soul of a champion who, shortly before the match, declared, "The way things are, I can beat any computer, if I concentrate simply on the computer's style of game. The computer can calculate billions of moves, but it is lacking intuition."

The world's most fascinating game has surely entered its most fascinating era. Though a man still stands on Everest, the mountain beneath him is steadily being eroded.

. . . Or perhaps one might better say that, some ways off from Everest, platoons of machines are working, night and day, to construct a mountain far larger than anything our wayward, tectonically restless planet has yet seen.

Introduction: A Mysterious Increase in Reality

You might say I was sheltered from the "underground" in two senses: both gangsters and ghosts were largely banished from my childhood. In many ways my parents viewed my brothers and me—we were four in all—as highly impressionable creatures requiring scrupulous protection from a world intent on scarring and brutalizing us. Our black-and-white television was an especially menace-laden object. Eliot Ness and his Untouchables were *not* for kids. Neither was "Shock Theater." Nor "The Twilight Zone." Today, in a society in which one sees children fresh out of toddlerhood being carted off to movies where they will witness decapitations, eviscerations, minutely rendered bludgeonings and blindings, acts of cannibalism and sexual maiming, etc., I look back on the vigilance of that vanished household with fond amazement. (Surely—I'd note in passing—it's a defining trait of our age, this process of *accelerated quaintness,* by which the mores of a mere two or three decades ago begin to look impossibly distant.)

The tameness of those forbidden television programs, when I chance upon one of them in reruns, renders sweetly comical my parents' once-infuriating proscriptions. Couldn't they see that this sort of thing couldn't harm *anyone?* But then I'll remember how I once suffered recurrent nightmares after exposure to the mere previews of *The Blob* (the original version, in which Steve McQueen helps rescue his fellow small-town folk from a big, mobile, hungry wad of bubble gum) and it occurs to me that maybe we *were* as impressionable as all that.

In any event, the ban on gangsters seems to have had its effect. I feel only a numb attraction—unlike a number of critics I admire—toward Hollywood's latest and bloodiest portrayal of organized crime. In my heart of hearts, indeed, I nurture a strong if unverifiable suspicion that these endless "explorations" of our country's passion for violence— *Goodfellas, Scarface, Bugsy, Godfather III*—do not merely fail to illuminate; they contribute, materially, to our deepening national tragedy. In regard to ghosts, on the other hand, parental prohibitions seem only to have enhanced their fluttering luster, their appalling appeal. I show no signs of outgrowing a taste for them.

It turns out that ghost stories themselves, like the spirits they traffic in, are not easily barred from a house. Tales kept creeping in, sometimes from peculiar sources. There was a man on our block who flew away one winter and shot a moose. Proof of his killing powers was unignorable. One snowy morning, walking alone to school, I discovered that the creature's furry, bloody, and altogether larger-than-life carcass—not much smaller than a compact car—had been deposited on his driveway. He'd had it shipped, by heaven knows what means, from the Canadian Rockies to our Detroit suburb.

Anyway, this big-game hunter one summer night set his sights, so to speak, on my brothers and me and some neighborhood kids. We were camping out in our backyard. He arrived just after dusk to narrate a tale about a woman with a golden arm, and by the time he departed, some fifteen, much-darker minutes later, we were, each of us, zipped tight in our sleeping bags, paralyzed with terror. It was a long time before anybody went to sleep, but when at last we'd all drifted off he returned to the backyard, this time to paw against our tent and make various sighing and searching noises. All in all, his was an unforgettable performance. . . .

It was some three decades later in my life, I guess, that I began systematically to connect my taste for the supernatural to my literary interest in imaginary lands, satire, folktales, and the surreal—and to my interest in various contemporary novelists (Evelyn Waugh, Flannery O'Connor, Shusaku Endo) who have embraced explicitly religious themes. At Mount Holyoke College, where I'd become a lecturer, I devised a course called Modern Alternatives to Realism. I assigned ghost stories and ghost poems and folktales, and also Wells, Stevenson, Lem, Kafka, Calvino, Borges, Abe.

I began to see that for me the course was meant as an antidote to a "realism" equated with the rational, the detached, the objective—the (at bottom) numerical. Some of my writers embraced mathematics, some fled from it, but in all cases there was likely to be an insistence on the primacy of a vague, visionary region beyond the reach of any *human* numbers, anyway. Wells may have equipped his Time Traveller with all sorts of scientific-sounding patter about fourth dimensions, but his novella takes off only when the numbers disappear, literally—when the Time Traveller hurls so rashly into the future that the dials of his chronometer blur.

In truth, I fail to see how any serious artist, whether a middling or a major talent, can avoid becoming something of a mystic. These days, his critics may coolheadedly inform him that the aesthetic hierarchy he subscribes to is arbitrary and relative and idiosyncratically value-laden. They may tell him it is merely—if intricately—the product of various economic, sociopolitical, religious, sexual, and cultural forces. And in this judgment they may well be correct. Indeed, the artist most of the time may well acknowledge their correctness, but in those instants when he authentically feels himself creating he will concede no such thing. Suddenly, he becomes an absolutist. The poet knows that one word is *better* than its synonym; the composer, that one modulation is *better* than another; the painter, that one shade is *better* than its near-neighbor on the spectrum.

If the creative spirit's intuition of some absolute *good-better-best* is at bottom illusory, it's nonetheless an essential illusion, for without this promise of perfection his quest is invalidated and necessarily collapses into—into criticism, I'm afraid. It used to puzzle me that most contemporary writers, even women and men of outstanding intelligence and sophistication, showed such scant sympathy for the waves of critical theory that have overswept English departments across the nation. Why were the writers so out of step? Eventually I came to see their seeming indifference as a self-defensive instinct: a visceral suspicion that many of theory's pervasive skepticisms (about the fixity of standards, the determinacy of language, the ranking of genres, the autonomy of art) were fundamentally at odds with their own creative methods and with what they saw as their own purest impulses. The artists simply couldn't afford to imperil their inklings of a transcendence into a "higher" realm.

How high is "higher"? Where is this realm to be found? Clearly, it's a place which, on the one hand, is not amenable to quantification and digitization, and which, on the other, is not wholly disjointed and haphazard. If no rule so confining as strict causation holds sway there, it's a place where strong principles of consecution obtain, so that one cluster of words (or pigments, or notes) compels another with firm particularity. It's a domain where Yeats's "monuments of unaging intellect" are the landmarks and we drift through a lush terrain where the dead are not dead; they are forever whispering. Within it, even the proudly rational novelist or poet, the one who has resolutely thrown off God, discovers himself an inhabitant not of a logical but of a pagan cosmos. The breezes are quick with spirits. The rivers murmur. The soil itself— the "underground"—yearns to speak.

DEAD FORMS:
THE GHOST STORY TODAY

Whether there is any *necessary* link between a devotion to afternoon sweets, queuing, and windowbox gardening on the one hand, and a passion for the ghost story on the other, would be hard to say. But one can assert without question about that puzzling thing, the English national temper, that it shows a deep affinity for the tale sprung from a restless grave.

In the last two centuries, beginning with Sir Walter Scott, the ghost story has flourished in England with an artistry and range unmatched throughout the world. Dickens, George Eliot, Gaskell, Hardy, Kipling, Wells, de la Mare, Maugham, and Elizabeth Bowen all composed ghost stories. And if in recent years the genre has not stirred the wealth of talents it once did, the ghost story in England continues to attract both sophisticated readers and discerning critical regard to an extent unknown in America. Last year saw the appearance in England of a host of well-produced and for the most part commendably sober-looking volumes, among them *The Oxford Book of English Ghost Stories, The Ghost Stories of M. R. James, The Mammoth Book of Classic Chills,* E. F. Benson's *Tales of an Empty House,* and *The Ghost Hunter's Guide* by Peter Underwood, who, according to the book's dust jacket, is president of the Ghost Club (founded 1856). These volumes come swaying lightly on the heels of *The Penguin Book of Ghost Stories* and *The Penguin Book of Horror Stories,* both of which—provided one ventures past the skulls and graveyards of their juvenile, lurid covers—turn out to be intended for the adult reader and to offer extensive and erudite introductions by J. A. Cuddon, who previously edited Penguin's *A Dictionary of Literary Terms.* And in recent months, Oxford has published a paperback selection of the ghost stories of M. R. James in its World's Classics series— to sit on the same shelf with Austen and Thackeray and Tolstoy.

If the English commitment to the ghost story is indisputable, some doubts may linger as to whether over the years an isolable genre, the English ghost story, was created—as Michael Cox and R. A. Gilbert assert in their introduction to *The Oxford Book of English Ghost Stories.* On the one hand, the tales they have assembled do display a range of penchants and preoccupations typically thought of as English: a fluent understatement; an imagination drawn to old manorial houses; a nervous harkening to ancestral claims and privileges; and a sense of uneasy doubt, of whispering guilt, about the entitlements and morals of the upper class (for it is almost invariably the moneyed and leisured who are visited by ghosts, those unruly guests who appear unannounced and without calling cards; the lower classes in these tales often serve as buffers, behind which the rich and normally powerful seek, vainly, to barricade themselves). On the other hand, American and Continental ghost stories have always displayed these elements, too, to varying degrees. That two Americans, Henry James and Edith Wharton, are included in the Oxford anthology, and mix harmoniously there, proves little either way, given how English were their lives and tastes.

The claims on behalf of the English ghost story as a distinct genre are methodically—and to my mind persuasively—set out in Julia Briggs's fine study, *Night Visitors: The Rise and Fall of the English Ghost Story* (1977). Tracing its origins to the eighteenth century and the rise of the gothic novel, she follows the ghost story as far forward as Kingsley Amis' *The Green Man.* But she devotes the bulk of her study to what she perceives as the tale's "golden age," a period extending roughly from the last two decades of the nineteenth century through the first two decades of the twentieth. She is categorically pessimistic about its current state and prospects: "Traditionally the form has affinities with mystery and detective stories and, more recently, science fiction, yet while these first cousins have maintained a certain vitality in the mid-twentieth century, the ghost story now seems to look back over its shoulder. It has become a vehicle for nostalgia, a formulaic exercise content merely to re-create a Dickensian or Monty Jamesian atmosphere. It no longer has any capacity for growth or adaptation." The reasons behind its decline are doubtless multiple and intertwined, although Briggs makes a good case that the primary one may have been the Great War, whose horrors eclipsed and rendered quaintly innocuous a genre associated with the Victorian fireside.

The rise of the genre, no less than its fall, is wrapped in mystery. On the face of it, the most surprising thing about the ghost story is that it took so long to emerge. In the theater, ghosts had held the stage since Shakespeare's day. And of course in England, as in the rest of the world, ghost stories in the form of folktales had been circulating since time immemorial. But not until the middle of the nineteenth century did the ghost story acquire both that union of authorial convention and readerly expectation which characterizes a healthy genre and that full expansiveness and sophistication which often mark the transition from the oral to the written tale. A number of nineteenth-century writers, Hardy most notably, drew on oral lore for their ghostly tales; and a return to the folktale may be useful as well to the reader of the modern ghost story, if he would view it with clarity. For whether produced in England, America, or the Continent, the modern—which is to say written—ghost story is apt to employ a pattern of literary conventions and aims whose very pervasiveness renders them obscure.

The ghost story in its folktale form usually divides neatly into two sections, which I shall call the Recognition and the Release. The former extends from the tale's beginning until that moment in which the protagonist first perceives himself unquestionably in the presence of a supernatural being. The Release, which comprises the rest of the tale, unfolds the precise manner of the protagonist's escape—or, in unfortunate cases, his failure to escape. This bipartite structure is a ubiquitous one, found in folktales throughout the world.

A choice instance (and my own favorite of ghostly folktales) is "The Deacon of Myrka," which comes from Iceland. (The richness of the supernatural in Scandinavian folklore, often attributed to sunless arctic winters, may have reached its culmination in Iceland, whose inhabitants had the additional creative boon of inhabiting a volcanic land that smelled of sulphur and looked like the moon.) A story with numerous international variants, "The Deacon of Myrka" is of the tale-type known to folklorists as The Dead Bridegroom Carries Off His Bride. In its Icelandic incarnation, it gives us hapless Gudrun, a woman who lives on the remote farm of Baegisa. Gudrun's lover, the deacon of Myrka, invites her to some Christmas festivities and promises to fetch her on his horse. On Christmas Eve, Gudrun is seen waiting for him. The reader knows, though, of a tragedy whose news has not yet reached this farm. The deacon was drowned a few days before, while crossing the Horga River, and has already been buried.

Burial is not the end of this deacon, however, who arrives as scheduled and knocks heavily on the door. Gudrun can hardly see him in the darkness, wrapped as he is in coat and hat, and he offers her no greeting. But—with what would seem like courtesy—he does lift her up to sit behind him on his horse. They ride in silence. One suspects that Gudrun may be feeling grave misgivings, although nothing of her mental state is disclosed. In any case, the transition from the dully menacing to the sharply horrifying comes abruptly: "They came to the River Horga, where ice was still piled high along the banks; and as the horse leapt down from the ice into the water, the deacon's hat was jerked forward, and Gudrun saw the skull itself laid bare." This moment of Recognition is brilliantly chosen: with the river raging below her, Gudrun cannot leap free of the horse, unless she would drown as her dead but mobile lover already has drowned. "At that very moment," the tale continues, "the moon came out from behind the clouds and the deacon spoke:

> "The moon glides,
> And Death rides;
> Don't you see a patch of white
> On this head of mine tonight,
> Garun, Garun?"

The deacon calls her Garun, a nonexistent name, rather than Gudrun, because he—this devout man, the former deacon—can no longer utter the sound *gud*, Icelandic for "god."

The rest of the story is given over to the details of Gudrun's Release—a protracted business, which includes the ringing of a churchyard bell, a physical struggle, the reading of psalms by a priest, and, finally, a magician's incantations and the rolling of a great rock over the deacon's grave. To the modern reader, the spirit's lengthy exorcism may seem anticlimactic. Certainly it is not the least bit scary, and the tale's concluding lines could hardly be more matter-of-fact: "After this, all the haunting stopped, and Gudrun grew more cheerful. A little later she went home to Baegisa, but people say she was never the same again." To stave off a sense of disappointment, the modern reader must remain mindful of the tale's intent: it aims, like so much folklore, at instruction. "The Deacon of Myrka" offers practical information about those exacting spirits which, as its listeners were well aware, surround us on all sides. It is a "how-to" story—advice on the best ways to de-spook yourself.

In the modern ghost story, the Release usually occurs very near the tale's close and arrives in a compressed, telescoped fashion—if it is not dropped altogether. The moment of Recognition, by contrast, which often met an abrupt and almost perfunctory treatment in the folktale, becomes the focus for all of the writer's ingenuity and craftsmanship. In its handling, more than in any other aspect of the tale, his artistry will be revealed and evaluated.

The shift in emphasis introduced by the modern story represented more than a mere alteration of the oral tale's tone: it signaled a realign-ment of authorial aims, and with it the possibility of a distinct new genre. The tale was changed throughout, but nowhere more strikingly than in its treatment of the ghosts that drive the plot. In folktales, ghosts are apt to step quickly into the foreground and to remain there; in the written tale, they are usually background figures, observed far less often than their handiwork is. When Elizabeth Bowen pointed out the artis-tic efficacy of a "series of happenings whose horror lies in their being just, *just* out of the true," she was only making explicit what most modern practitioners of the ghost story had been implicitly expressing for years; but it is useful to recall that here is a method that springs from a comparatively recent aesthetic and that applies to what is, historically speaking, a narrow range of tales. Only when placed in the sophisti-cated trappings of the written ghost story do spirits become, so to speak, insubstantial.

A ghost that hangs in the background is often a vulnerable creature, bred for a doubting public; by and large, the modern tale emerges out of and depends upon a healthy skepticism. The connection which numerous critics have seen between the eighteenth century's "age of rationalism" and the nineteenth century's hankering for the ghost story makes a good deal of sense. A vapor of skepticism helps to create, somewhat paradoxically, an atmosphere in which the literary ghost can thrive. The written ghost story is likely to falter wherever ghosts are either believed in too unshakably (constraining an author's artistic liberties) or dismissed outright (leaving the genre ripe for the condescensions of an author who would "go slumming"). The best stories often seem dark, pagan counterparts to conventionally religious cautionary tales. In both cases, rationalism is a besetting sin that calls for prompt punishment. (In Bowen's "The Cat Jumps," we know that Mr. and Mrs. Harold Wright are headed for trouble as soon as we read that they had "light, bright, shadowless, thoroughly disinfected minds.") For the ghost story, this need to answer rationalism's doubts, to summon the faithful back into the flock, has a bracing effect. It compels the author to present that moment when doubts are likely to be most intense—the Recognition—as powerfully and vividly, as *undeniably*, as possible. The result is an artful strengthening of the tale in a way that would once—in an earlier and more credulous age—have been unnecessary.

A second and closely related change in public attitudes was reflected in the explosive growth of supernatural literature in the late eighteenth and early nineteenth centuries. The ghost story is close kin not only to the gothic novel but also to the horror story, as developed by E. T. A. Hoffmann in the early nineteenth century and perfected by Poe a few decades later. Collectively, the three genres suggest a radical shift in literary aesthetics and, hence, in world view. All are grounded in an appreciation of the pleasures of fear. They engender uneasiness, terror, distress, not merely as tools of edification or of moral injunction but also as self-justifying pleasures. This is an aesthetic with underpinnings in the theories of Edmund Burke, whose essay on "The Sublime and the Beautiful," published in 1756, praises "delightful horror, which is the most genuine effect and truest test of the sublime." Mary Shelley struck a similar line when recalling her aims for *Frankenstein:* she wished to "speak to the mysterious fears of nature and awaken thrilling horror." As she recounts in her introduction to the novel's second edition (1832), *Frankenstein's* genesis lay in an extended visit which she and her husband paid Byron in Switzerland: "But it proved a wet, ungenial summer, and incessant rain often confined us for days to the house. Some volumes of ghost stories translated from the German into French fell into our hands. . . . 'We will each write a ghost story,' said Lord Byron, and his proposition was acceded to." This suggestion antedated by about a decade Scott's "invention" of the English ghost story, and shows that the form was stirring uneasily in its womb, or tomb.

. . .

If a thing of beauty is a joy forever, a thing of thrilling fear is often a short-lived pleasure. Which is to say, the ghost story proves a perishable commodity. What stirs shivers in one generation may well elicit titters in the next, since a ghost story that fails to frighten usually seems ludicrous. We read it with unavoidable condescension. Few other genres, if any, are so unextenuatingly hit-or-miss. And a ghost story that "misses" in this crucial matter of awakening our fears has little to offer. It is no longer interesting (in the sense of lively or engrossing), but is condemned, at best, to be "interesting" (in the academic's sense, meaning sociologically instructive, or illuminatingly primitive, or some such thing). In that elemental cosmos which the ghost story erects, the reader typically sees one of two things happen. Either "they" beat "us" (superstition momentarily triumphs, as the spirits of the dead, overmastering our every doubt, assert their existence) or "we" beat "them" (rationalism remains unshaken, and we can laugh at another clumsy attempt to play upon our childish fears).

A genre that aims at the sublime (in Burke's sense) will differ radically from one that pursues the conventionally beautiful. It is illogical, then, to suppose that a talent for realistic fiction will necessarily carry over into the realm of the supernatural. In his introduction to *Roald Dahl's Book of Ghost Stories* (1983), Dahl turns to a different genre for an instructive anecdote: "Quite a long time ago, a New York publisher . . . had what they thought was a brilliant idea. They decided to invite all the most celebrated writers in the English-speaking world to write a children's story. They would then combine all the results in one volume and they would have a classic on their hands. . . . The stories came in. I saw each one of them. Only one writer, Robert Graves, had any conception of how to write for children. The rest of the stories were guaranteed to anaesthetize in two minutes flat any unfortunate child who got hold of them." The ghost story, like the children's story, is a genre to itself. Seeking literary respectability, anthologists of ghost stories often make the mistake (which Dahl in his collection avoids) of going for "big names." But a mediocre story is a credit to no one and to nothing. The resulting anthologies are a disservice both to their readers and to those lesser-known writers who have created some of the most accomplished pieces in this singular genre.

One cause of its singularity—and a cause, as well, of many unwittingly comic moments—is the central place that it must give to the
indescribable. In no other genre does the reader stumble so frequently
over phrases like "no one can convey" and "there are no words" and
"an inexpressible feeling." Of course, the reader must sympathize with
the writer's task—to depict the walking dead is no humdrum undertaking—even while wincing at such stock phrases (or at a kindred infe-
licity, the desperate overuse of italics). In the work of adept writers,
much artistry goes into this task of expressing the inexpressible, which
is often facilitated by means of a narrative frame; the tale will be told
by someone without firsthand experience of ghosts, someone who may
echo, at least at first, the reader's own skepticism. Obliquity of this
sort often enhances the reader's uneasiness; he is apt to feel cut off,
uninformed. In a story like A. M. Burrage's "One Who Saw," for example, we are not told what Simon Crutchley beheld that made his
hair go white. We only know, teasingly, eerily, that it left "one or two
peculiar aversions. . . . He can't bear to be touched, or to hear anybody laugh."

The ghost story is singular, too, in its tendency to disappoint the
reader time and again in its last few paragraphs. Perhaps no other literary form can be depended upon so reliably to leave the reader feeling
let down. According to one of its conventions (a sensible rule, ignored
at the author's peril), whatever mysteries the story advances must be
explained; the ghost's behavior must finally conform to some pattern
of motivation. Unfortunately, such explanations are rarely so satisfying
as the edgy wonderment of the mysteries it would clarify. Although
the reader of a ghost story wants everything "tied up" in the end, the
tying up is not itself a primary appeal of the genre (as it is, say, in the
murder mystery). No, the reader comes to the ghost story for that
uncertain, skittery sensation that arises when the laws of science no
longer seem to apply but nobody can say what has supplanted them.
In a story like Robert Aickman's excellent "Ringing the Changes," for
example, one thrills as the heroine calls nervously across a dark beach,
"What sort of seaport is it that has no sea?"—even as one recognizes
that no explanation which would account for a missing ocean could
ever equal the high-strung splendor of this moment.

A principle of strict accounting obtains in the ghost story. With few exceptions, any ghosts that are promised must in time be delivered. Those stories in which the supernatural ultimately yields to the natural, in which all spirits dissolve in the light of science, are unacceptable almost without qualification. In this sense, the ghost story runs strictly counter to a genre like the bedroom farce, whose conventions require that an unpleasant possibility (typically, a wife's infidelity) should be made to look mountingly irrefutable, only to be cleared spotlessly away at the finish. In the bedroom farce, the fun lies in the certainty that all will come right before long. But in the ghost story, we feel displeased, almost resentful, if a promised unpleasantness turns out to be anything other than unpleasant.

L. P. Hartley, a gifted writer of ghost stories, made on their behalf what sounds like a wildly exorbitant claim: he called them "certainly the most exacting form of literary art." But if one considers how many first-rate writers have attempted the form, and how few first-rate stories have resulted, Hartley's pronouncement sounds reasonable. Unfortunately, it is only the rarest of ghost stories that repays a second reading. And this is hardly surprising, given the demands one asks of the form: at the very least, a discriminating reader requires a clever and fresh relationship between haunted and haunter; a lively manipulation of the genre's clichés; and an effortless transcending of everyday reality. In addition, one hopes for all those virtues that make the writing of an "ordinary story" so difficult: deft pacing, sharp dialogue, a felicitous way with words.

If, as Julia Briggs asserts, the genre is moribund and irrecoverable, the aficionado's largest regrets must be that so few masterpieces emerged from its brief heyday. Collections like the Oxford or Penguin anthologies leave the reader tantalized by the genre's untapped (and now, perhaps, untappable) potential. Time and again, one comes upon a story that hints of unexplored pathways. Somerset Maugham's "The Taipan," for example, although a predictable and at times maladroit tale, reverberates with lost promise. It is set in China, where its unnamed English protagonist has lived for so many years that the Orient has become his true home. For him, there will be no final, twilight return to England: "he had seen too many men do that and he knew how often it was a failure; he meant to take a house near the racecourse in Shanghai. . . . But he had a good many years before he need think of retiring." He feels himself at home, anyway, until he encounters one morning some coolies digging a grave that inexplicably unnerves him (it turns out, not surprisingly, to be his own). A sense of painful, fuddled isolation suddenly flows through his expatriate's soul: "He felt a horror of the winding multitudinous streets of the Chinese city, and there was something ghastly and terrible in the convoluted roofs of the temples with their devils grimacing and tortured. He loathed the smells that assaulted his nostrils. And the people." The dislocations of Empire, and especially those of colonists in torrid climates, destined to feel haunted by a cool, misty country thousands of miles away, would appear to be an ideal matter for ghost stories. Similarly, Kipling's wonderful "The Return of Imray" (one of his few successful ghost stories) leaves a lingering sense of the sadly unrealized. A man named Imray, a minor officer at a small Indian station, disappears and a police officer named Strickland eventually rents Imray's vacated bungalow. When Imray's murdered body is found perched on a beam in the roof, one realizes that although his affronted soul has been trying to communicate with Strickland, it has had greater success in reaching Strickland's dog. In its counterposing of Christian and pagan beliefs, imperial rationalism with a subjugated colony's mysticism, "The Return of Imray" creates another of those uneasy borderlands which would appear to be a perfect breeding ground for ghosts. It seems a shame that the English ghost story has so often confined itself to the English country house. Rich as England's treasury of ghost stories may be, it might have been far richer still.

Few writers of ghost stories have proved insightful analysts of the genre. The most incisive theorizing—what little there is of it—has been done by writers who wrote few if any ghost stories. Virginia Woolf, for instance, offered some lively, scattered observations about what she called "the strange human craving for the pleasure of feeling afraid." She observed that "It is pleasant to be afraid when we are conscious that we are in no kind of danger." This interplay between danger and safety suggests that one of the genre's appeals is the power it temporarily conveys: one calls up demons purely to exult in their helplessness. This is a thrill which, I suppose, also feeds on a peculiar form of nostalgia. Most of the adults who enjoy ghost stories probably also enjoyed them—but more dynamically, with a potent blend of pleasure and affliction—as children. The adult reader may bring to the ghost story an odd self-congratulation—the sweetness of returning, fortified by the certitudes of adulthood, to those creatures who were our bullies and tormentors during the suggestible nights of childhood.

Freud's venturesome essay on the "uncanny" ("Das Unheimliche") was a pioneer attempt to probe systematically our peculiar feelings about, among other things, the "return of the dead." The essay may suffer, as Freud concedes at the outset, from what he calls his "special obtuseness in the matter, where extreme delicacy of perception would be more in place. It is long since [I] had experienced or heard of anything which had given [me] an uncanny impression." His examples are likely to seem, to those either blessed or persecuted by greater "delicacy of perception" in this unsettling area, rather limited in scope. But in the depths of its ideas, and the breadth of the connections it makes, the essay lays a solid-seeming groundwork upon which any more thorough and ambitious study is likely to stand.

Freud located the source of most uncanny feelings in the uneasy cohabitation within us of rational judgment and a "residue of animistic mental activity." (One recalls Samuel Johnson on the existence of ghosts: "All reason is against it, and all belief for it.") At the outset of his essay, Freud offered a brief definition of the uncanny ("that class of the frightening which leads back to what is known of old and long familiar"), which in subsequent pages he elaborated in ways that touched directly on the ghost story: ". . . this uncanny is in reality nothing new or alien, but something which is familiar and old-established in the mind and which has become alienated from it only through the process of repression. . . . Many people experience the feeling in the highest degree in relation to death and dead bodies, to the return of the dead, and to spirits and ghosts. . . . Considering our unchanged attitude toward death, we might rather inquire what has become of the repression, which is the necessary condition of a primitive feeling recurring in the shape of something uncanny. But repression is there, too. All supposedly educated people have ceased to believe officially that the dead can become visible as spirits, and have made any such appearances dependent on improbable and remote conditions. . . ." Here is an explanation for that dizzily involuted confusion that is the hallmark of the uncanny: given the underlying familiarity of the uncanny object, we feel strange because we feel that we shouldn't feel strange. And although Freud's essay sought chiefly to identify the uncanny's sources rather than to take up the related question of why some minds are drawn so profoundly to a zone Freud himself characterized as one of "repulsion and distress," he did—like Virginia Woolf—imply that the tale provides an arena for expiation. In summoning that "surmounted" world of animistic thought, we are given a chance to reconcile ourselves to guilts that may be inaccessible to rational probing.

The ghost story would seem also to have a sizable but elusive sexual component. Rarely are ghost stories overtly sexual. (In A. S. Byatt's fine story "The July Ghost," the reader experiences a shock on coming across even this relatively demure passage: "She hissed at him 'Don't talk' between clenched teeth, so he stroked her lightly, over her nightdress, breasts and buttocks and long stiff legs, composed like an effigy on an Elizabethan tomb.") But the experience of reading them often feels oddly racy, and the language commonly employed in their description seems to parody a sexual encounter, often of a violent sort— "ravishing fear," "panting, helpless excitement," "innermost secrets," and so on. Any literary genre grounded in the aesthetics of fear rather than beauty will likely partake of some sort of alternate, parodic sexuality. Just as the conventionally beautiful has its goal and culmination in an experience—the catharsis—not entirely separable from sexual pleasure, the sublime has its own purgative climax, endearingly referred to as "the creeps": that thrillingly cold wash of fear which leaves the hairs on one's arms and neck on end. For children, whose appetite for ghostly tales is insatiable, this experience may serve as a foretaste of consummated adult sexuality. No wonder, then, that the child responds to these tales that Robert Louis Stevenson called "crawlers" with a wide-eyed, breathless ambivalence—a mix of signals that says "Please, don't tell me any more" and "But what happened then?"

This is an ambivalence paralleled in the minds of the tales' creators, regardless of when and where they live. Whatever the reigning system of belief, animistic or rational, the dead are approached uneasily; we have no comfortable way to deal with them. In the oral ghost stories, sprung from cultures pervaded by supernatural beliefs, one hears yearnings for a world free of all spirits, where the living can walk undisturbed. In the written tale, often composed for a skeptical audience by a skeptical author, one detects a different sort of wistfulness, a longing to see the dead reassert themselves. It seems there is a child inside us who, after complaining of a Spook in the closet, is rather disappointed when Science, that parental figure, comes along with its flashlight to prove there's nothing there. In its own way, a night cleansed of spooks turns out to be an unnerving, a discomposingly empty, place. For the skeptic, as for the believer, feelings of oppression are the common lot. The creator of ghost stories is forever trapped (and happily so, from the viewpoint of those for whom such tales are an endless delight) inside an unease that will find no tranquility on this side of the grave.

(1987)

COLD LAUGHTER

From the Introduction to

The Norton Book of Ghost Stories

In one of M. R. James's most celebrated ghost stories, "Count Magnus," a moment arises that, for me, strikes to the thrillingly cold heart of this peculiar genre. An innkeeper re-creates an evening in which his grandfather nervously awaits the return of two men who have trespassed into what some consider a haunted wood:

> My grandfather was sitting here in this room. It was the summer, and a light night. With the window open, he could see out to the wood, and hear.
>
> So he sat there, and two or three men with him, and they listened. At first they hear nothing at all; then they hear someone—you know how far away it is—they hear someone scream, just as if the most inside part of his soul was twisted out of him. All of them in the room caught hold of each other, and they sat so for three-quarters of an hour. Then they hear someone else, only about three hundred ells off. They hear him laugh out loud; it was not one of those two men that laughed, and, indeed, they have all of them said that it was not any man at all.

The scream is a simple but pitiful thing, a cry of pure animal terror, but the laughter's a good deal more complex. Just why are they so effectively unnerving—these final, gloating explosions of merriment from a supernatural agent (whether ghost, vampire, genie, or the Devil himself)? Most of us have heard the sound so often—in films, in television skits, in written stories, in oral childhood tales—that we ought by now to be immune to it. Yet it still lays an arresting hand upon us.

Surely, such laughter is chilling partly because of the rich range of messages it manages so compactly—wordlessly—to convey. It speaks volumes. In "Count Magnus," as in many ghost stories, laughter first of all evokes for us an adversary of striking self-possession; this is somebody who not only snares his human prey but all the while has the distance and detachment, the diabolical *leisure,* to draw amusement from doing so. The laughter also implies that all human calamities— even the loss of one's life, sanity, or immortal soul—are trifling affairs; its eruption abruptly, viciously transforms tragedy into comedy. In this transformation, the doomed is denied what seems the final entitlement of any doomed soul: a lingering moment of pity before his headlong tumble into hell. The laughter usually carries, in addition, an echo of self-satisfaction, of vindication, as though the protagonist's fall were inevitable, his stratagems and evasions foreseen and forfended from the outset. Lastly, the laughter may seek to prompt in us an altogether different show of mirth—the reader's nervous chuckle at having himself survived the tale.

One might say, in comparing the ghost story to a sibling genre, that science fiction typically seeks to elicit from the reader a "Wow" of surprise and wonderment, while the ghost story aspires to a "Whew . . ." We are meant at the denouement of most supernatural tales to feel relief. Ghost stories reflect a variety of aims, of course, but in its essential form the tale undertakes a careful sortie into a landscape of terrors—a cyclical journey (from the natural world to the supernatural and back again) that promises to release us, chastened but intact, at its close.

It's a journey with more than its share of pitfalls. Anyone who would compile a ghost story anthology—as I have recently done for Norton—faces a number of stiff tasks, chief among them being the wretchedness of so much of the material; is there any other genre whose failures are quite so impossibly godawful? But the anthologist ought to enjoy one considerable boon. Since this genre is a sort of back lot, an ancillary literary form, he surely needn't be overly respectful of it— need not make inclusions based upon a tale's date of origin, or its historical sway, or the repute of its author. Many an illustrious writer, justly renowned for accomplishments in mainstream genres, has stumbled when attempting a ghost story; not surprisingly, it calls for talents that are exacting, narrow, and quirky. It may well be the case, for instance, that Sir Walter Scott invented the modern ghost story in English, and duly deserves a place of preeminence in histories of the genre, but to my mind all the ghosts in his tales have, long ago, shifted from a sleepless to a tranquil grave. They're twice—doubly—dead. The same could be said of stories by Brontë, Dickens, Gaskell, Cather, Bierce, Hardy, Wells, De la Mare. If ghost stories are all about durability—the spirit that will not quit—they are themselves, as a genre, a highly perishable commodity, and the anthologist must aspire not only to include a number of strange "animals," but to ensure that his book feels less like a museum than a zoo: he must seek to avoid the once splendid but now dusty stuffed beast in its glass case, in favor of the restive creature that even yet breathes and eats and watches.

The late Raoul Dahl was expressing a widespread opinion when, in the introduction to his *Raoul Dahl's Book of Ghost Stories,* he wrote that "Spookiness is, after all, the real purpose of the ghost story. It should give you the creeps and disturb your thoughts." I take a broader view of the genre than that. I have a good deal of patience with ghosts that are other than malign—with benign ghosts and forgetful ghosts and needy ghosts and ghosts that may or may not be ghosts. I feel the genre ought to mirror the whole outflung gamut of our feelings about the dead.

If mere spookiness is one's objective, a ghost story anthology may not be the best place to look. If the virtue of any artwork that deals with the supernatural is to be directly correlated to adrenaline production—if its aesthetic value could be tabulated by wiring up its audience in a laboratory—surely one would be better off looking to film rather than typescript. When it comes to the sort of fear that thumps the heart and dampens the temples, horror movies are hard to beat.

My hypothetical laboratory of course raises a host of qualifications. The measuring of any audience response, even one as purely primal as terror, is a problematic undertaking. Spookiness might be evaluated not merely by intensity but by duration. In the long run, no horror film I've ever seen has unsettled me as have the stories of that "other" James—Henry—particularly his "The Turn of the Screw." On the other hand, no ghost story has ever made me literally jump from my seat—as George Romero's low-budget black-and-white cult classic, *The Night of the Living Dead,* once did.

For many of us who, like me, have little taste for horror films but a bottomless appetite for ghost stories, the written tale offers various pleasures only loosely linked to terror. We relish those delights that are innately literary: the author's ability to dart in and out of a character's head; an employment of language's inherent ambiguity in order to shift artfully back and forth between revelation and concealment; the gradual warming of diction as a climax nears; the odd aesthetic tuggings inherent in an art form that is at once unsettling in its aims and comfortingly old-fashioned in its conventions; and the playful, often ironic refurbishing of those conventions.

In their artful ambiguity—their simultaneous existence as studies of madness and of the supernatural—the ghostly tales of Henry James can create problems for two kinds of readers. In one camp are those (frequently undergraduates, my teaching experience tells me) who come to a ghost story looking for tangible spirits; they have little patience with the coy dancing of Henry's shades. In the other camp are those readers and critics for whom the ghostly is instantly reducible to psychological components. For them it is a truism that one's demons are always internal, that the "other" afloat out there represents only some form of ourselves. Neither type of reader is temperamentally adapted to a two-tiered tale—although, since the underpinnings of the entire ghost story genre are inherently primitive and superstitious, a naïve reader probably does less violence to Henry's stories than an overly sophisticated critic.

This sort of critic often lacks that mobility of imagination needed to understand that what individuates the genre is precisely the fear that our nervous forebodings are *not* all reducible to inner trauma and turmoil. To conceive the ghost story purely as a battle with inner demons, however terrifying such may be, is to denature it. Henry took his ghosts seriously. (One thinks of his long attendance on posthumous communications from his brother William.) Ghostly horror hinges upon this issue of *ex*ternality—the fear of something out there that is *not* oneself, something wholly independent of one's wishes and feelings. It's the suspicion that, to rephrase Roosevelt, we have more to fear than fear itself.

I've occasionally been asked, by someone who had heard that I was assembling a supernatural anthology, whether I myself believe in ghosts—to which I've replied, less facetiously than might first appear, "Everybody does." I can't believe any of us, if we dig deep enough in our psyches, is utterly free of a suspicion that the dead continually attend the living. Where is the person who has not resurrected them in dreams? At *this* level of the psyche—where dreams are bred and cultivated—there are no dead.

. . .

Ghost stories are inextricably bound up with notions of Justice. It is rare for ghosts to prey upon the wholly blameless. Most of the time one must infract a rule or injunction in order to provoke them. However heartless a ghost may be, he or she will likely respect any sort of compact or bargain. Justice is blind in the next world, too—it binds the living and dead alike. Often the ghost story can be seen as a bizarre gloss on English contract law, in which what the law calls "consideration" has been expanded to encompass one's sanity or immortal soul. What is so harrowing about ghostly Justice is that it appears at once fair and ferocious. True, we have the security of knowing that some transgression is usually required in order to bring down a ghostly reprisal, and yet punishments are brutally disproportionate to offenses. It takes so little to summon up one's doom! M. R. James's characters typically go astray through peccadilloes: somebody kicks open a lock on his own property; or, while seeking hidden treasure, reaches into a niche he has been warned against; or ignores a servant's misgivings about the placement of a rose garden. The reader protests, with a shudder, *But I would have done the same thing.*

One of the genre's great charms is its way of regularly reaffirming and upending orthodox social arrangements. (This might help to explain why women have traditionally found the form congenial. The ghost story is slyly insurgent.) In M. R. James's stories, one never doubts that the world properly revolves around comfortably situated dons and gentlemen scholars. (He spent his entire adult life in two august English educational institutions—King's College, Cambridge, and Eton.) Almost everyone else—loquacious rustics, struggling civil servants, solecism-prone foreigners, shrieking children, occasional domineering aunts and wives—is an amiable joke. But if his oeuvre flattered his colleagues, it also reprimanded them. The men he writes about are lacking in a kind of native wit or mother wit; their strict rationality will cost them. In the main, ghost stories rebuke and admonish those at the top of the pyramid, who are warned to pay closer heed to their pets, servants, wives, children.

Whomever a ghost chooses to pursue, the genre can hardly help being subversive of established religions. Its mere existence testifies to the emotional inadequacy of divine justice. In theory, any faith that pledges fairness on an eternal scale—with the wicked consigned to Hell and the virtuous ensconced in Heaven—ought to be enough for us. Yet it seems that the prospect of Justice in the next world is insufficient. We summon up supernatural agents in order to ensure that retribution is effected on earth. Human courts of law are fallible, and too often allow the wicked to disport with impunity; divine justice is presumably unerring, but takes too long. We need something else, something faster, and this is where the supernatural obliges us.

Ghosts are a sort of proto-religion ("Do you believe . . ." we ask each other), and, as such, they play an uneasy, interstitial role beside any larger, more fixed faith. Their long association with Christmas Eve—a final flurrying of spirits before the advent of the Christ Child—reminds us that they are kin to those minor deities and idols that monotheistic religions insist we abjure. If, individually, ghosts symbolize the lingering potency of a particular deceased, collectively they stand for the deathless power of the pagan. They particularly like to materialize when and where they are least welcome—on Sunday, in churches. Religion has suppressed them and they are resentful. They are on the look-out. They have all the time in the world.

(1994)

GAYS AND GHOST-WRITERS

We are in the midst of a centenary of sorts. Throughout the nineties—the eighteen-nineties—the English-language ghost story flourished as never before or since. The genre is often considered to have begun with Sir Walter Scott's "Wandering Willie's Tale," published in 1824, and in the sixty-five years that succeeded it—before the advent of the nineties—many tales were written that still compel our loyalties. These include stories by Charles Dickens, J. S. Le Fanu, Elizabeth Gaskell, Robert Louis Stevenson. (Poe is usually regarded as a pioneer in the field not of ghost stories but of horror tales—a distinct if close enough sibling that occasional confusions inevitably ensue.) But it was in the nineties that, its energies and sophistication gradually mounting, the developing genre attained a summit. Today, the stories of that decade hold us more powerfully than their predecessors, and—allowing for the musty trappings that cobweb the entire genre—speak with an arresting immediacy that remains coldly thrilling.

Since the genre is rife with inexplicable affinities and odd twists of fate, there is something quite pleasing in the coincidence that the two men commonly deemed the greatest practitioners of the form happen to share, though unrelated by blood or nationality, a surname. As masters of supernatural fiction, both the American Henry James and the Englishman M. R. James came into their own in the nineties. It was, far and away, Henry's most prolific decade as a writer of ghost stories. And while he was composing "The Turn of the Screw" and "Owen Wingrave" and "The Real Right Thing," his namesake—whose initials stood for Montague Rhodes, and whose devotees often refer to him as Montie—was beginning to compile *Ghost Stories of an Antiquary*, his first, most celebrated and richest collection.

The two were writers whose principal energies lay in other literary disciplines, and the peripheral place of supernatural fiction in each man's oeuvre carries a good many ironies. In Henry's case, even now his ghost stories suffer from the brilliance of his nonsupernatural fiction. For readers to make their way merely through those of his volumes that have legitimate claims to be called masterpieces (*Washington Square, The Bostonians, Portrait of a Lady, The Ambassadors, Wings of the Dove, The Golden Bowl*—the list proliferates) is so sizable a task that we may get around to various branches of his "minor fiction" belatedly, if at all. While it may sound absurd to say of the author of "The Turn of the Screw"—surely the most extensively analyzed piece of modern supernatural fiction in the language—that his ghost stories are neglected, the truth is that although some are indefatigable anthology pieces ("The Beast in the Jungle," "The Jolly Corner"), others are little seen or discussed. Certainly, it's not easy to view his ghost stories in their entirety. The book that gathered and introduced them—*Henry James: Stories of the Supernatural,* edited by Leon Edel—has drifted out of print. The scattered fate of Henry's ghosts has distorted the robust role they had in his creative life. In my preoccupation with some of his lesser-known ghost stories, I've discovered that even academics who have taught James and generally know his work well are often surprised to learn that the output of his supernatural fiction runs to some seven hundred pages. Ghosts were for him a lifelong obsession. One of his earliest stories, "The Romance of Certain Old Clothes," published when he was twenty-five, was a ghost story, and the novel he was working on when he died, almost a half-century later, had a supernatural theme.

As a fiction writer, M. R. James has the advantage of not competing with himself. He published no stories that weren't supernatural. His primary literary endeavors were abstrusely scholarly: he was a medievalist and paleographer and biblical scholar, based at King's College and later at Eton, who devoted nearly two decades to cataloguing the manuscript collections at Cambridge University. His ghost stories had an intimate and informal origin: most were written to be read aloud to colleagues at King's, in candlelit performances on Christmas Eve. It was a small circle destined to widen immeasurably. Montie's thirty-plus ghost stories, released in four volumes, have never gone out of print. His fans are legion.

The two writers shared a precocious appetite for the supernatural. In Henry's case a taste for the mystical seems to have been family-bred;

his father, Henry Senior, immersed himself in Swedenborgianism, and his brother, William, the psychologist, helped found the Society for Psychical Research, in London, in 1882—the world's first attempt to bring scientific investigatory techniques to the study of the paranormal. Montie's penchant for the supernatural might have been expected to sit less easily with his family. His father was an Evangelical clergyman in a small town in East Anglia. But the family seems to have relished the immensely bright, well-behaved boy's appetite for the queer and unearthly.

The two writers shared a good much else besides: punctilious manners; an appetite for the drawing-room refinements of tea and sherry and biscuits; a physique brimming with unathletic energy; a gift for languages; conversational panache supplemented by a flair for mimicry; and a confirmed, sociable bachelorhood. In their wifelessness lies perhaps another, deeper affinity: both appear to have been latent or at least nonpracticing homosexuals. Whether their sexual tendencies ought to be regarded as a further coincidence, akin to their common surnames, or should be viewed as vitally linked to their distinctive achievements in the realm of supernatural fiction is an issue best addressed through a look at the peculiarities of this lively little genre.

The ghost story, like most minor art forms, has a limited number of motifs, and the aficionado eventually comes to relish this very limitedness. I'm reminded of one of the world's most appealing and narrow literary forms, the sunny social comedies of P. G. Wodehouse. One of the great charms of Bertie Wooster and Mr. Mulliner is what tireless, timeless *bores* they are, and there's a kind of perverse satisfaction in rolling one's eyes on being informed, for the thousandth time, that Bertie once wrote an article called "What the Well-dressed Young Man Is Wearing" or that Mr. Mulliner would indeed this evening favor a hot Scotch and lemon. Likewise, the ghost story connoisseur delights in the creaking stair in the family manse, the rumble of distant thunder, the unplaceable odor in the parlor.

But anyone who plunges deeply into ghost stories (and I estimate I've read over a thousand, first as a simple fan and later, doggedly, as the editor of an anthology) must recognize that the common elements extend beyond a threadbare grab-bag of creaks, rumbles, odors. The traditional ghost story employs various hierarchies, and its unfolding plot might be seen as a complex ascent. Time and again the stories reflect a kind of biological and social pyramid of perception. The lower your position, the quicker you are likely to be in sensing a ghost's arrival. Animals, the lowest beings in the pyramid, will dependably recognize a visitant long before their owners do. Higher up are children and servants and people of "exotic" backgrounds. Still further up are women (feminine intuition) and the Irish (that mystical Celtic blood!). Generally, at the apex stands an upper-class man—a rational being who "knows better" than to believe in spooks. But in the domain of the ghost story, those who know better are usually the last to know.

The five senses generate a second hierarchy. Ghosts are wont to announce their arrival first through a smell, or perhaps a distant cry. Gradually, they impinge on senses we consider more reliable—sight and, culminatingly, touch. They are immaterial entities who are forever solidifying, and the climax of a story often arrives when flesh at last encounters something not quite flesh—something simultaneously human and inhuman.

These two progressions are usually played out in what turns out to be a three-part drama. The stories work with, and at times against, a formula. A generic ghost story typically devotes its initial paragraphs to creating a scene or landscape which looks sedate and secure—but which is underlain with subtle presentiments of unease. Montie, especially, aimed in his opening lines for that zone where the innocuous edges into the soporific:

> Those who spend the greater part of their time in reading or writing books are, of course, apt to take rather particular notice of accumulations of books when they come across them.

> Some few years back I was staying with the rector of a parish in the West, where the society to which I belong owns property.

> Mr. and Mrs. Anstruther were at breakfast in the parlour of Westfield Hall, in the county of Essex. They were arranging plans for the day.
> "George," said Mrs. Anstruther, "I think you had better take the car to Maldon and see if you can get any of those knitted things I was speaking about which would do for my stall at the bazaar."

The middle, climactic section of the typical ghost story encompasses that crowning moment when even our thick-skinned hero or heroine encounters incontrovertible evidence of the supernatural—evidence which may include physical contact or may merely threaten it. The generic story's final section represents a sort of exorcism or purification. The old crypt is freshly padlocked, the spook-ridden house razed to the ground, the queer manuscript incinerated, and so forth. By such means, our chastened hero liberates himself from his otherworldly encounter.

The psychological progression in this tripartite structure seems wonderfully suited for the playing out of a vexed, guilt-laden homosexuality; it seems suited, that is, to men who might be expected to show an especially keen sensitivity—compounded of fear, desire, and a need for dual outlets of expression and suppression—to the images and implications of "aberrant" encounters. The quiet opening simulates a seduction—we are drawn in despite ourselves. In the best stories, we move gently, and yet steadily and ineluctably, toward a physical contact we feel helpless to prevent. For those authors whose insurgent minds are abuzz with images at once "unnatural" and irrepressible, what literary analogue might have richer allures than this one, whose climax is a contact of the most unnatural sort imaginable—that between the living and the dead? When these ghostly meetings are lifted from their ambience of terror and set down in isolation, it is striking how frequently they suggest an amorous encounter, as in these climactic moments from Montie's stories:

> One body had the arms tight round the other.

> It hung for an instant on the edge of the hole, then slipped forward on to my chest and *put its arms round my neck.*

> . . . two arms enclosing a mass of blackness came before Eldred's face and covered his head and neck. His legs and arms were wildly flourished, but no sound came.

> I was pursued by the very vivid impression that wet lips were whispering into my ear with great rapidity and emphasis for some time together.

The ghost story has innate attractions to the sensibility that inwardly yearns, despite itself, for a touch so overmastering that one's scruples or inhibitions are as nothing, so sweeping that one cannot help succumbing. Who among us, after all, is equipped to reject the advances of the dead? And to the mind stretched between desire and guilt, between the outreaching hand and the locked door, what form more satisfying than one whose conventions outfit it with provisions both for forbidden touch and for subsequent purification?

My focus leads me to stress the appeal to the homosexual imagination, but the form holds, of course, inviting elements for any author of thwarted sexuality wishing to play out, symbolically, a prohibited contact. In the genre's profusion of stories about demon lovers—typically, a vampiric figure if male, an angel of death if female—one senses an ongoing uneasiness about that perilous business in which men and women briefly mingle and blur bodies. Both of these demon lovers upend conventional sexual functions. The vampire departs from one of his trysts having been not the depositor but the repository of bodily fluids; the angel of death is a creature whose womb brings forth not creation but destruction.

The ghost story might also be expected to hold a mesmeric fascination for the sensibility raised in the shadow of child abuse, whether actualized or not. The typical ghost—a nocturnal, larger-than-life visitor bent on unspeakable mischief—might well possess a horrific vividness for a child threatened by a parent's invasive attentions. When we pick up an old collection of supernatural tales and scan its table of contents, we know that we will never know precisely what private terrors prefigured the terrors chronicled within. But the suspicion is strong that the stories reflect not only adult repressions but childhood violations. These are knotted sensibilities. There are ghosts behind their ghosts.

Any attempt to examine the supernatural fiction of Henry James and M. R. James based upon assumptions about their clandestine desires runs into difficulties commonly encountered in the burgeoning academic field of gay studies. This is a discipline where both postulates and conclusions must be advanced with great hesitancy; unless we are dealing with a modern writer of forthright candor, we are likely to be trafficking in evasions, lies, and obfuscations, both deliberate and subconscious. Given the dangers of exposure—the 1890s marked not only the acme of the ghost story but Oscar Wilde's trial for crimes against nature—a "deviant" sensibility had every incentive to conceal its promptings from others and, if possible, from itself.

The result is a literary discipline whose boundaries are more suscep-tible to revision than any we're accustomed to. The borders of tradi-tional literary studies, fixed through chronology and nationality, are stable. One can work a few minor adjustments (Was Shakespeare born on the 24th of April or the 26th? Just how Polish *was* Joseph Conrad?), but most of the milestones are lodged immovably in the earth. Things are otherwise when our measuring device is something as amorphous and fleeting as sexual desire; the landscape suddenly blooms with fog. If incontestable evidence were to turn up tomorrow that Henry James or Montie James had fathered a passel of children with a chambermaid, I suppose most of us would be deeply surprised but not, in the end, astounded. Life conspires to teach us that even people we know long and well are least to be predicted when we contemplate their sexuality. The end result of our various uncertainties, then, is the certainty that at times writers will be taught and studied under a gay fiction rubric who were, if the facts were better known, of another temperament altogether, and that others belong under it whom we would never dream of placing there.

A second difficulty concerns questions of privacy. Henry James and M. R. James illustrate the problem with striking acuteness. However each man may have accommodated himself to his sexual yearnings, their lives were a strong, implicit affirmation of the notion that the matter was no one's business but their own. Imagine their incredulous horror, their sense of outraged violation and bitter betrayal, on dis-covering that their *admirers* would bandy their private lives in a public forum. It's an issue that has special poignancy in regard to ghost stories, so many of which are rooted in the premise that the dead find no repose because their wishes are heartlessly rebuffed by the living.

Given such obstacles, what justification might there be for analyzing the ghost stories of Henry James or M. R. James in the light of their alleged homosexuality? To my mind, it's simply a matter of the impos-sibility of reading meaningfully at least *some* of their fiction outside a homosexual interpretation. Montie's "'Oh Whistle and I'll Come to You, My Lad'" seems unignorably a tale of homosexual panic—just as unignorably as Henry's "The Great Good Place" seems an arcadian fantasy of guiltless homosexual dalliance. With such stories, the author's sexual orientation is not an extraneous or even a penumbral aspect of their creation; the tales themselves are sexual entities, sexual enactments, and to partake in them fully, as an ideal reader, is to immerse yourself in their carnal anxieties and longings.

The panic of " 'Oh Whistle and I'll Come to You, My Lad' " originates in a comic fluster. When we're introduced to Professor Parkins (who is "hen-like" and "something of an old woman"), he quivers and blushes at the prospect of sharing a room at the seaside with his "bluff" younger colleague Rogers. Parkins reaches the inn a few days before his friend, and his vacation begins auspiciously. Walking on the beach he finds what seems to be a mysteriously inscribed pagan whistle. He blows upon it excitedly: "it had a quality of infinite distance in it, and, soft as it was, he somehow felt it must be audible for miles round."

Yet as he awaits his friend's arrival, Parkins is repeatedly visited by a waking nightmare. He beholds a man on the seashore running from a "figure in pale, fluttering draperies." The pursued takes shelter in the lee of a groyne. When he is eventually discovered, his pursuer darts "straight forward towards the groyne" (a pun of such flagrancy that one marvels its author could have overlooked it), at which point "Parkins always failed in his resolution to keep his eyes shut." The next morning he discovers that the sheets in the neighboring bed are twisted as if someone had "passed a very poor night" (or, the reader wryly observes, a very wanton one). In the story's culminating scene, the hapless Parkins is attacked by—what else?—the sheets of the bed his friend is meant to occupy. He screams. Fortunately, a fellow vacationer (ideally suited to play the dual paternal role of protector and disciplinarian—he's a retired military man, no less) bursts into the room and disentangles Parkins from the sheets.

By sober morning light, the military man ensures that the whistle is tossed into the sea and the offending sheets burned. Significantly, although Parkins is undone by his experience, the author himself realizes that "it is not so evident what more the creature that came in answer to the whistle could have done than frighten." The ghost had, after all, "nothing material about it save the bed-clothes of which it had made itself a body." At some level, anyway, Montie recognized that the dread of the encounter he could not bring himself to visualize was a greater threat than the encounter itself. " 'Oh Whistle and I'll Come to You, My Lad' " allows its author to contemplate a forbidden embrace—one initiated with a sort of wolf-whistle—and then to detach himself from it. The story is suffused with a sexuality all the more powerful for its unselfconsciousness; it is no coincidence that Montie regarded the insertion into a ghost story of any overtly sexual element as "a fatal mistake." The story is at once licentious and chaste; it caters to both the libertine and the ascetic in each of us.

" 'Oh Whistle and I'll Come to You, My Lad' " neatly embodies Montie's characteristic strengths and shortcomings. He was a master of atmosphere and pacing, whose concise, well-plotted stories deliver their little wallop of terror with dependable efficiency. For the most part, he kept things simple. While Henry's people were marvels of depth—personalities as many-layered as a slab of fossiliferous limestone—Montie's cast of characters consisted almost exclusively of stick figures: timid bachelor dons, malapropism-spouting rustics, sinister landholders.

Montie spent little time pondering the literary form in which his enduring fame was won. What he left us by way of prefaces and introductions is modest, casual, unreflective. Apparently, it never occurred to him that the ghost story as he constructed it is an especially problem-ridden form, that he had barred himself, in embracing his bookish bachelor dons as heroes, from many of the most reliably fruitful devices of the genre. Ghost stories commonly strike at us "where we live." In many—perhaps most—tales, the ghost takes on the role of an intimate: one's spouse or betrothed is revealed as a demon lover (as in Henry's "The Friends of the Friends"), or the family unit is infiltrated (as in "Turn of the Screw"). But Montie's heroes are likely to have no lovers (and to meet no temptresses), and to be without close family (or distant family either). They are solitary men, whose pared lives offer supernatural agents precious little purchase.

It was Montie's instinctive genius to understand that such men are most productively haunted—are most exquisitely vulnerable—within the two institutions toward which any upright turn-of-the-century English don might reasonably look for impregnable sanctuary: the library and the Anglican church. Wherever books are gathered in his stories, there's a risk of infernal subterfuge—frequently taking the form of some craftily coded message that only the most adroit scholar might decipher. And wherever a church stands, there's the danger of some kind of satanic interloping, sometimes in the form of a stealthily evil clergyman (like Archdeacon Haynes of "The Stalls of Barchester Cathedral," who arranges to send headlong down a flight of stairs a ninety-two-year-old rival) and sometimes in the form of the various residues—pagan rites, Hebrew texts, or, most threateningly, "papist designs"—of some stubbornly unexpunged faith. His ghosts may trespass simultaneously into both realms, as is presaged in the first sentence of "An Episode of Cathedral History": "There was once a learned gentleman who was deputed to examine and report upon the archives of the cathedral of Southminster."

Haunted archives? Well, they turn out to be a natural lair for ghosts. . . . What is a library, after all, but a place where the dead, tidily coffined in their separate volumes, continue to speak? Montie's stock hero is likely to be culpable of no crime more grave than that of scholarly inquisitiveness. Libraries are irresistible to him. He desires merely to *know,* and yet in so desiring may lure catastrophe to himself. The title of one of Montie's stories, "A Warning to the Curious," cuts to the core of the matter. He was forever notifying his original audience—that group of dons whose Christmas Eves were consecrated not to families but to colleagues—that their solitary, sedentary livelihood was strewn with hazards. It's a risky business, this process of extracting information from dusty old tomes! Montie's bespectacled heroes are, willy-nilly, intrepid voyagers into the unknown.

He was also advising his colleagues to keep their skills honed. His heroes are forever finessing their way out of a jam by decoding a garbled message, tracking down a rogue citation, locating an obscure medieval document. His tales are part detective story and part brain-teaser. It would not be enough for the reader merely to crack the cryptogram in "Abbot Thomas"; he or she must also know some French *and* Latin to make it out fully. Montie's are Sherlock Holmesian stories in which Moriarty (a nebulous figure, anyway, in the Conan Doyle series) has been transformed into a wind from the crypt.

In the supernatural world of Henry James, by contrast, the intellect solves nothing. Rather, it engenders its own family of difficulties. His ghost stories repeatedly point out the danger of reason's ascendancy in the mind that has divorced itself from feeling—his characteristic preoccupation with the unlived or unintegrated life. Often the intellect has become derailed; there is a hint of madness in the air. The stories traffic concurrently in apparitions and pathology.

The out-of-print Edel collection, in its persuasive bulk, leads us to suspect that for Henry this may have been the chief reward of the genre: the opportunities it presented for radically bifurcated discourse. Many of his stories are two-tiered. On one level, the workaday world that most people commonly regard as "real" is shown to be starkly dismissible, for ghosts are afoot in its shadowed purlieus and byways. On another, any reports we're given concerning supernatural doings are themselves to be dismissed, for they can only be delusional ravings; since the ghosts aren't genuine the madness has to be. Either way, the reader is unmoored. This is the state of affairs in "The Turn of the Screw," and in the near-century since its publication hundreds of critical pages have been devoted to "proving" either the authenticity of the ghosts or the insanity of the governess who is the tale's primary narrator. It was Edmund Wilson, writing in the twenties, who most prominently advanced the insanity thesis, and his essay might still serve as a prime illustration of how on occasion even the most brilliant thinker can become, in the fervent pursuit of a half-truth, a half-wit. His was the folly of trying to solve what was left intentionally ambiguous. No one has written odder supernatural fiction than Henry James, but his stories nonetheless are genre pieces and partake of a good many of the genre's distinguishing characteristics, including a resistance to sweeping explanations that eliminate all mystery. To find a solution to "The Turn of the Screw" is to miss what is perhaps its principal gratification: that of watching its author deftly mediate between the plausible and the fantastic.

Despite their tenuity, Henry's here-and-not-here ghosts often represent lives more freewheeling and rugged than those of the people they haunt. The ghosts tend to be the victims of their own audacity and tempestuousness—they are souls who risked romance and found heartbreak, who chased after military glory and met only defeat. Spencer Brydon's maimed ghost, in "The Jolly Corner" (one of a number of Henry's stories concerned with alter egos), is the "blatant, vulgar" figure Spencer might have become had he pursued the sullying rough-and-tumble of commerce rather than the genteel pastimes of a man of leisure.

We need not stretch very far to see that Henry's fascination with "blatant, vulgar" alter egos may be a logical by-product of a man's commitment to an unrequited sexuality. Indeed, despite their differences, the work of both of our "ghost-writers" might be viewed as highly nuanced meditations by bookish, brilliant men on the decision to forsake the life of the body for the life of the mind. Their tales are cautionary examinations of the phantoms—grim and yet oddly beguiling—that may pursue those who choose for themselves a life of solitude and find they are not alone.

Academe's curious disregard of so fertile a literature suggests that the image of a pyramid or hierarchy might usefully be applied here as well. At a time when English departments throughout the land are bent on rattling orthodoxies and reworking critical assumptions, it is interesting—if sometimes a little alarming—to observe how certain wayworn assumptions persist. If one contrasts the multitudes of critical studies focussed on the English gothic novel, as exemplified by Horace Walpole, Ann Radcliffe, M. G. Lewis, to the few spare examinations of the supernatural fiction of M. R. James or Edith Wharton or Elizabeth Bowen, the conclusion is inarguable that novels continue to be esteemed as "higher"—farther up the pyramid of genres—than short stories. Because there are so few modern ghost novels of note (the list thins precipitously after Kingsley Amis' *The Green Man* and Shirley Jackson's *The Haunting of Hill House*), ghost fiction can hardly be taken seriously by anyone not first willing to take the short story seriously. Having immersed myself for some time in the literature of the supernatural, I frankly can't imagine anyone who wouldn't trade away a shelf of sagging old gothic novels for the sharp-angled brilliance of Henry's "Maud-Evelyn" or Montie's "Casting the Runes"—or Elizabeth Bowen's "The Cat Jumps" or Muriel Spark's "Portobello Road" or John Cheever's "Torch Song." This is "small" art only in terms of size. The strength of these last three stories, all of relatively recent vintage, attests to the form's ongoing vitality. It continues to provide far more than a hospitable environment for the writer of troubled sexuality: it remains one of the best media we have for exploring our most primitive, irrational attitudes toward the dead. Every literary genre, obviously, negotiates with death, but the ghost story elevates those moments in which, distorted by yearnings or misgivings so potent as to be well-nigh uncontainable, our reason attenuates: we enter a realm in which no insurmountable barrier obtains between the living and the deceased. All the old borders, all the old protections, are down. . . .

I remember once walking a country road on a viciously icy winter night. There was a car parked some ways ahead, and, my eyes teary with the cold, I didn't immediately notice the human shape behind the steering wheel.

When I did, my step faltered. It *spooked* me, having thought myself alone, to have to accommodate myself so unexpectedly to a night in which I had company. But moments later, my vision clearing, I had a second surprise. The human shape was merely the driver's-side headrest.

The second jolt was stronger than the first, for this time around a sort of death had unfolded: where there had been life, there now was none. In a few seconds I'd been twice uncentered. It was an experience familiar to devotees of the ghost story. In their bones they know that the universe is unsettling whether it is inhabited by spirits or whether we—lone walkers on a bitter night—are alone in the windy darkness.

(1994)

LAWYER'S ISLAND
Austin Wright's *Islandia*

Now and then, on a day when no big news is breaking, local television may bring you a story like this:

We enter the modest home of a stoop-shouldered middle-aged man. He's a pedestrian figure by profession (a mail-sorter, maybe), and yet he's in possession of a larger-than-life secret. Clandestine knowledge flushes his rapidly blinking face as the camera zeroes in upon him— renders him bashful and exultant and gawky. We follow him as he clumps down into his basement, where for the last twenty-four years, it is now revealed, he has been erecting a medieval village out of tooth-picks. Here are stables, and taverns, and a gabled manor. He is at work now on the ogival cathedral, which he expects will occupy him for another five or six years. . . .

Or perhaps the story goes like this:

We are shown into the cramped apartment of an elderly widow. She's a creature of simple, severe tastes, to judge from her no-nonsense bun and black sweatshirt, but she, too, harbors an extravagant revela-tion: she, too, is in possession of an alternative world. For the last two decades, ever since the death of Ronny, her bail-bondsman husband, she has been working on a needlework quilt of a square footage nearly equal to her apartment's. Thread by thread, thread *over* thread, she has constructed an Inuit fishing village, complete with igloos, dogsleds, seals, glaciers, breaching whales, and the aurora borealis. . . .

While such stories appeal to everyone, they probably hold a height-ened interest to viewers who make their living as creative artists. The professional novelist or musician or painter may well look on such projects with a mixture of envy and incredulity and admiration at an aesthetic passion so pure, so removed from the imperatives of the mar-ket and from conventional routes to recognition. The life of the artist is supposed to be free (isn't that its great appeal?), but might there not be something freer still in those artists who don't see themselves as such—but merely as people who enjoy working with toothpicks or thread?

I recently finished rereading the book that, far and away of the novels I know, comes closest in spirit to the postman architect of Toothpick Town, the widowed seamstress of Polar Panorama. It's a huge book with a small cult following, Austin Tappan Wright's *Islandia*. It was first published in 1942, eleven years after its author's death. I have a later paperback version, which describes the book as an "underground classic," but I fear it subsequently went so far underground as to be better described as long-buried. It has drifted out of print, and even among acquaintances with esoteric literary tastes, a mention of its title often elicits a look of puzzlement.

The novel details the benign adventures of young John Lang, Harvard '06, who shortly after graduation is sent as consul to Islandia, a nation that "lay, facing the Antarctic, on the edge of the Karain semicontinent in the Southern Hemisphere." Lang enjoys an extended, mostly leisurely sojourn in this large, illusory country of some three million inhabitants. I suppose *Islandia* might be classified as a utopian novel. Or it might be deemed a fantasy, or a social satire. Whatever it is, it presents us with a country of almost mind-boggling detail and verisimilitude. The poet-critic Randall Jarrell once spoke in praise of the wayward book that "does a single thing better than any other book has ever done it," and I would be amazed if there exists, among all the novels ever written about imaginary places, one that creates a more total, tactile environment. To read *Islandia* is to venture convincingly into a remote and intricate land. Readers who ramble for a couple of weeks through its thousand-plus pages are likely to feel they have a more intimate knowledge of the place than they would have of, say, France if they were to spend a similar length of time motoring around the French countryside.

Just as the creator of Toothpick Town can be expected to toil painstakingly over sections of the cathedral vault that will not be visible to the onlooker, so did the creator of Islandia variously labor in ways indiscernible to its readers. To begin with, the book in typescript was far longer than the novel as eventually published; after Wright's death, in a car accident at the age of forty-eight, his daughter, Sylvia Wright, pruned the manuscript to commercially feasible proportions. Hundreds of pages were cut.

But that's just the start. Austin Wright also compiled a document, never published, entitled "A Description of Islandia," which purports to be a scrupulously researched treatise written by the imaginary nation's French consul. Wright also compiled, independent of the novel, a glossary of Islandian words, an Islandian calendar, a number of extraordinarily detailed maps, an illustration of the Islandian duodecimal number system, population graphs, land-use tables, and so forth. The "Description" includes nearly two hundred dense pages of Islandian history, originating more than a millennium before the novel actually opens. It devotes seven pages, for instance, to the history of the year 1328. Typical in its comprehensiveness is this brief aside about King Alwin XVIII, who reigned from 1281 to 1292: "His appellation—'lotas' in Islandian—is not quite aptly translated 'lazy.' True laziness is 'ston.' 'Lotas' is vicious laziness." Similar profusions of detail surround Islandia's geological evolution ("At the same time, probably, were formed by igneous activity in the ocean then lying south and west loccoliths of harder felsitic magma, which today appear in the Hills of the City, in Lower Doring, and possibly elsewhere"), its agricultural animals, its dress and customs, system of governance, educational policies, literary tradition. (Actual samples of the literature were also provided in Wright's papers, in the form of verses "translated from the Islandian," one of which runs more than twenty pages.)

From what sort of imagination did such things spring? Who was Austin Tappan Wright? The novel offers an affectionate, unhelpful introduction by a colleague and friend of Wright's, Leonard Bacon, which includes a barebones sketch of the author's life. Wright was a New Englander by birth. He was a law professor, first at Berkeley and later at the University of Pennsylvania. He left at his death a "beautiful, entertaining, and highly intelligent" widow. He was "engaging" and "friendly"—but how intimate were his friendships, one must wonder, given that he never confided to Bacon that for decades he'd been amassing an immense novel set in an imaginary land?

Who was Austin Tappan Wright? I took this question over to Harvard's Houghton Library, where a number of his papers are stored. He was the son, on his father's side, of a distinguished classics professor at

Harvard, and, on his mother's, of a now-forgotten novelist. His brother was an esteemed geographer who was the subject of a *New Yorker* profile. After graduating from Harvard in 1906 (along with Lang, *Islandia's* hero), Wright attended Harvard Law School, where he was an editor of the *Law Review* and graduated among the top ten students in his class. He then went to work in Louis Brandeis' firm, at least during the days; nights, he became the founding father of Islandia.

As to how often and how steadily he wrote, the record remains unclear. Wright was a self-contained man. An atypically self-probing passage in a letter to his brother after his daughter Sylvia's birth, in 1917, speaks volumes about his temperament:

> I feel that I can do much for a girl. Our family code, or philosophy, or whatever it is, is peculiarly helpful to women I think. I never before thought much about it until the last few years, and now I see it for what it is (rather brought into relief by various things) and I admire it immensely and want to perpetuate it. . . . It is very simple.
>
> 1. No religion but fair play.
> 2. Plenty of devil but fair play.
> 3. Don't be a slacker in your interest and love of life.
> 4. The aristocrat is simple, not complex. The lower you go, the more complex you are.
> 5. The "primitive man" is the most complexly sentimental brute-cad of all.
> 6. If you suffer, that is your own affair—keep the pain of it to yourself.
> 7. Never bleed others for sympathy.
> 8. Moodiness is merely lack of self control.
> 9. Self control and fair play.
> 10. And what is fair play?
>
> Don't go bothering God to tell you. Make the best of yourself, keep yourself clean, don't turn your eyes inward perpetually and you will find your instincts an infallible guide.
>
> A sort of 10 commandments.

The Houghton Library materials include forty-four letters from Austin to his brother—graceful, cheerful letters that are generous in their evocations of Austin's sailing, hiking, and tennis-playing, and niggardly in their supply of literary appraisal or of anything resembling earnest soul-searching. There are also two letters to his mother, minutely concerned with his new housing arrangements in California. He must have been an affable mystery to everyone around him. "His library was large and varied in its contents," his obituary in the University of Pennsylvania *Law Review* noted. "One was given the impression that he was preparing to try his hand at some form of belles lettres if time and opportunity occurred."

Islandia is a country of pared, simplified wants. It is a monarchy that has turned its back on technology. Although its people are well educated, they pursue lives all but unstamped by machinery. They do not have watches; they pace themselves by water-clocks. They prefer horses to cars. They are mostly farmers. Their days are tranquil. They are fond of sailing. Foreign nations tend to regard Islandia as a global backwater, peopled by pagans. The Islandians themselves are unvexed by the world's condescension—provided the world leaves them alone. For the nation has made it a policy to restrict foreigners, whose visits are rigorously limited and monitored. At the time the novel commences, a number of great powers—Germany, France, the United States—have grown resentful about being barred from Islandia (whose mineral wealth is reputed to be vast), and are pressuring its government to open itself to the forces of "civilization."

Pre-Meiji Japan—a "closed" nation likewise perceived as refined, pagan, affluent, and secretive—seems to have figured largely in Wright's imagination. And in the leafy landscapes of Islandia, its every valley a haven to the contemplative, one hears as well the measured reflections of Thoreau. Some other influences were tentatively put forward in a letter that Wright's brother addressed to an admirer of the novel more than two decades after its author's death:

> Austin was a voracious and rapid reader and had many passing enthusiasms for particular writers and subjects, which tended to be writers and subjects in which most people are not particularly interested.
>
> Among his early enthusiasms were Mallory's Morte d'Arthur, Spenser's Faerie Queen, Sienkiewicz' novels of Poland, George Meredith, the Mongol invasions, the history of Greece and Byzantium in the Middle Ages, the origins of Gothic architecture, Swinburne, Herman Melville (then a "discovery"), sailing in small boats, collecting books on yachting and especially on voyages in small boats around the world.

One might also plausibly detect—though I came up with no hard evidence for it—the influence of D. H. Lawrence. *Islandia* reflects, in any event, an impulse to subject sexual mores to a steady, thoroughgoing examination. Indeed, if this sprawling story might be said to have one overarching theme, it would be that of a man's awakening and accommodation to his own sexual impulses. For all the book's abundance of dry, reportorial facts, the country of Islandia turns out to be a place of carnal fulfillment—or, at least, the place to which an inexperienced turn-of-the-century upper-class New Englander voyages in order to explore his sexuality.

As he sets off for Islandia, Lang is a sexual naïf. (Unsympathetic readers might call him a prig.) He's a man who, in his late twenties, finds the taking of a woman's hand a bold and marvelous stroke; a kiss positively bedazzles him. The sexual code that he embodies, with its heated strugglings between "base" temptation and "difficult" virtue, may seem cloyingly quaint to modern readers. Nonetheless, it feels genuine. We gather something of the life Lang has led—something of an entire generation and social milieu—when he is aroused by the sight of an Islandian woman's foot: "Her feet were still bare. How rarely had I seen a girl's bare feet! They did not seem natural. These pink-soled things with toes were not the proper way for a girl to end off."

Since the unraveling of every other strand of plot in this colossal novel asks patience of the reader, it's hardly surprising if the book proceeds slowly when treating of sexuality. But, in time, Lang not only loses his virginity—in a prolonged and passionate premarital affair with a younger Islandian woman—but comes around, with Lawrentian earnestness, to a radical critique of contemporary American sexual mores. Why, he asks, can't an unmarried man and woman travel together? Why do American women need so many undergarments? Why must it be the man who takes the physical initiative? John Lang, our dry stick of a hero, begins to sound like a bohemian.

Wright is hardly the first man to have populated a deserted island in order that he might incarnate his sexual fantasies. One of the charms of *Islandia,* though, is that its women are not the compliant, complaisant creatures of the formulaic male fantasy. In most ways they are tougher and more logical than Wright's American hero, and, in the clinch, more forthright in their physicality. Another charm is that far more is going on than mere dalliance; Wright is resolutely attempting to integrate the sexual into the rest of the psyche. There turn out to be four words for "love" in Islandian: *amia*, nonphysical love; *alia*, love for family and place; *ania*, the desire to marry; and *apia*, sexual passion. They are subtly interwoven. Lang eventually learns that, even when the clothes come off and inhibitions tumble, complexity still abounds.

Many children, perhaps most, inhabit for a while a rococo fantasy world. But these places almost invariably fade with time. Wright managed not only to hold on to his but to induce it to ramify—succeeding in doing so, perhaps, by fusing the child's appetite for a private kingdom with an adult's intense hunger for sexual daydreams of a realistic, workaday texture. Throughout the novel, Lang is seeking a suitable wife. The book examines four possible solutions—each representing, from the author's standpoint, a different reconciliation with his romantic kingdom. Lang could marry an American woman and settle permanently in America—which would be, for Lang's creator, an embracing of the familiar and an ultimate renunciation of the "unreal." Or Lang could marry an Islandian and bring her to America—the importing, from Wright's perspective, of the exotic feminine into a homegrown world of masculine commerce. Or Lang could marry an Islandian and remain in Islandia—a full capitulation to the dream. Or Lang could marry an American and settle permanently in Islandia. Eventually, he takes the last of these paths, and the book might finally be seen as a story of a successful adoption—whereby Wright, in the person of his hero, induces his beloved to accept as her own his most personal, precious possession: his Toothpick Town, his Polar Panorama, his Islandia. He manages to draw her fully into the terrain of his dream—the only zone where he can possess her, and she him, utterly.

That branch of the modern novel devoted to imaginary countries may represent a minor genre, but it's a vivacious and fruitful one. I'm thinking of books like Butler's *Erewhon* or Hilton's *Lost Horizon* or Bellow's *Henderson the Rain-King* or Updike's *The Coup* or Spark's *Robinson*— novels in which the author seeks to build something from nothing. These are far removed in spirit from a book like Waugh's *Black Mischief*, which purports to be about an imaginary country (Azania) but satirizes a real place (Ethiopia). Bellow had never seen Africa when he created the Wariri tribe of *Henderson*; he made it a point of *not* going, lest the facts interfere with the verity of his imagination. For all their touches of realism and fussing over minutiae, novels of this type may be closer kin to elaborate works of fantasy, like Tolkien's *Lord of the Rings,* or of science fiction, like Lem's *Solaris,* than to books grounded in a particular, visitable place.

According to Sylvia Wright, "Islandia started when my father was a small boy, when it was 'my island.' " She went on:

> I have been told that he used occasionally to shut my uncle out of it, so my uncle then created his own country, which was called Cravay. Cravay, like Islandia, was thoroughly mapped, and I think had a peerage. When my grandfather, who was a classical scholar, died, they discovered an imaginary country among his papers.

My island is by nature the sort of place one reveals to the outside world charily, with some reluctance. Wright's premature death leaves the matter unclear, but apparently he had no intention of publishing the book he'd labored over for a quarter of a century. Had his car not skidded on a rain-slicked road in New Mexico on September 18, 1931, a family pattern might eventually have surfaced: once more, Wright children would have discovered in their deceased father's papers the trappings of another world.

It's a rare and, I suppose, inessential talent among novelists—this flair for creating alternative societies. Certainly there have been wonderful writers who, in terms of place, invented practically nothing, doing little more than affixing new name-tags to the world they lived in. But for most novelists, probably, the impulse to create from scratch is at least skeletally present, and while they may never construct an entire country, they will revel in going part of that distance: in fabricating a village, a country house, an apartment building.

As *Islandia* makes clear (and the unedited manuscript of *Islandia* makes clearer), there are all sorts of novelistic talents that Wright mostly or utterly lacked: he had little gift for pacing, for concocting vivid minor characters, for determining what was and wasn't germane to his larger story. On the other hand, such shortcomings serve only to throw into greater relief his outstanding virtue. It would be hard to argue that *Islandia* is a better novel than *Henderson the Rain-King,* which evinces a structural intelligence and a suppleness of prose that *Islandia* cannot begin to match. But Islandia is a realer place than Bellow's African kingdom—or than Butler's Erewhon, or Hilton's Shangri-la, or Updike's Kush. It's the realest imaginary place I know.

At times, readers may feel as though Wright is less the nation's author than its discoverer—as though he can no more alter its characteristics than we can. This is felt particularly when something delays the story. Perhaps a spell of rain detains the hero on his journey. Lang chafes impatiently, and the reader chafes impatiently—and one imagines *Wright* chafes impatiently. You can almost see him remarking, "Pity about this rain. I'm as eager as you are to get on with the story."

A taxonomist of the novel might conclude that Wright is someone who developed a virtue to the point of hypertrophy. Among nature's creatures he is kin to the Irish elk, whose outsized antlers may have contributed to its extinction; or to the bird of paradise, whose elongated plumage proves an encumbrance; or to the calvaria tree, which developed a germination technique so specialized it hinges on the existence of the nonexistent dodo. We cherish and seek to preserve such creatures in the wild, and I don't see how we can do anything less in the wilds of American literature; it's time for *Islandia* again to see print.

One of the great satisfactions of Wright's life is that this man who lived so minutely in the domain of the imagination simultaneously throve in the "real world." His career as a teacher and legal scholar looks exemplary—and he seems as well to have been a contented father and husband and friend. A near-contemporary of Wright's at Harvard, E. E. Cummings, once defined art as the place where two and two make five. It's the domain where, happily, things don't add up. Austin Wright presents us with the model of a man who gave himself exclusively, one hundred percent, to two contrary worlds.

(1994)

ANY PLACE YOU WANT
Thomas Pynchon's *Vineland*

The further I ventured into Thomas Pynchon's new novel, *Vineland,* the more pressingly I found myself wondering: For whom is this intended? What sort of sensibility would, on turning page 200, say, of this nearly four-hundred-page book, find itself cheerfully hoping to be introduced to yet another character who boasts both a funny name and a taste for folksy facetiousness? For this is what, like as not, you'll get at any given juncture. (On page 200, incidentally, one reads about Zipi Pisk, Frenesi, Darryl Louise Chastain, and Krishna.) Pynchon introduces by name a cast of well over a hundred, including Scott Oof, Moonpie, Isaiah Two Four, Willis Chunko, Morning, Chef Ti Bruce, 187, Meathook, Cleveland ("Blood") Bonnifoy, Baba Havabananda, Ortho Bob Dulang, Dr. Elasmo, Chickeeta, and Sid Liftoff. Needless to say, the result can be confusing, and prospective readers might find useful my eventual realization that the names of pets and cars (for cars, too, are christened) tend to be less outlandish—marginally—than those of the people associated with them. Hence, "Bruno" will be the car and "Rex Snuvvle" its owner, "Desmond" the dog and "Prairie" its master, and so forth.

Lest all of these details sound disastrously coy and cloying, I hasten to note that *Vineland*—although it tries one's patience at nearly every turn—is far from a disaster. It is manifestly the work of a man of quick intelligence and quirky invention. Many of its episodes flicker with an appealingly far-flung humor. And Pynchon displays throughout *Vineland* what might be called an internal loyalty: he keeps the faith with the generally feckless and almost invariably inarticulate misfits he assembles, tracking their looping thoughts and indecisive actions with a patience that seems grounded in affection. He is true to his creation until the finish; the book's closing pages strike a moving note of sweet inconclusion, of curiosity grading not into enlightenment but into wonder. Nonetheless, such virtues having been tallied, one must note that in view of our expectations the book is a disappointment.

One's sense of letdown derives in part from a condition extrinsic to the book itself: seventeen years have elapsed since Pynchon last released a novel, *Gravity's Rainbow,* and hopes naturally run high, perhaps unreasonably so. But in the end *Vineland* falters in a convincing variety of ways—perhaps chiefly through its failure in any significant degree to extend or improve upon what the author has done before. In its style and diction, in its satirical targets, in the techniques of its plot unfoldings and outreachings toward illumination—in practically everything—*Vineland* marks a return to what was weakest in his patchy novella, *The Crying of Lot 49,* published in 1966. But whereas the earlier book offers the virtue of compression—and, with it, the thrill of watching, at the book's denouement, as the pent-up becomes the pell-mell—*Vineland* is a loosely packed grab-bag of a book. And there is no pleasure in *Vineland* to compare with the one great delight of *Lot 49*—its madman-in-a-library's hunger for arcana, as the century-long development of the postal service is pursued with a diligence worthy of a superhuman mailman.

Vineland opens to opening eyes—those of Zoyd Wheeler, a largely unemployed, pot-smoking, fortyish Californian who wakes up one morning in the summer of 1984 to the realization that he must perform "something publicly crazy," preferably before a television camera, if he is to protect his "mental-disability" stipend. He resolves to secure his money, as in years past, by leaping through an enormous plate-glass window, a scene to be rendered visually all the more striking by his first having got himself up as a woman.

Although he passes through the window unscathed, Zoyd is, we gradually discern, a wounded man. He has never recovered from the disappearance, many years before, of his wife, Frenesi, who abandoned him for a federal prosecutor named Brock Vond. When the reader meets up with Frenesi, he discovers that she, like Zoyd, is on the public payroll, though not in any humorous, harmless way. A student revolutionary in the sixties, she has since become an FBI informer and lackey, shuttling from place to place at the behest of her increasingly ruthless and indifferent employers.

Zoyd and Frenesi have a teen-aged daughter, Prairie, who lives with her father and dreams of being reunited with her mother, whom she has not seen since she was a little girl. Her quest is, in fact, one of the book's main themes, for at one point or another most of the principal characters seem to be on the trail of a missing woman. Another theme is the centrality in our culture of television, which is generally referred to as the Tube (capital "T") and which inspires meditations on Tubal abuse and Tubaldetox and Tubeflicker. Whatever the disparities in their outlooks, Pynchon's characters are united in having television serve as their communal well of learning, from which they draw their humor, morality, locutions, analogies. No one reads; everybody watches; and what binds us, soul to soul, is "Wheel of Fortune," "The Flintstones," "Phil Donahue," "Alvin and the Chipmunks," "The Mod Squad," and (a special favorite) "Gilligan's Island."

At the book's heart—the one theme without which *Vineland* wouldn't be *Vineland*—is political paranoia. The novel asks us to entertain the notion that, beginning with Nixon and culminating with Reagan, our government came to regard its subclass of easy-doping layabouts—its Zoyd Wheelers—as meriting not merely contempt but brutal repression and, perhaps, extermination. Deep in the hills of northern California, in the imaginary county of Vineland, from which the book draws its title, a military installation has gone up for the evident purpose of sowing domestic terror.

The book's title recalls, of course, the Norse adventure sagas and the North American expeditions they chronicle, but little is made of this connection. A tighter literary link is fixed when Pynchon evokes the white man's discovery of Californian Vineland:

> Someday this would be all part of a Eureka-Crescent City-Vineland megalopolis, but for now the primary sea coast, forest, riverbanks and bay were still not much different from what early visitors in Spanish and Russian ships had seen.

Hovering in the background here, needless to say, is Nick Carraway and his celebrated lament at the close of *The Great Gatsby:*

And as the moon rose higher the inessential houses began to melt away until gradually I became aware of the old island here that flowered once for Dutch sailors' eyes—a fresh, green breast of the new world.

Pynchon's passage rings a dirgelike note of corroboration. Out there at the New World's newest New World—the coast of California—one catches an echo of hopes mislaid, a continent betrayed.

But to set the two books side by side is unavoidably to highlight one of *Vineland*'s gravest deficiencies: the absence in it of natural beauty. Certainly it contains nothing even remotely as lovely as Nick's passage by train through a Midwestern snowfall:

> When we pulled out into the night and the real snow, our snow, began to stretch out beside us and twinkle against the windows, and the dim lights of small Wisconsin stations moved by, a sharp wild brace came suddenly into the air.

Compare a kindred moment in *Vineland*:

> Zoyd must have dozed off. He woke to rain coming down in sheets, the smell of redwood trees in the rain through the open bus windows, tunnels of unbelievably tall straight red trees whose tops could not be seen pressing in to either side.

At various points in *Vineland* (beginning with the marvelous photograph on its dust jacket, which depicts a hill of evergreens savagely reduced to clipped and smoking rubble) Pynchon asks us to ponder the rape and poisoning of our environment, but how are we to summon any deep consternation when Nature in these pages engages us so thinly? Pynchon characteristically renders natural detail in a tone of pop flippancy—a "golden pregnant lollapalooza of a moon," a "sun just set into otherworld transparencies of yellow and ultraviolet, and other neon-sign colors coming on below across the boundless twilit high plain," a "squadron of bluejays stomping around on the roof."

In 1982, not long before he died, John Cheever published a short book, *Oh What a Paradise It Seems,* that likewise treats issues of paranoia and environmental vandalism within a tale of antic folly and reversal. But one of the many lessons offered by that fine, valedictory novel was that contemporary fiction of a comic, even slapstick kind has ample room for the humbling grandeurs and outsize poetry of the natural order. When Cheever informs us that quaint Beasley's Pond, on which the book's New England hero likes to skate, has been poisoned by unscrupulous businessmen, the reader feels heartsick, for Cheever's is a world where "a traverse of potable water" can represent "the bridge that spans the mysterious abyss between our spiritual and our carnal selves." In *Vineland,* one could witness the dynamiting of the entire state of California, redwoods and all, and remain unaffected.

What one longs to meet in *Vineland,* and never does meet, is some moment when Zoyd or one of his buddies would find the stars overhead cutting so deeply into his psyche, or the wave before him breaking with so plaintive a collapse of voices, or the ground underfoot releasing so tangy a mixture of surge and decay that all wisecracks die aborning in the throat. One longs for a sweeping crack of thunder. The rain-whetted smell of toadstools. The shifting flank of a startled deer.

A feeling for the natural world may be welcome in a satirical novel, but it is hardly essential—as is demonstrated by Evelyn Waugh, who in a masterwork like *A Handful of Dust* can hurl the reader into the feverish Amazon jungle without ever evoking much of its infernal beauty. What is essential, however, is freshness; even if the targets that one aims at are in tatters, the darts that one tosses at them must be sharp. When Pynchon takes on laid-back California ("The little portable sign read OPEN, KARMOLOGY CLINIC, WALK RIGHT IN, NO APPT. NECESSARY") or outdoorsy chic ("He wore sunglasses with stylish frames, a Turnbull & Asser shirt in some pastel plaid, three-figure-price-tag jeans by Mme. Grés, and après-logging shoes of a subdued, but incontestably blue, shade") or a Mafia thug (an "oversize gorilla") or militant feminism (" 'It was sleazy, slippery man,' Rochelle continued, 'who invented good and evil, where before women had been content to just be' ") or made-for-television movies ("Pee-wee Herman in *The Robert Musil Story*") all we can give him is a weary smile. This humor has no bite; we've heard it all before.

He's even less successful when he bundles off one of his heroines to Tokyo, where she is sold into white slavery by a bunch of inscrutable technocrats. Lord knows that modern Japan is ripe for satire, and perhaps in time, as the Japanese bury us economically, we may abandon our solicitous but condescending notion that they—unlike the British, the French, the Soviets—are not hardy enough to withstand our chiding. But even if one applauds Pynchon's recognition that to lampoon the Japanese is not necessarily "Japan-bashing," what he actually presents here is not merely bathetic and inane but ("Girl, you have never seen picky till you've been in one of these Jap meat shows") ugly and offensive.

In short, his aim is off. What could be a more rewarding adversary than television, provided you actually had something novel to say about the ways in which it alternately stupefies and imbrutes us? But what Pynchon offers has already been said better in Cheever, in Updike's Rabbit novels, even in Kosinski's *Being There*—and, daily, in the parodies that television unselfconsciously makes of itself. And with his icon of governmental coercion, Brock Vond, he creates somebody who, even by cartoon standards, looks insubstantial. Cartoons operate in two dimensions, anyway, whereas Vond is strictly one-dimensional. Trousers perpetually askew with the upthrust of his desire, he is a sort of ambulatory erection, who reduces poor Frenesi to a love slave:

> Brock Vond had reentered the picture, at the head of a small motorcade of unmarked Buicks, forcing her over near Pico and Fairfax, ordering her up against her car, kicking apart her legs and frisking her himself, and before she knew it there they were in another motel room, after a while her visits to Sasha [her mother] dropped off and when she made them she came in reeking with Vond sweat, Vond semen—couldn't Sasha *smell* what was going on?—and his erect penis had become the joystick with which, hurtling into the future, she would keep trying to steer among the hazards and obstacles. . . .

As satire, *Vineland* is a case not of "too little, too late," but of too much, too late. Given the book's length, there is simply not enough originality to sustain it. Most of it, particularly the sending-up of California, feels a little stale. One is left with a troubling image of an author supplying what he thinks his audience wants, based upon what it embraced in the past. Do his readers like to meet rock bands with unpalatable names, like the Paranoids of *The Crying of Lot 49*? This time around he'll give us Billy Barf and the Vomitones. Have we shown a liking for portentous aphorisms? Okay, then how about "Life is Vegas"? In the end, it's hard to quell a suspicion that Pynchon is—either deliberately or through a sort of unguarded psychological seduction—playing down to his audience.

Although *Vineland* tilts at grand issues, the book is actually at its best in little, unforced moments in which Pynchon puts a spinning zap on his language:

> Why, the man had me scared spitless.

> They arrived at the mouth of an oversize freight elevator, scrambled inside, and began to plunge earpoppingly hellward.

> Dangerous men with coarsened attitudes, especially toward death, were perched around lightly on designer barstools, sipping kiwi mimosas.

Pynchon's style everywhere courts ungainliness. He pursues dissonance over euphony, roughness over smoothness, and, often, confusion over lucidity. For one thing, he adopts into his own expository prose some of the awkward contractions employed by his characters: "to've," "might've," etc. For another, his almost exclusive reliance on the comma, and his penchant for breaking phrases unidiomatically, leads to a prose of jumpy, tumbling disclosures:

> He didn't get to the Cuke quite in time to miss Ralph Wayvone, Jr., in a glossy green suit accented with sequins, who was cracking jokes into the mike to warm this crowd, who in Ralph's opinion needed it, up.

> Not long before this her period, a major obsession by then, had arrived at last, plus lately she felt washed under by these long, sometimes daylong, waves of inattention, everybody looking at her weirdly, especially boys.

This is writing with a lot of clangor, a lot of racket, in it—as in these thumping repetitions of "out" and "out of":

> Somewhere down the hill hammers and saws were busy and country music was playing out of somebody's truck radio. Zoyd was out of smokes. On the table in the kitchen, next to the Count Chocula box, which turned out to be empty, he found a note from Prairie.

This sort of discordancy can hardly be attributed to oversight, since it is drawn from the novel's first page and since each succeeding page turns up similar effects. No, Pynchon deliberately hits the ear harshly; reading him is like listening to a song on the radio with the volume cranked up to the point where, now and then, static crackles.

Among contemporary writers Pynchon is, of course, hardly unique in cultivating disharmony. J. D. Salinger and Flannery O'Connor owe many of their most winning effects to an ear attuned to the preposterous ways in which words get mangled around them and to a tongue prepared to go the manglers one better. But both of them reserve such effects until something truly choice happens by. For all the malformations of speech that Pynchon records in *Vineland* (all the phrases like "actin' like a li'l fuckin' army o' occupation") none is so felicitous as when Meeks, in *The Violent Bear It Away,* with a misguided stab at formality, declares, "You figure he might have got aholt to some misinformation"; nothing is so inspiredly garbled as this moment in Salinger's "Just Before the War with the Eskimos":

> He inserted the nail of his uninjured index finger into the crevice between two front teeth and, removing a food particle, turned to Ginnie. "Jeat jet?" he asked.
> "What?"
> "Jeat lunch yet?"
> Ginnie shook her head. "I'll eat when I get home," she said. "My mother always has lunch ready for me when I get home."
> "I got a half chicken sandwich in my room. Ya want it? I didn't touch it or anything."

Why is a surreal, madcap novel like O'Connor's *The Violent Bear It Away* so much more satisfying than a surreal, madcap novel like *Vineland?* In part because O'Connor's careful clumsinesses are always bumping up against something graceful, or Graceful: human fumbling is set off against divine agency. By contrast, there is little "behind" all the clatter in *Vineland,* nothing transcendently spiritual or beautiful or numinous—or even overarchingly malignant, unless one is prepared to take seriously its (surely satirical?) suggestion that Reagan and his cronies were only a step or two removed from committing Ceauçescu-like pogroms against their own people. *Vineland* lacks the huge, desolating disillusion of, say, Beckett; the abyss that it contemplates is, simply, not very deep.

For some readers, such shortcomings will scarcely matter. *Vineland* by mere virtue of its arrival qualifies as a phenomenon—one that releases, in some quarters, an almost irresistible impulse to announce a masterpiece. How else to explain why a highly intelligent critic like Sven Birkerts, reviewing the book for *USA Today*, would liken it to the *Divine Comedy*? Or why Salman Rushdie, in *The New York Times Book Review*, would proclaim it "a major political novel about what America has been doing to itself, to its children, all these many years"? Pynchon inspires cultists, and a cult that has waited nearly two decades for word from its leader will naturally feel uncontainable pressures to declare the wait worthwhile. (Just how powerful this impulse can be was crystallized for me when I discussed *Vineland* with an academic friend. When I complained that most of the book's jokes fall flat, he readily agreed—but added that Pynchon surely had trafficked to such length in leaden humor for some aesthetically sound, if as yet undetermined, reason.)

The cult is fueled, naturally, by Pynchon's celebrated, and greatly refreshing, anonymity. In an era in which the writing of books begins to seem, for many prominent writers, an adjunct to the business of promotion—talk shows, readings, signings, "appearances"—he somehow contrives to make even Salinger look like a party animal. No one appears to know where he lives and how he spends his time; what may be his most recent available photograph dates to his 1953 high school yearbook. The blankness that enfolds him allows each of us to make of him what we will—to convert him into a species of ideal artist or secret friend. In addition, by setting so much of *Vineland* in a sixties' dope haze, he taps into what for many people remains an era of indestructible nostalgia. How delightful it is as one's joint-passing youth is now revealed to be no mere idyll but—wow! neat!—the stuff of great art.

The common tendency to overrate Pynchon reflects as well his admirable fascination with the ways in which science and technology daily refigure our lives—a subject of curiously little urgency for many American writers, whether traditional or avant-garde. This has been a preoccupation of his from the outset; one of his earliest stories, written when he was little more than twenty, was a meditative piece entitled "Entropy." In *Vineland* he muses repeatedly upon the nature of the computer. But if we look outside America to a writer like Stanislaw Lem, we see just the sort of sparks that can fly when a first-rate creative temperament truly immerses itself in scientific issues. In his native Poland in the fifties—a milieu in which computers were but a distant rumor—he discovered in cybernetics "a new era not just for technological progress but also for the whole of civilization." Time and again, he has demonstrated a genius for focussing on new or potential technological breakthroughs and teasing from them one implication after another, each more striking than its predecessor. After the dizzying meditations on theology and artificial intelligence in a book like *The Cyberiad, Vineland* can look embarrassing:

> We are digits in God's computer, she not so much thought as hummed to herself to a sort of standard gospel tune. And the only thing we're good for, to be dead or to be living, is the only thing He sees. What we cry, what we contend for, in our world of toil and blood, it all lies beneath the notice of the hacker we call God.

Over the years, Pynchon has clearly established himself as our foremost "experimental" writer—but isn't it equally clear that our country in recent decades has not produced anyone who can compare to Borges, Calvino, García Marquez? Many wonderful things have emerged from those American writers who are regularly grouped, in both age and aims, with Pynchon. Donald Barthelme, for instance, brought to the short story a distinctively oddball humor—his "The King of Jazz" is a gem—but does anyone sincerely wish to hold up one of his collections beside Borges' *Ficciones?* John Barth can be marvelous—particularly in *The Floating Opera* and some of his short stories—but who would set his oeuvre beside Calvino's? Where are the recent American novels that one would want to stack up against García Marquez' *One Hundred Years of Solitude?* Or Lem's *Solaris?* Or Kobo Abe's *Woman in the Dunes?* Or Halldor Laxness' *The Atom Station?* Or Juan Rulfo's *Pedro Paramo?* (Ironically, some of the best antirealist American fiction in our time belongs to writers who are generally classified as naturalists. Who would have supposed that Cheever, often dismissed as a chronicler of suburban quandaries, would write some of the best American ghost stories since Henry James?) These are the books against which *Vineland* must be matched; we do no favor to Pynchon when we allow him to flourish in a critical vacuum.

If I concentrate on *Vineland's* shortcomings, and underplay its considerable charms (and how unlikable can a book be in which one character's haircut was apparently "performed by someone who must have been trying to give up smoking"?), I do so in an attempt to counterbal-ance its idolaters. For all its dark moments, the book is closer to farce than tragedy, and to herald it as some sort of weighty masterwork is to place a king's crown on the head of a jester. And although I have no more idea than anybody else about how Pynchon spends his days, I have trouble believing that during the last seventeen years he has de-voted himself exclusively to *Vineland*. My guess—and my hope—is that time will reveal this book to have been a lighthearted interlude, one completed while its author was intent on a more substantial, if not necessarily more voluminous, work. Peering hard at that high school yearbook photograph—its pair of earnest probing eyes, its appealing buckteeth—one longs to be able to say, as Prairie says in the last spoken words of the novel, "You can come back. . . . Come on, come in. . . . Take me anyplace you want."

(1990)

DEMONIASIS

Salman Rushdie's *The Satanic Verses*

🌀

What has befallen Salman Rushdie in recent months defies encapsulation. Time and again, the furor surrounding *The Satanic Verses* apparently crested, only to erupt in a more vehement, madder guise. One can usually depend on a loose network of contemporary social conditions (among them, the primacy of film over written works, the accelerated turnover of news in our media, and the general din of modern life) to dilute and diffuse any literary controversy, but things have gone otherwise with this novel. When, three months ago, the Ayatollah Khomeini issued his "sentence of execution," a sort of infernal standoff was forged: somewhere, in hiding and under police protection, Mr. Rushdie goes on living, but those who would annihilate him remain unplacated. Meanwhile, borders of all sorts—of national sovereignty, of logic, of civilization itself—have given way.

The horrors that have grown up around *The Satanic Verses* make it almost impossible to recollect the time when Rushdie's book seemed merely one controversial novel among many new novels. Yet less than four months ago (to Rushdie, it must seem like four lifetimes ago) he felt free to compose a spirited self-defense for the London *Observer,* in which he lashed out at both the "Thought Police" of militant Islam and the Labour Party politicians who stood ready, in his view, to bargain away creative freedom in a pandering to ethnic voters. But that was before the Ayatollah's decree.

If the various counterdemonstrations in support of *The Satanic Verses* have been heartening reassertions of an artist's right to unfettered expression, Rushdie's sympathizers are left, nonetheless, with a sense of ultimate impotence. In the face of the Ayatollah's pronouncement that the "blasphemer" should be sent "to hell," and that every Muslim should "employ everything he's got, his life and wealth" toward that end, who can grant Rushdie the security of mind and movement which he, as both man and artist, requires? At the moment, little can be done except to comply with his repeated request that his novel be considered as a novel—and that, as such, it be evaluated on its literary merits.

The Satanic Verses picks up where Rushdie's last novel, *Shame,* left off: in the clouds. *Shame* concluded with a billow of smoke that gradually rose and coalesced into the torso of a man. *The Satanic Verses* begins with a literal bang—the explosion of a hijacked jet as it cruises 29,002 feet over the English Channel—that sends cascading down through a cloud bank "reclining seats, stereophonic headsets, drinks trolleys, motion discomfort receptacles, disembarkation cards, duty-free video games, braided caps, paper cups, blankets, oxygen masks." Among the wreck's "titbits" are "two brown men"—Gibreel Farishta, who was for fifteen years the leading star of Indian cinema, and Saladin Chamcha, who, as the Man of a Thousand Voices, has made a fortune in the British film industry, chiefly in commercials. ("If you wanted to know how your ketchup bottle should talk in its television commercial, if you were unsure as to the ideal voice for your packet of garlic-flavoured crisps, he was your very man.") The two men, neither of them equipped with a parachute, manage not only to survive the descent (they are the disaster's sole survivors) but to bicker and sing and remonstrate with each other on the way down. With characteristic bravado, Rushdie at one stroke casts off the constraints of realism and rings the note of fabulism that echoes throughout this outflung, ambitious novel: "Let's face it: it was impossible for them to have heard one another, much less conversed and also competed thus in song. Accelerating toward the planet, atmosphere roaring around them, how could they? But let's face this, too: they did."

Gibreel and Saladin are linked, it becomes clear, by more than a miraculous escape, careers in film, and Indian ancestry. Their passage together through five and a half miles of sky initiates a number of complementary, surreal transformations. The first of these seems a purely lighthearted touch. Gibreel has long been notorious for what one of his leading ladies has described as "breath of rotting cockroach dung"; but after the two men find themselves deposited, bones unbroken, on an icy stretch of Sussex coast, it is Saladin whose exhalations suggest "ochre clouds of sulphur." It isn't long before other, queerer changes surface: Saladin begins to grow horns and a tail, while Gibreel's head emits a halolike glow. We have entered the realm of Milton's *Para-dise Lost;* the novel's opening detonation, the reader comes to see, was nothing less than a fall of angels.

The nascent halo serves as confirmation to Gibreel, who for many months has suspected that he is an incarnation of his namesake Gabriel, the archangel who was sent to Daniel to explain the vision of the ram and the he-goat, who served as the agent of the Annunciation to Mary, and who—more to the point in this novel—revealed to Muhammad the principles of Islam. Large portions of the book are set in Arabia in the early decades of the seventh century A.D., during those incendiary years when Muhammad—who is here called Mahound—became a prophet, attracted a small cadre of followers, time and again eluded and outwitted his persecutors, and eventually invested himself with suffi-cient authority, both moral and military, to ensure the ongoing life of his new faith. One measure of the book's ambition is that it chronicles the founding of a world religion as a sideline to its primary plot.

I might alternatively say that the whole of the book takes place in the twentieth century, since the sections that depict Muhammad arrive by way of the archangel Gabriel by way of the film star Gibreel. Gabri-el's revelations come to Gibreel in dreams. The first dream begins after Gibreel, repudiating the dietary laws of his Islamic upbringing, indulges in what must be called a swinish repast: "He loaded his plate with all of it, the pork sausages from Wiltshire and the cured York hams and the rashers of bacon from godknowswhere; with the gammon steaks of his unbelief and the pig's trotters of secularism." Overindulgence of this sort is commonly associated with bizarre dreams, but Gibreel's dreams continue—steadily, in serial fashion—for months on end. He grows convinced of his celestial nature, and who's to doubt him? Readers who would interpret the dreams as guilt-engendered delu-sions have that troublesome halo to explain away.

Dreams of one sort or another suffuse the novel. There are violent dreams, paradisal dreams, daydreams and nightmares, and dreams within dreams. They take on a life of their own. This is a world of permeable sensibilities, in which dreams often "leak" from one state of consciousness into another, from one person to another.

Whether one ought to view the Muhammad of *The Satanic Verses* as an impressionistic dream amalgamation or as the solid historical figure who founded Islam, it is difficult to square Rushdie's portrait with the international turmoil that the book has produced. Although there is much here to offend the faithful—Rushdie's Muhammad is a manipulative, lecherous, and somewhat cynical man, and the novel also depicts a brothel that becomes an "anti-mosque" when its dozen prostitutes adopt the names and mannerisms of Muhammad's wives—the book, when taken in its entirety, is so dense a layering of dreams and hallucinations that any attempt to extract an unalloyed line of argument is false to its intention. Rushdie, who was raised a Muslim but says he now holds no religious beliefs, pointed out in his *Observer* article that Muhammad always discouraged his followers' attempts to apotheosize him, and argued further that the portrait in *The Satanic Verses* is consonant with a man who continually stressed his own humanity.

Most American readers, I suspect, will feel unqualified to sort through the byways of the debate. To take but one example, many Muslims are enraged by Rushdie's practice of referring to Muhammad as Mahound—a name, Rushdie acknowledged in his article, "which, long ago, was indeed used as a derogatory term." He justified himself with a passage from *The Satanic Verses*: "To turn insults into strengths, whigs, tories, Blacks all chose to wear with pride the names they were given in scorn; likewise, our mountain-climbing, prophet-motivated solitary is to be . . . Mahound." Whether Rushdie's analogy is apt or his choice of names is simply, maliciously offensive (that pun on "prophet" does give one pause) remains—for me, anyway—an unresolved issue. But if the American reader is likely to feel removed from the controversy's intricacies he will probably enjoy, by way of compensation, an ability to form artistic judgments the more lucidly for not being embroiled in religious issues—to see, specifically, that the weakest portions of the book are those dealing directly with Muhammad. A bridge of dreams, it turns out, is too flimsy and insubstantial a structure to support heavy traffic between the seventh century and the twentieth; the two worlds never completely fuse. In any final accounting, *The Satanic Verses* must stand or fall according to aesthetic criteria. And when the dust settles (or perhaps one should say, given the book burnings, when the smoke clears) it will be evident that *The Satanic Verses* is a book of splendid but segmental components that do not quite cohere into a satisfying whole.

Rushdie is a writer fond of and occasionally besotted with excess. In *The Satanic Verses* he disregards E. M. Forster's distinction between "flat" and "round" characters and seeks to infuse the fullness of life even into peripheral presences. The result is not a sense of enhanced dimensionality so much as of clutter; the propulsion of the tale is forever being retarded by obstructions of its own making. When, for instance, the penmanship of a secondary character is described as "large, looping, back-leaning, left-handed," one can't help thinking that we've been given two, and perhaps three, adjectives too many. A writer blessed with an omnivorous eye, Rushdie at times succumbs to his gift and lets himself be waylaid by any number of things—furniture, faces, advertisements, bibelots, graffiti—that have little bearing on his story.

Still, you must admire the man's titanic energy, proof of which is that his novel, though it runs to more than five hundred pages, often seems too packed but seldom padded. Rushdie has a rare talent for surrealistic invention—an ability to pursue chains of causation and contingency without regard to where they cross or recross the boundary separating the plausible from the fantastic. Curiously, then, the best part of *The Satanic Verses* is a somewhat conventional, thoroughly realistic story. Over the years, Saladin Chamcha, the Man of a Thousand Voices, has grown more English than the English (he weathers his miles of free-fall without losing his bowler), and on one of his trips back to India he is unnerved when a woman named Zeeny Vakil, the first Indian he has ever taken as a lover, speaks of his eventual "reclamation." She prophesies that India is "going to get you back."

Which in some sense it does. After Saladin sheds his satanic horns and tail—his demoniasis (as he thinks of it) departs as mysteriously as it came—he makes another journey to India, to attend to his father, who is dying and from whom he has long been estranged. In the daily business of ministering to a helpless old man—shaving the gaunt cheeks, hauling the atrophied body to the toilet—Saladin discovers a filial love that was lost, seemingly forever, in adolescence, and, what's more, he learns to accept his native country as never before. If the theme of divided loyalties is what might be expected from Rushdie, who was born in Bombay, in 1947, and has spent more than half his life in England, it nonetheless provides the book with the one extended section where the reader's respect and admiration freely give way to something better: empathy.

. . .

At times, the punctuation available to writers who work in English looks inadequate to Rushdie's needs. When he composes a novel, the bottom row of his typewriter, where the comma, period, virgule, and question mark are found, gets a heavy workout. He's also keen on dashes, hyphens, colons, semicolons, exclamation points, and parentheses. Literary English has undergone a streamlining of punctuation in this century, of course, which can make the reading of fiction written only a hundred years ago seem a slow business—often pleasurably so. Rushdie offers a kindred typographical density. One is not surprised to come across in his fiction an ellipsis followed directly by a question mark and a dash:

> Then whose head, in my own lap, with my own hands . . . ?—who received caresses, spoke of nightmares, and fell at last singing from the sky?

Or, in unbroken succession, an ellipsis, question mark, quotation mark, and dash:

> "Then how can *I* . . . ?"—With which he snatched up his clothes in an untidy bundle, and fled from her presence.

Or an Emily Dickinsonian onslaught of dashes:

> —And someone else, too,—the one with whom our Saladin fell to earth,—has come; is wandering within.—Chamcha enters the arena; and is amazed.

In other spots he jettisons most punctuation ("Unable to muster the smallest scrap of dignity, he blubbers whimpers pleads beats his breast abases himself repents"), and even tosses out the spaces between words, thereby coining compounds by the dozen ("redwhiteblue," "goodandproper," "whatstheword," "justlikethat," and so forth).

Rushdie's experiments with punctuation reflect his handling of larger questions of style. He treats the language as though he owned it. At his best, he can wrench syntax to the teasing verge of incomprehensibility without losing his reader, or can burden a sentence with such a weight of clauses that it threatens to collapse and yet stands firm. He is a writer of inspired violence. One feels on every page how much he loves to read and write. His books brim with rapid, glancing allusions. In *The Satanic Verses* he nods at—among others—Ovid, Lewis Carroll, Coleridge, Walt Disney, T. S. Eliot, the Wizard of Oz, Shelley, Forster,

Little Black Sambo, and Kafka. (Kafka was probably bound to materialize in a book so devoted to physical metamorphoses; in any event,
Chamcha's name seems a thickened variant of Kafka's man-turned-
beetle Gregor Samsa, and at one point Chamcha is referred to as "the
insect on the floor.")

Shame, which was Rushdie's third novel, was a considerable feat, and
Midnight's Children, his second novel, was probably better still—but it
may be that, so far, his most significant accomplishment lies not in
narrative but in language, not in an individual book but in the evolution of a nonesuch style. In borrowing easily from Western and Eastern
sources and in experimenting so broadly—with punctuation, sentence
construction, abrupt shifts of viewpoint, deliberate incongruities of
tone—he has developed a voice we haven't heard before.

As one would suspect, he brings to the English-language novel an
invigorating influx of Indian cadences (the Bombay interludes of *The
Satanic Verses,* particularly when Zeeny Vakil speaks, have an irresistible
bounce and sparkle), but he does far more than that. His prose blends
elevated diction, an exclamatory, cartoony collection of words like
"zap" and "boom" and "pow," clanging rhymes ("the jouncing and
bouncing of youth," "arms wide, feet with the beat"), reportorial flat-
ness, and a jazzy spontaneity:

> So maybe someone should have been able to forecast, only nobody
> did, that when he was up and about again he would sotospeak succeed
> where the germs had failed and walk out of his old life forever within a
> week of his fortieth birthday, vanishing, poof!, like a trick, *into thin air.*

> The city—Proper London, yaar, no bloody *less!*—was dressed in
> white, like a mourner at a funeral.—Whose bloody funeral, mister,
> Gibreel Farishta asked himself wildly, not mine, I bloody *hope* and *trust.*

> The moment Saladin Chamcha got close enough to Allie Cone to be
> transfixed, and somewhat chilled, by her eyes, he felt his reborn animos-
> ity towards Gibreel extending itself to her, with her degree-zero go-to-
> hell look her air of being privy to some great, secret mystery of the
> universe; also, her quality of what he would afterwards think of as *wilder-
> ness,* a hard, sparse thing, anti-social, self-contained, an essence.

In his fondness for needless, playful abbreviations ("as to omnipres-
ence and -potence," "what was possible was possible and what was
impossible was im-," "yielding or un-," "whether mortal or im-"), he

can even wind up sounding like—of all people!—P. G. Wodehouse;
we are not far from Bertie Wooster, lounging in bed while Jeeves carries in "the eggs and b."

The effect of this heterogeneous mixture can be a little wearing. As
a stylist, Rushdie is continually breathtaking—and a breathless reader
is likely to feel winded at times. There are moments, frankly, when
one wishes he would get on with it. Now and then, a sentence slips
utterly away from him. His parentheses, in particular, have a python's
tendency first to engorge whatever wanders into proximity and then
to lie there in a digestive slumber. And his naturally arch temperament
has a way—as archness naturally does—of becoming cloying. I don't
see how anyone could read the following passages without feeling an-
noyed by them:

> Love, a zone in which nobody desirous of compiling a human (as
> opposed to robotic, Skinnerian-android) body of experience could
> afford to shut down operations, did you down, no question about it, and
> very probably did you in as well.

> Of the fruit of the tree of the knowledge of good and evil they
> shouldst not eat, and ate. Woman first, and at her suggestion man, ac-
> quired the verboten ethical standards, tastily apple-flavoured: the serpent
> brought them a value system.

Finally, one might wish that Rushdie displayed a greater flair for that
variety of beauty whose essence resides in brevity. Although he can
produce ravishing imagery, rarely is it of the concentrated type found
in those novelists we praise for having a poet's eye. Another novel with
an Eastern setting, Forster's *A Passage to India*, offers an instructive contrast. It runs about half the length of *The Satanic Verses,* and yet no
single passage in the latter possesses the distilled beauty that Forster
commands when, for instance, he ventures into the Marabar Caves:
"There is little to see, and no eye to see it, until the visitor arrives for
his five minutes, and strikes a match. Immediately another flame rises
in the depths of the rock and moves towards the surface like an imprisoned spirit: the walls of the circular chamber have been most marvel-
lously polished. The two flames approach and strive to unite, but
cannot, because one of them breathes air, the other stone." Rushdie, it
is true, can enter the mind of either Easterner or Westerner with a
conversancy that the more circumspect and wholly English Forster

lacked. Still, one sometimes longs, amid the impressive clangor of Rushdie's prose, for the hushed, suspended moment that comes when loveliness is wed to concision.

In the light of such reservations, and of the tragedy and fear that have recently engulfed Rushdie's life, it seems worthwhile to point out that even before this book appeared Rushdie was perhaps the only young novelist in the English-speaking world to have legitimate claims to an international reputation. He is prodigiously gifted. He is especially good on the subject of racism; the reader burns with freshened, reawakened indignation, as though apprised of prejudice for the first time. And in the meeting of East and West he appears to have sufficient subject matter for a couple of dozen novels. One of the strengths of *The Satanic Verses* is the way in which his "East" encompasses not merely India but—in its range of subplots and allusions—Southeast Asia, the Middle East, even Morocco. Worlds within worlds, dreams within dreams . . . One comes away from *The Satanic Verses,* as from *Shame* and *Midnight's Children,* with an inspiriting sense of multiplicity.

(1989)

A NASTY DOSE OF ORTHODOXY
Flannery O'Connor

❦

"I reckon you think you been redeemed," Hazel Motes, who is the young hero of Flannery O'Connor's earliest book, the novel *Wise Blood,* remarks in the first chapter to a Mrs. Wally Bee Hitchcock, who sits across from him on a train. Hazel's observation, coming as it does out of nowhere—up to this point their scrappy conversation has turned on travel plans and family matters—presents the opening surprise in a tale that eventually unveils a talking ape, a blind man who can see, the theft of a doll-size mummy from a museum case, a breathtakingly cold-blooded murder, a feud between the newly formed Church Without Christ and the even newer Holy Church of Christ Without Christ, and the donning of a barbed-wire shirt. But all these things lie some way off for Hazel Motes, who has just returned to the South after four years overseas in the Army. Hazel is awkward and headstrong and proudly unsuperstitious, and as he watches the landscape roll by, a price tag for $11.98 still stapled to his new suit, he has no inkling of the oddities and reversals in store for him.

I reckon you think you been redeemed is also what, in effect, all of O'Connor's books—*Wise Blood* and her second novel, *The Violent Bear It Away,* her two collections of stories, her letters and essays—say to the reader. Hazel Motes proclaims the notion scornfully, since he is an atheist of such impregnable skepticism that he wouldn't believe in Jesus "even if He existed," and O'Connor offers it concernedly but respect-fully, since she was a woman who could not, in her own words, "be-lieve Christ left us to chaos," but in each case it comes as a challenge: Motes and his author share a sort of incredulous horror of those people for whom theological questions are not "a matter of life and death." Together, they ask you the reader to appraise your soul; plainly, nothing else will do.

Although O'Connor wrote most of her mature fiction under a death sentence—in 1951, when she was twenty-five and ailing, blood tests confirmed that she suffered from disseminated lupus erythematosus, the incurable degenerative disease that had killed her father ten years before—one hesitates to attribute the soul-searching fervency of her fiction to her physical infirmities. The illness may have compelled her to leave New England, to which she had moved after three years of graduate study at the State University of Iowa, and to settle in her mother's home, in Milledgeville, Georgia; it probably ended any thoughts she had of marriage and children; in time, it crippled her; but it does not appear to have preyed constantly on her mind. The woman presented in the Library of America's new *Flannery O'Connor: Collected Works,* which concenters the two novels, twenty-eight stories, eight essays, two hundred and fifty-nine letters, and a helpful chronology, had little use for self-pity, or even for the self-congratulation common to those who believe they have triumphed over self-pity. To an extent that might appear dissembled or contrived if the genuineness of her feelings were not repeatedly manifested within these pages, she accepted her life as a blessing. A few years after the lupus was diagnosed, she wrote to a friend, "I have never been anywhere but sick. In a sense sickness is a place, more instructive than a long trip to Europe, and it's always a place where there's no company, where nobody can follow. Sickness before death is a very appropriate thing and I think those who don't have it miss one of God's mercies." Though she enjoyed recalling a period in her youth when religious doubts afflicted her and she fought her guardian angel—"From 8 to 12 years it was my habit to seclude myself in a locked room every so often and with a fierce (and evil) face, whirl around in a circle with my fists knotted, socking the angel"—she did so with the tranquil savor of someone who has outbraved a grave peril; she remained at peace with God until her death, in 1964, at the age of thirty-nine.

Whatever the ways in which O'Connor's illness may have altered—or failed to alter—her spiritual vision, one can say confidently that no other major American writer of our century has constructed a fictional world so energetically and forthrightly charged by religious investigation. In the main, readers of contemporary fiction are accustomed to seeing religious issues treated obliquely—when they are treated at all—and to having them take shape negatively, as a gradually felt absence. O'Connor's characters, by contrast, confront religion squarely, contentiously, and obsessively. In how many other recent writers might one expect to confront—as one does in *The Violent Bear It Away*—the Devil himself? The spirit that shadows the novel's adolescent hero is not a camp figure of fun, or an allegorical symbol of man's inhumanity to man, or a literary allusion, but a familiar who is very little altered from the one who exhorted Christ to "command that these stones be made bread." He becomes the boy's "friend," and solicitously invites him to demand of the Lord an "unmistakable sign, not a pang of hunger or a reflection of himself in a store window, but an unmistakable sign, clear and suitable—water bursting forth from a rock, for instance." O'Connor's letters reveal, in a tone of amusement whetted by an underlying dismay, her sense of how peculiar is the "de-Christianized" modern reader's inability to "recognize the Devil when he sees him." Our forebears, she suspected, were not so undiscerning. She felt herself radically out of step with the "modern, sick, unbelieving world." In another of her letters she sounds gleeful in describing a literary symposium at which "the Devil had his day" amid talk of "liberal religion" and "new symbology," and she herself "waded in and gave them a nasty dose of orthodoxy."

O'Connor would be only sixty-three if she were alive today, and it seems unlikely that the last couple of decades would have tempered her outrage and foreboding. She would have recoiled, surely, both at the legalization of abortion and—given her continual harping on the aesthetic and moral dangers of pornography—at the legal and social collapse of obscenity prohibitions. In her unbending Catholicism she can make a troublesome ally for the liberal, the feminist, the ecumenicist. On the other hand, her penchant for the grisly, which inspired some of the most hauntingly brutal stories in our literature, and her irreverence toward a wide variety of social conventions prove sizable obstacles for those who would translate her moral conservatism into support of "traditional family values," or anything of the sort. It would be tempting to say that she stood alone, if it were not so apparent that she saw nothing solitary about her spiritual life. Every Catholic, she explained to a friend who was contemplating conversion, is "a part of the Body of Christ and a participator in the Redemption." Her essays and letters display scarcely a minim of impatience with the Church's elaborate strictures and reluctance to change. Quite the contrary. She insisted that the Church "has done more than any other force in history to free women," that its position on birth control "is the most absolutely spiritual" of all its stands, and that writers should welcome religious censorship, since "the business of protecting souls from dangerous literature belongs properly to the Church." She was simply unable to imagine her existence outside of her religion: "I write the way I do because and only because I am a Catholic. I feel that if I were not Catholic, I would have no reason to write, no reason to see, no reason ever to feel horrified or even to enjoy anything."

What makes this intertwining of her religious and aesthetic beliefs so convincing is, of course, the fiction she produced in accordance with it. A story like "The Artificial Nigger" speaks at every turn of her piety, even while it traffics constantly in unpleasantness, from its offensive title to its improbable close. It recounts a Southern white boy's first journey to "the city," in the company of his racist grandfather. The two of them, Nelson and Mr. Head, meander lost through black neighborhoods and white. They quarrel, briefly separate, angrily reunite, and are finally reconciled in mutual surprise at the sight, in a white neighborhood, of a lawn decoration: "the plaster figure of a Negro sitting bent over on a low yellow brick fence," eating "a piece of brown watermelon." Neither had ever supposed that the world contained such a thing, and Mr. Head feels challenged by it:

> He looked at Nelson and understood that he must say something to the child to show that he was still wise and in the look the boy returned he saw a hungry need for that assurance. Nelson's eyes seemed to implore him to explain once and for all the mystery of existence.
>
> Mr. Head opened his lips to make a lofty statement and heard himself say, "They ain't got enough real ones here. They got to have an artificial one."
>
> After a second, the boy nodded with a strange shivering about his mouth, and said, "Let's go home before we get ourselves lost again."

But if there is humor in their backwoods benightedness it soon grades into something far more rewarding: a state of holy grace. On the face of it, both grandfather and grandson appear all but impervious to subtle or elevated feelings; the reader knows within a few paragraphs that these are not sensibilities that could ever be uplifted by music, by painting, by the written word. But their minds crackle with wonder at the discovery that some unknown team of manufacturers would actually have undertaken to design and cast and paint anyone so beneath consideration as a black man or boy, and wonder leads the grandfather to a sense of "what mercy felt like," as he "saw that no sin was too monstrous for him to claim as his own, and since God loved in proportion as He forgave, he felt ready at that instant to enter Paradise."

"The Artificial Nigger" is a story as daring today as it must have been when it was written, three decades ago. In fact, I have trouble imagining any nonreligious writer, then or now, showing so much of this particular audacity, by which an object at once inflammatory and abhorrent, and ultimately a reminder of slavery, becomes an agency of positive good. The strength that O'Connor showed in writing the story (and in sticking to the story she'd written—she demurred when John Crowe Ransom, who had accepted it for *The Kenyon Review,* asked her to soften the title) was that of a person for whom questions of race, like all other earthly concerns, must remain a secondary matter. If, sadly, a quarter century after O'Connor's death we continue to inhabit a world in which the gap between blacks and whites—or, for that matter, between women and men—can seem unbridgeable, she offers us the liberation of an alternative prospect, where neither race nor sexual identity represents the essential human division. The great divide for her was the one that separates the believer from the unbeliever. In her view, blacks and whites alike, women and men alike, will in time enter Heaven—or Hell. And anyone wishing to ponder a true division would do well to cast an eye upon the differing eternities reserved for the saved and the damned.

Although O'Connor complained little about her crippling disabilities, she lamented often the artistic difficulties she faced as a religious writer in a secular age. She beheld everywhere a decline of religious sentiment, and a chief virtue for her in being a Southern writer was the region's comparatively slow-changing, "Christ-haunted" quality: "Ghosts," she pointed out in one of her essays, "can be very fierce and instructive." To her way of thinking, this sensation of a growing distance between the believer and the unbeliever rendered necessary "ever more violent means" on the writer's part: "To the hard of hearing you shout, and for the almost blind you draw large and startling figures." She found comfort in the notion that, historically speaking, not she but the age was the aberration—that only in recent times would an explicitly religious writer face a "hostile audience." She was linked in this belief to another Catholic, Evelyn Waugh, whose work she admired, and who once made a kindred point in a letter to his mother, while discussing *Brideshead Revisited:* "The general criticism is that it is religious propaganda. That shows how opinion has changed in 80 years. No one now thinks a book which totally excludes religion is atheist propaganda. 80 years ago every novel included religion as part of the normal life of the people." (Waugh admired O'Connor as well, even though she, as a woman, a stranger, and an American, was triply suspect to his insular sensibility. Of *Wise Blood* he wrote, "If this is really the unaided work of a young lady, it is a remarkable product"—an observation whose skepticism, as though she might be some sort of female impersonator, pleased and amused her.)

She was like Waugh, too, in frequently stressing the artistic remove of the Catholic artist. She resisted being classified as a Christian writer; she was always brooding about Christianity's "terrible division," and was far more eager to point out differences than to assert similarities within the branches of the Christian faith. She was also fiercely partisan and took to heart her friends' conversions and apostasies. She grieved when the poet Robert Lowell, a friend of hers since Iowa days and a Catholic convert, abandoned the faith. And few things in this world so irked her as critics—especially friendly critics—who treated her religious preoccupations as adventitious or tangential to her artistry. She wrote in a letter to a friend, "Many of my ardent admirers would be roundly shocked and disturbed if they realized that everything I believe is thoroughly moral, thoroughly Catholic, and that it is these beliefs that give my work its chief characteristics." She made a similar point, less coolly and wryly, in another letter, this one written after she received a "moronic" review: "It was a case in which it is easy to see that the moral sense has been bred out of certain sections of the population, like the wings have been bred off certain chickens to produce more white meat on them. This is a generation of wingless chickens, which I suppose is what Nietzsche meant when he said God was dead."

O'Connor was an eccentric stylist. Like the poet Elizabeth Bishop, with whom she corresponded for years, she prized the maladroit. Her

novels and stories come laden with constructions that would be routinely excised by most teachers of expository composition. Her un-
gainlinesses at times reflect the locutions of her characters, who were
almost universally the rural poor of the Deep South; at times they serve,
with their homespun finish, as a highly effective, covertly sophisticated
method of conveying sincerity and rectitude; and at times they seem
mere lapses. (For all her endless rewriting, she had difficulty identifying
her stylistic overdependencies. She had been "blissfully unaware" of
how many "*seems* and *as-if* constructions" had crept into one of her
manuscripts until Caroline Gordon, a longtime friend and mentor, uncovered them for her; their removal was, O'Connor observed, "like
getting ticks off a dog.") She delighted in the sort of word cluster that,
if extracted from its surroundings, looks almost unworkably misshapen:
"had he had had," "doing all right with what I was doing with," "got
off on was," and so forth. One measure of her mastery of the colloquial
is the way in which these virtually unutterable mouthfuls manage to
blend in, unobtrusively supporting the longer cadences of her writing.

She could be deliberately rough-hewn, too, in her visual descriptions. She was forever mentioning colors, for the most part in starkly,
almost defiantly unadorned terms: the "white moon," the "yellow sun,"
the "brown soil." One thinks, by way of contrast, of Marianne Moore,
who pursued chromatic distinctions of such liminal nicety ("calla or
petunia white," "amanita-white," "white with white spots," "ivory
white, snow white, oyster white"—to name just one color!) that they
seem both risible and heroic. In a story like O'Connor's "A Good Man
Is Hard to Find," which may well be her masterpiece, the gruesome
action—six people, including two children and an infant, are murdered
within its seventeen pages—unfolds in a landscape lit with the vibrancy
of a child's drawing. There's scarcely an object that does not come
tagged with a pure, crayonlike color. A family from Atlanta—a father,
a mother, their three children, and a grandmother, who carries "a big
black valise"—leave by car for a Florida vacation. As they are driving
down a pink road, between blue trees, the family cat, who has a white
face and an orange nose, leaps on the shoulder of the father, who is
driving, and a minor accident results. The father has a yellow face and
blue eyes. In a few minutes, another "big black" object, this one a
"hearselike automobile," materializes. The car stops and three men get
out. The first is wearing black trousers and a red sweatshirt. The second

is wearing a blue-striped coat and a gray hat. The third, who is wearing tan-and-white shoes and has a black hat and red-rimmed eyes, is named The Misfit. He's a notorious killer, and he is carrying a gun. All this is as painfully simple as it might be, and equally simple and raw is the ensuing carnage. But the accompanying dialogue is of a different nature entirely. The Misfit may be a psychopath, but he is also, it turns out, something of a theologian.

If this is a common enough literary strategy—the placing of profound philosophical queries in the mouth of a social outcast and near-illiterate—it's also a device that is almost unfailingly destined to seem artificial, condescending, or strained. But—to this reader, anyway— The Misfit's spiritual hunger is as real as his pointy tan-and-white shoes, with which he makes little incisionlike holes in the sand, and as unforgettable as his taking the family cat into his arms after shooting the grandmother. He seeks to explain himself before gunning her down:

> "Jesus thown everything off balance. It was the same case with Him as with me except He hadn't committed any crime and they could prove I had committed one because they had the papers on me. Of course," he said, "they never shown me my papers. That's why I sign myself now. I said long ago, you get you a signature and sign everything you do and keep a copy of it. Then you'll know what you done and you can hold up the crime to the punishment and see do they match and in the end you'll have something to prove you ain't been treated right. I call myself The Misfit," he said, "because I can't make what all I done wrong fit what all I gone through in punishment."

Things are no longer black and white, or even black and white and red and yellow and blue; the colors here are no longer simple. The man is a monster, and—amazingly—one pities him.

The decision to publish O'Connor in the Library of America, a series that comes as close to embodying an official national canon as anything could in these fractious and revisionist times, is unexpected, even startling. Most of what has already appeared in the series belongs to the nineteenth century, and in order to enlist O'Connor the Library's selection committee had first to leapfrog over a generation or two of commanding literary presences—including Anderson, Hemingway, Fitzgerald, Dos Passos, and Lewis. The business of securing rights and permissions for so monumental a series (which advertises itself, incidentally, as "the only definitive collection of America's greatest writers") will naturally create scheduling irregularities, and at this point the shape of the whole can only be guessed at. But in approving O'Connor the committee relinquished what seemed its staple criterion: the test of time. Hefty portions of this volume—her letters and essays—were published only in the last two decades; their staying power remains unverified. Yet, while greatly troubling as a precedent, the book satisfies as an independent object. O'Connor's work may be unseasoned, but hers are materials that should weather well. And if she is—at least, in the difficulties of categorization she poses for the critic—something of a misfit herself, she appears to line up quite comfortably on the shelf with such misfits as Poe and Melville and Twain and Whitman.

To see O'Connor so prepossessingly assembled in one volume is, however, to raise small but unavoidable doubts about the possible exhaustibility of her gifts. Could she—health permitting—have gone on to write half a dozen fine and varied novels? Did she have another twenty stories resonating within her? How great, in short, was her potential range? One discerns with some misgivings the twinlike kinship of her first and second novels. In each, the young hero is raised in the shadow of a brimstony family preacher, whose teachings he eventually forswears. He leaves home, wanders about, proves an easy mark for hucksters, loudly deplores the meaninglessness of sacred ceremony, and at last commits, as an act of ultimate religious repudiation, a murder—only to discover that even mortal sin is an insufficient refuge from the power of God's calling. The similarities extend to small details—to anecdotes, to metaphors, to quirks of speech. Indeed, in some cases— as in the pivotal significance each novel reserves for the hero's hat— the similarities suggest an endearing act of obduracy: the author appears to be saying, *Well, I liked this touch before and I like it still.*

Even gingerly qualifications of this sort, however, become possible only when one steps backs a good distance from O'Connor's work. Up close, she can seem so onrushing—so revolting, so humorous and heartbreaking, so spiritually tempestuous—that the repetitions go unnoticed and one's reservations dissolve. Confronted by the religiosity of her work and the inspiring speed with which her seemingly earthbound characters again and again soar toward infinite divinations, most readers would forgive literary shortcomings far graver than any she displays. O'Connor felt little appetite for most contemporary fiction—she found it empty of soul—and she devoted many of her reading hours to Catholic theology. Perhaps in the end one praises her work most powerfully by acknowledging that it leaves one, if only temporarily, sharing her sense of the inanition around her. When you're under her spell, most other works of contemporary fiction can seem denatured or dilute. They do not satisfy as she satisfies. And whether or not you care to define this dissatisfaction in religious terms, it's momentarily clear that in those other writers something—maybe even everything—is missing.

(1986)

PLACES

Introduction: Far East

So upending were the changes in our lives that I don't think either of us was at first quite aware how much of our past we'd left behind us. It took some weeks fully to sort out that we had no telephone, no washing machine, no stove, no car, no stereo, no bed, no sit-down toilet, no bath or shower—indeed, no hot water. We were living in a papery house that, I liked to think, I might have torn apart with my bare hands had I come home one night in a rage. But there were no rages. We made do and counted ourselves lucky. We went to the public baths. We ate out. It was a boon to have lost so much.

We had no monthly bills, a heady lack that did take some getting used to. We lived by cash—queer-shaped new coins and festive, particolored notes. We were renting the vacant portions of an old wooden house in western Kyoto for one hundred dollars a month. Two rooms were ours. The other two were devoted to storage and to tea ceremony; our landlady, a doctor's wife who lived across the street, used our house as a sort of annex. It was to her that our few bills—taxes, electricity, water—were sent, and she, as often as not, would pay them herself. We were her strays, her pets—this pair of gaijin newlyweds who had, in effect, materialized one morning under a bamboo tree in her cramped but graceful garden. Clearly we needed looking after.

It wasn't long before we began to feel we'd been adopted, and, dutiful children that we were, we couldn't think of abandoning our new mother by moving elsewhere. Instead, we bought a boom box and a water heater (for one sink) and an old washing machine (which, for lack of room, ran in our backyard) and an old stove (which, for lack of room, sat under the stairs). It turned out that our paper house was piercingly cold in winter—mornings, we'd regularly see our breath— and its buckling walls were open to incursions of mice, snails, and cockroaches, surrealistically winged. We stayed on anyway, for three years.

The doctor and his wife showed us home movies of their trip to China, to which they had journeyed in the mirroring comfort of a large party of other doctors and doctors' wives. They had glimpsed many unforgettable marvels but they wanted us chiefly to understand how *strange* a country it was. They were not like us—"they" in this case being the Chinese and "us" those brave new hybrid creatures, the Nippo-American men and women of advanced technology and hygiene whose clear destiny it was to guide the emerging twenty-first-century world.

A few weeks before my wife and I moved to Japan, when we were still living in Boston and I was studying for the Massachusetts Bar, I took a trip to Chinatown as a way of forefeeling what it might be like to be surrounded by Asian objects and faces. I wandered into an overloaded grocery store and there, amid a chaos of cries I couldn't understand and packages I couldn't decipher, an icy surge of panic went through me. It would all be too much—too alien to be borne!

This was a feeling, though, that never once touched me after we'd actually arrived in Japan. The queer—the lovely—surprise was just how *right* it all felt. The whole package made beautiful sense: to be travelling everywhere by bicycle, to be editing legal articles about Japanese commercial law by day, to be sleeping close to the floor at night, to be writing a novel—my first—while constantly being made to feel like an illiterate. I couldn't read the street signs and billboards that pressed me on all sides. I was travelling blind, which should have been regularly disastrous but rarely was. We were being watched over not merely by our landlady. The nation itself seemed to be promoting our well-being. People were so solicitous, it was hard to go far astray. Now and then I'd take a bus and discover I was the only gaijin aboard. This, too, was unexpectedly reassuring. External reality had seemingly come to correspond with an inward image—less self-pitying than self-congratulatory—of myself as an odd man out.

To be sure, these were congratulations laced with an oblique form of self-dislike. If another gaijin happened to board the bus, I'd meet my counterpart with a twinge of instant, instinctual resentment. I was fearing a dilution, I suppose—as though my authentic Japanese experience were being undermined. Or fearing perhaps a confrontation with my own beggarly helplessness. In any case, these fears of mine, as I quickly came to see, were widely shared. In fact, they were a defining characteristic of Japan's gaijin community. In no other foreign land I've visited have my fellow expatriates viewed each other with quite so much distrust and disdain. Obviously, wherever you go, those who consider themselves old hands in their adopted country will shudder at the arrival of fellow countrymen bearing maps and train schedules and shopping bags. But in Japan the tension among gaijin went far beyond the dismissal of the tourist by the long-term resident.

Why was this? It's hard to say, but it's clearly a long-standing attitude. One senses it even in the pieces Lafcadio Hearn was publishing in *The Atlantic Monthly* a century ago. In those essays Hearn is forever hankering after that outflung island or temple where gaijin are absolutely unknown; he would, if he could, free Japan from the taint of himself.

No doubt, this is an unease bolstered by a quiet Japanese insistence on the gulf between themselves and their gaijin visitors. For it turns out there is another "us" and "them," and while a Japanese man or woman can become an American—can in time be accepted in America as such—the American can never quite become a Japanese. It's an embittering realization for the long-term American expatriate, whose response occasionally takes one of two extreme forms, neither very seemly. He may seek to out-Japanese the Japanese: to wed himself almost religiously to futon and geta sandals and green tea even among those of his hosts who have abandoned such things for beds and Adidas running shoes and cappuccino. Or he may wind up, pointedly unshaven and slovenly, idling away his hours in endless railing against Japanese "narrowness" and "uptightness."

Admittedly, these are traits which sometimes can hardly be overstated. I seem these days to come upon a steady stream of magazine pieces and newspaper articles all resolutely downplaying the rigors of Japanese conformity. The authors in question are apparently operating on that hallowed journalistic guideline which says that any widely held conclusion for which the evidence is extensive and well documented must be a "myth" in urgent need of being "exploded." It's worth bearing in mind, then, that recently some Japanese public high school girls were ordered by school authorities to dye their hair—a demand all the more piquant since their school absolutely prohibited hair dye. But the girls in question had been born with a faint henna tinge to their ebony hair—as sometimes happens among the Japanese—and this condition naturally called for forced concealment, that they might more success- fully blend with the crowd.

Needless to say, such coercions never touched a gaijin like me. My quirks of appearance and behavior were to be expected, and indulged, with the result that I came away with an overriding impression not of narrowness but of an elongated breadth. Vistas not so much of space but of time had opened up for me. Now and again I felt I'd stepped into the future. Tokyo, especially, in all its burnished newness and daz- zling gadgetry, must be the closest thing the planet offers to a twenty- first-century city. Japan was, among other things, a time machine.

Evelyn Waugh observed in his autobiography that if he were given a time machine he would feel no curiosity about the future; the past alone would summon him. Unexpectedly, I seem to find myself mostly in agreement with him; it's certainly true that the time-journeys I most often sought to induce were backward-looking. I was particularly drawn to the mountainous countryside, where on occasion the mist and the centuries would seem to dissolve away together. For the hiker in those hills, time can be a sort of backpack—heavy but removable.

Just as the walls of our home in Japan were porous, so too for me were the partitions dividing past from present. The remote felt near at hand. This wonderful sense of connection—of the past's proximity— obviously has less to do with the age of the buildings ranged before you, or their place in history, than with the subtle interaction of ambi- ence and temperament: in the end, it's perhaps a physiological matter of the parts-per-million of enchantment in the air.

I read recently that the latest generation of Japanese schoolchildren is nearly a head taller than its grandparents. Maybe these young people— beefed up, like us, on opulence—will come to survey their country's history from a gaijin's perspective of themselves as outsize and mal- adroit. The past will look smaller to them. And by this odd means, anyway, the gulf between future generations of Americans and Japanese might be temporarily bridged. They will share a perspective. In those moments when the present fades away and the past beckons to them, they will step into it as twins—tall, broad-shouldered, well inten- tioned, tentative—to walk as foreigners there.

ALONE AND EXTREMELY ALONE
Lafcadio Hearn

He was named, in part, for an island he could not remember. He was born, in 1850, on the Ionian isle of Leucadia, which gave birth to "Lafcadio": his parents christened him Patrick Lafcadio Hearn. He was two when he left Leucadia for good, moving with his mother to the British Isles. He seems to have shed his first name by the age of nineteen, when he emigrated, alone, to the United States. By the time he died, in 1904, he had managed to drop his other names as well, in order to become Koizumi Yakumo, a Japanese citizen. "Lafcadio Hearn" had evolved into little more than a pen name—though an illustrious one, for he was by then a journalist and essayist of international renown. In the Western continents he had abandoned so long ago (Hearn spent the last fourteen years of his life in Japan), he counted among his staunch admirers William Dean Howells, Stefan Zweig, and Hugo von Hofmannsthal.

His Anglo-Irish father, Charles Bush Hearn, was a surgeon with the British Army Medical Staff who was posted to the Ionian Sea in 1846. His mother, Rosa Cassimati, was an illiterate Greek of unstable temperament who spent the last decade of her life in an asylum. It was at her husband's urging that, after he was reassigned to the Caribbean, she took their son to live with the boy's grandparents in Dublin, where Rosa—with her dark features and fervent Greek Orthodox practices—apparently excited suspicion and disdain. She was desperately unhappy (she tried at least once to kill herself), and wound up returning to Greece, leaving her son, then four years old, behind. The marriage was annulled, and the boy never saw his mother again. In later years, she, like his birthplace, lingered in his psyche in a sort of incandescent mist, a zone where primal impressions dissolved into heartsore fabrications. At the age of forty-three, he wrote of her, "I have memory of a place and a magical time in which the Sun and the Moon were larger and brighter than now. Whether it was of this life or of some life before I cannot tell. . . . And all that country and time were softly ruled by One who thought only of ways to make me happy." He also called her the source of "whatever there is good in me." That Hearn reposed his deepest faith in a disturbed woman who had abused and abandoned him says a great deal about this inconsistent, headstrong, pettish, and often touching man.

Hearn's unshakeable sense of an initial calamitous loss—a fall from paradise early in childhood, before there were words enough to interpret or temper it—ensured that he would never feel at home anywhere. He seems to have come closest in Japan, where he was beringed by alien customs and a language he never mastered sufficiently to converse with subtlety and nuance. By nature a man who kept his distance, he chose to live much of his life within recesses of memory and appetite inaccessible to those around him. He often felt, as he wrote once to a friend, "alone and extremely alone." Needless to say, he makes a difficult subject for a biography, though something like half a dozen have appeared over the years. The latest, Jonathan Cott's barely serviceable *Wandering Ghost: The Odyssey of Lafcadio Hearn,* is a handsome package, with some appealing drawings and photographs.

Hearn, it seems fair to say, loved Japan not with his intellect so much as with his soul—and it might fairly be added that Japan requited him in kind. Perhaps, among modern Japanese, an eagerness to embrace this early "friend of Japan" has resulted in some distortion, in a scanting of Hearn's oddities and dishonesties, but there is no question about the firmness of that embrace. Now largely unknown in the lands he lived in before he crossed the Pacific, he remains a colossus in Japan: one of the most famous of modern Western writers. A Hearn museum has gone up beside his former home in Matsue; he has inspired movies and television programs; his books are quoted in the newspapers; schoolchildren study him.

But what are those who haven't embraced Hearn wholeheartedly to make of him? In America, our confusion is partly nationalistic. Is he one of our own? Technically, no, for he was never an American citizen. And yet he lived in America for nearly twenty years. He began his writing career here, in our sensationalistic "penny papers," to which he took naturally; as a word painter, Hearn gravitated toward a lurid spectrum, and both yellow journalism and purple travel pieces came easily. Even after he moved to Japan, many of his closest personal and professional ties remained American.

The canon of nineteenth-century American literature contains a number of outsized oddballs (Poe, Dickinson, and Whitman foremost among them), but even in such singular company Hearn often succeeds in looking sharply eccentric. In his fifty-four years, this British-Irish-Greek-American-Japanese essayist, fiction writer, folklorist, and translator clashed with our country's miscegenation laws (in 1874, with a black clergyman presiding, he married Mattie Foley, an eighteen-year-old mulatto who had been born a slave); denounced Christianity and pursued Buddhism; composed journalism of such raw gusto that even in our unbuttoned age it can still jangle the nerves (here is Hearn quaffing a glass of blood at a kosher butcher's: "No other earthly draught can rival such crimson cream, and its strength spreads through the veins with the very rapidity of wine"); talked to ghosts in mediums' dens; and became, possibly, a bigamist (his marriage, in 1891, to a Japanese woman was evidently not preceded by a divorce from Mattie). Given a life so contrarily colorful and so charged with explosive social issues, it is surprising that Hearn has not found his way onto more English-department syllabuses. It would be heartening to suppose him excluded on strictly stylistic grounds; much of his early work, especially, is so clumsy and overwrought as to be almost unreadable. But the eager acceptance into the canon of (among others) Hearn's near-contemporary Frank Norris—who, for all his likeable intensity, was often a laughably unsteady craftsman—renders this interpretation doubtful.

If the tradition of Japanese literature offered any precedent for the admission of foreign-language writers, one would readily slot Hearn into its English-language division. Japan did more than provide him with inexhaustible subject matter; it seems to have taught him how to write. Of course, literary criticism abounds in speculations about the influence of place on a writer's style. We may be told, for instance, that Wordsworth's burly verse reflects the ruggedness of the Lake District, or that Hemingway's cadences echo the lappings of the tides. Most of the time, though, purely literary influences can be found that will account for the trait under examination and any recourse to the extra-literary seems a dubious business. In Hearn's case, however, one turns up no literary forebears that explain the retooling his writing underwent after his arrival in Japan. He pared his prose and showed himself increasingly capable of an almost epigrammatic finish:

> Until you can feel, and keenly feel, that stones have character, that stones have tones and values, the whole artistic meaning of a Japanese garden cannot be revealed to you.

> Certainly Japanese poets have not been insensible to the real melancholy inspired by autumn—that vague strange annual revival of ancestral pain.

> Yet, after all, to devour one's own legs for hunger is not the worst that can happen to a being cursed with the gift of song. There are human crickets who must eat their own hearts in order to sing.

Hearn joyfully adopted Japanese ways—dressed in obi and yukata, frequented his neighborhood shrines and temples, lived on rice and pickles and fish, slept on a futon. Ironically, one of the few aspects of Japan's culture that did not immediately touch him was its literature—which he could not read, and most of which had not yet been adequately translated. It was by means of something vaster than literature—an overarching aesthetic, a subsuming ethos—that Hearn learned both to savor "the ancient charm" of Japan and to disparage "the utterly commonplace Western taste." Japan dismantled his prose—stripped it of much of its clutter. By the end of his life, certainly, he would have been unlikely to write anything so execrable as this passage from "Three Dreams," which he composed a few years before he left for Japan:

> Then the eyelids opened widely, horribly; and the dead Shape quickly leaped; and Myself,—my cadaveric Self,—snatched at me, clutched me,—tearing, rending, shrieking—striving to bite, to gnaw, to devour! And I, with the rage of fear, with the fury of hatred, with the frenzy of loathing,—I also wrestled to destroy.

Hearn went to Japan in 1890, at the suggestion of an editor at *Harper's*, and, although he subsequently became an English teacher, he continued to look to American periodicals for his livelihood. Catering to a public almost wholly unacquainted with the Orient, he found himself in a complicated, often compromised situation. Sound instinct told him that what his readers craved were articles swaddled in the "exotic."

These were easy enough to supply at first, while Japan yet seemed a "World of Elves," wherein everything was "delicate, exquisite, admirable." As his familiarity with the country deepened, however, and inward reservations inevitably multiplied, he began to entertain a host of unsaleable convictions. It would perhaps be an overstatement to say that Hearn became disillusioned with Japan, but toward the end of his life he was unquestionably desperate to leave it, and he did once confess in print that the country's "magical atmosphere" had "totally faded out at last." For the most part, though, Hearn kept his disgruntlements from his public; they are expressed only tacitly, in the vacant gesturing and windy puffery of some of his later pieces.

Hearn's view of Japan was also complicated by the driving psychological needs he brought with him. With a transparency gratifying to the amateur Freudian, he initially disembarked in Yokohama intent on recovering the Greece of his infancy; Japan was to be, in short, a reunion with his mother. Hearn was—whatever his far-flung destination—always heading home. Cott's assertion in *Wandering Ghost* that Hearn wrote about Japan "without prejudice or preconceptions" is therefore puzzling.

Although Cott's affection for his subject suffuses nearly every page, softening a reader's censures, his biography can hardly be recommended. The book feels oddly unsure of its audience (as when Cott explains that Maupassant was a "French writer"), and it is laced with repetitions. Cott displays no gift for surmise, for penetration beyond the often scanty facts available to him. And he is hopelessly credulous, time and again incorporating Hearn's narrations or descriptions unhesitatingly. Credulity is a danger even for biographers working with dependable subjects, and it is fatal when applied to someone like Hearn, who as a guide was unreliable both psychologically (if not a pathological liar, he was certainly a habitual one) and physically (he was blind in one eye and severely myopic in the other). As the sad, wearying record of Hearn's blasted friendships makes clear, he was someone who detected slights everywhere; he was a paranoid, whose interpretations were patently untrustworthy. By the end of his life, when he often withdrew into a sullen reclusiveness, he may well have been gravely disturbed.

Cott, who is a contributing editor of *Rolling Stone,* would portray Hearn as a nineties-style "lefty"—and in fact he was, but his nineties were the eighteen nineties. *Wandering Ghost* reveals little sensitivity to historical nuance. True, Hearn's skepticism about industrialism, his open-mindedness about race, and his repeated journalistic crusading on behalf of the downtrodden have the earmarks of a contemporary liberal—but Hearn, in all sorts of interesting, unplumbed ways, was enmeshed in the attitudes of his era. Cott treats his subject's sexuality, for instance, as a kind of deliberate political subversion: Hearn becomes a stainless fighter against racial prejudice. And, indeed, there is some-thing bracing in the air—a jangling of liberty bells—when Hearn speaks of "the beauty of colored skins," or when, with a boldness that was later bowdlerized by his would-be protectors, he writes to a racist friend of liking to "eat and drink and sleep with members of the races you detest." Yet Cott fails to probe with any psychological acuity the possibility that for Hearn the sexual allure of the outcast had its origins in a tormented uneasiness. His penchant for whores, in combination with his paralysis around women of his own social milieu, bespeaks a hunger for women as "debased" as he was. His dealings with women were far sketchier than his dealings with men (predictably, since his first wife was illiterate and his second knew no English), but it would be surprising—to say the least—if the cruelty and hectoring that Hearn inflicted on his male acquaintances did not carry over into his behavior with women. It seems a safe bet that marriage to Hearn was often pretty hellish.

Readers keen on venturing off in quest of Hearn's questing soul are probably best advised to begin with Robert A. Rosenstone's *Mirror in the Shrine*. Rosenstone, a professor of history at the California Institute of Technology, focusses on three varied Westerners (a missionary and a scientist in addition to Hearn) whose lives were altered by extended sojourns in Meiji Japan. Fixing Hearn with a sympathetic but unsenti-mental eye, Rosenstone gives us a more complex and arresting figure in about a hundred pages than Cott does in four hundred plus. Rosen-stone seems to grasp intuitively the degree to which Hearn's Japan was a place of Hearn's own making.

Cott is particularly unsatisfactory in his handling of Hearn's final years. He conveys almost no sense of their turmoil. Inexplicably, Hearn's attempts to secure a lectureship at Cornell—a prospect that frantically enticed him—are dismissed in a sentence. It's difficult to escape the impression that in the book's concluding chapters, which have a cursory and truncated feel, Cott's patience or interest has waned. This is a biography that expires before its subject does.

Our difficulties in placing Hearn within a literary context find an echo in the curiously parallel career of a contemporary, Robert Louis Stevenson, who also was born in 1850 and died in the Pacific. (He succumbed to a cerebral hemorrhage in 1894, in his house on Samoa.) Stevenson spent his early life in Edinburgh, and he has naturally been championed by those who would define and promote Scottish literature. A number of his books, including the late, unfinished *Weir of Hermiston,* do fall comfortably under that heading. But others—among them one of his last completed projects, the novella *The Beach at Falesá,* which he judged "nearer what I mean than anything I have ever done"—do not. *The Beach at Falesá* is set in the South Pacific. Some of the themes it takes up are the commercial exploitation of natives by whites, sex between the races, the tenuousness of Western law and customs in remote places, and the extirpation of native culture. Like Hearn, Stevenson felt compelled to chronicle a mode of life that was passing away before his eyes.

Stevenson's tales commonly have a way of degenerating into yarns, and *The Beach at Falesá* ends disappointingly, with some conventional adventure-story explosives. But it is a strong enough book, rich in humor and sense of place, to leave a reader rueing Stevenson's premature death. He had come to the South Pacific for good and all ("I love the land," he told a friend, "and I have chosen it to be my home while I live, and my grave after I am dead"), and the letters of his last years reveal a heady exultation in having hit upon a "whole new society to work." The ghost of Robert Louis Stevenson inevitably trails behind it the string of sun-blazed turn-of-the-century Pacific novels that, had he been granted health enough and time, he might have bequeathed to the world.

A similar poignance attends Hearn. He, too, was presented with a matchless, since vanished, opportunity. There he was, footloose in Meiji Japan at a time when disenfranchised samurai were still walking the streets, when women were blackening their teeth to render themselves attractive, when forests were falling to make way for telephone lines, and one cannot help thinking of the irreplaceable novels he might have given us. Before coming to Japan, Hearn had, in fact, written a few short novels, but he was by no means up to the creative challenges now before him. (The one novel of his that I dipped into—*Youma: The Story of a West-Indian Slave*—was so dry and wooden that it might well be labelled a fire hazard.) He embodies the particular pathos that arises when a writer of talent meets a challenge that demands genius.

Unfortunately, no one else was on the scene to seize the opportunity. Japan boasts no figure comparable to Kipling in India, or Conrad or London or, somewhat later, Maugham in the South Seas. Indeed, we can only speculate about what Kipling—whose brief visits to Japan, in 1889 and 1892, kindled some marvellous letters and commentary— might have made of a lengthy residency. Or, if we truly wish to indulge in hypotheticals, we might ask what another contemporary of Hearn's, a genius who specialized in the revelatory tensions and befuddlements that spring out of transoceanic exchanges, would have made of Hearn's opportunities: why wasn't Henry James in Kyoto when we needed him?

Elegists often—in time, posthumously—wind up lamenting more than they intended to. Hearn repeatedly sought to memorialize the "astonishing fairy-land" of Japan before the "barbarian" West intruded upon it; he was, one might say, bent on the creation of a world in which he would be expunged. He once asked, "What is there, finally, to love in Japan except what is passing away?" And yet, as a result of forces he couldn't have foreseen, he symbolizes for us the death of quite different things. How could he have known, as he rhapsodized about the view of Mt. Fuji from the streets of Tokyo—a vista that represented for him a spiritual unification, the balancing of the modern and the timeless—that eventually we would sully the atmosphere and lose that prospect utterly? Tokyoites have suffered a severance that would have broken his heart. He also symbolizes for us the death of the amateur Japanologist. Gone are the days when a passionate but uninitiated Westerner might cross the Pacific and immediately expect people to hearken to him as he held forth on Eastern conceptions of religion, marriage, sex, and art. Such pronouncements now belong, as they should, to specialists—to holders of advanced degrees in Eastern studies and sociology and anthropology, who bring to their disciplines amassings of erudition that Hearn (always happiest when negotiating with the inchoate: with spiritual affinities, intuitions, verses, dreams) could not begin to match.

Elegists likewise have a way of bringing us unexpected cheer. On the face of it, Hearn's vision is bleak. One of the reasons he resonates for us is that he took up so convincingly the theme of relentless depletion—the day-by-day, decremental receding of what in his eyes had been a gentler and more civilized way of life. Well, who among us hasn't sometimes viewed depletion as the hallmark of our age? We seem, in a bitter paradox, to face an ever-expanding list of diminishments—the decline of animal species, rain forests, nonrenewable resources, even water to drink and air to breathe. But isn't there also something buoyant in the contemplation of those novels-that-might-have-been which would have lastingly placed before us the fumbling, gingerly minglings of East and West in Meiji Japan? Barring the arrival of someone with an unparalleled gift for spiritual and intellectual exhumation, they will never be written. But who could fail to take heart at this vision of a world that, in its tireless unfoldings, is forever offering us more tales of wonder than we have geniuses equal to their telling?

(1991)

BLACK SHIPS
Toson Shimazaki's *Before the Dawn*

🦋

Western friends of the modern Japanese novel are accustomed to slender volumes. With some sizable exceptions, like Yukio Mishima's *The Sea of Fertility* or Junichiro Tanizaki's *The Makioka Sisters,* most modern Japanese novels—or, anyway, most of those exported through translation—are tersely told tales. Long on beauty though they may be, the books of Soseki Natsume, Yasunari Kawabata, and Kobo Abe generally demand little shelf space; and both Tanizaki and Mishima, for all their drives toward amplitude, worked most commonly with forms closer in length to the novella than to the novel. Into this august but austere company now emerges Toson Shimazaki, whose *Before the Dawn* runs to more than seven hundred and fifty pages, not including a generous introduction by its translator, William E. Naff; various maps; a list of principal characters; an extensive glossary; and a bibliographical note. With what might seem an un-Japanese lack of delicacy, the book arrives here with a startling, satisfying thump.

Before the Dawn, which was first published in 1935, was Toson's sixth novel, and the last he completed before his death, in 1943, at the age of seventy-one. (Toson was born Haruki Shimazaki; the ideographs of his pen name suggest a wisteria flower and a village.) It is also the first of his books to be published in this country—a fact that would probably surprise most Japanese readers of fiction, for whom he is one of the century's most prominent figures. Naff notes in his introduction that in Japan a mountain of literary exegesis—more than a hundred and thirty books and some seven hundred articles and essays—has been erected in commemoration of Toson.

Many, perhaps most, of those modern Japanese novels which find an English translator take as their theme the effect of the West on traditional Japanese ways and outlooks. Frequently handled in tacit fashion, with little recourse to Western characters, the theme may be presented as a confrontation between duty and liberty, or the old and the new, or the intuitive and the rational. *Before the Dawn* is striking in its attempt to treat the pressures of West on East frontally, minutely, and from their outset. The prologue opens in the spring of 1853, a few months before a mysterious, minatory cluster of "Black Ships"—those of Commodore Perry—are spotted near Yokohama. The epilogue closes in 1886, within the graveyard of a Buddhist temple. In the three decades and seven hundred pages that intervene, scarcely an incident arises that is not touched by those Black Ships and the colorful, confusing world they bring as their enduring cargo.

Before the Dawn tells the story of the Aoyama family, who for seventeen generations have lived in the village of Magome, one of eleven post stations in the deep Kiso Valley of central Japan. Magome lies on the Kiso Road, which winds through the valley and, although tortuous and often snowbound, is of vital military significance; it is the only inland route linking western with eastern Japan, the imperial court in Kyoto with the Tokugawa shogunate in Edo (modern-day Tokyo). At the time of Perry's arrival, Kichizaemon Aoyama is fifty-five and—though he feels his years a little as he maneuvers around the steep environs of Magome—he is still vigorously serving the village in the hereditary positions of *shoya* (tax and labor administrator), *toiya* (freight official), and *honjin* (keeper of the posthouse, in which high-ranking official travelers are lodged). He is also the head of what is by long tradition Magome's leading family; the village was founded by an Aoyama in the sixteenth century. In the nicely calibrated society of mid-nineteenth-century Japan, Kichizaemon is at ease in his dual role as a kind of country squire to the other villagers and an unquestioning subordinate to the distant shogun. (Kichizaemon is hardly unusual in bending unresistingly to the shogunate; for centuries, even the emperors were reduced to mere figureheads in the face of its military might.) Unfortunately for Kichizaemon, his only son, Hanzo, seems temperamentally unsuited to the positions of authority he is meant to inherit. Hanzo is contemplative, restive, feckless, and imprecise. Also unfortunately for Kichizaemon, the Black Ships signal the advent of revolutions along the Kiso Road, which would upend a far steadier sensibility than Hanzo's.

Toson's decision to center his novel in a far-flung mountain village, rather than in one of the big cities where face-to-face contacts with

Westerners quickly became common, proves an artistically liberating choice. The impact of the "red-haired barbarians"—as early Westerners were sometimes known—is felt the more powerfully for their invisibility. Most of the villagers have never seen either Kyoto or Edo. In fact, communities in the Kiso Valley are so insular that slight variations in pronunciation can be heard between neighboring villages lying only five miles apart. Life is given over to subsistence farming and vague, fiercely nervous speculation about the various samurai and lords whose elaborate, palanquin-equipped processions pass "one after another like waves of cloud in a storm front." One day, a few weeks after Perry's arrival, heavy cannons are dragged laboriously through the village— and what could this mean? All the great political upheavals of the age are much too distant for the villagers (with the exception of Hanzo) to think of influencing or interceding in them—but not so distant, it seems, that their aftershocks will not come rumbling through like one of those earthquakes that, in this precariously vertical mountain community, are a continual source of terror.

In deciding to write a historical novel, Toson unwittingly did the Western reader a great favor. The need to reconstruct a vanished world seems to have led him naturally into an expatiating, comfortably didactic tone, and the reader receives much more in the way of background information than he generally expects to be given in a Japanese novel. He may feel, indeed, that he is sometimes given more than he can usefully absorb. Toson discourses, occasionally at great length, on the politics of the era, paying particular attention to military campaigns. He is also copious—more helpfully and proximately so, in terms of the plot—in his exposition of the functioning of the transport network along the Kiso Road. Page after page, the book bespeaks a dogged aptitude for historical research, by which a vanished world becomes a gratifyingly palpable one.

If the Western reader finds the tangled, faction-ridden history that Toson presents a little bewildering, he can take consolation in the thought that bewilderment of this sort has a long history; as Toson points out with some amusement, early Western officials often failed to distinguish between the imperial and the shogunate court. But, whatever small confusions Toson may cause the reader unversed in Japanese political history, he succeeds completely in what Naff singles out as one of the book's primary objectives: a vivid demonstration of the richness and ferment of Japan's intellectual life during an age when most outsiders would have deemed the country only recently and partly "opened." Japan's initial American visitors naturally had little chance to perceive that they had irrupted into one of the most literate and vigorously scholastic countries in the world—or that they had happened to arrive at a moment when the shogun was being undermined by renewed moral and political claims on behalf of the emperor. From the Japanese point of view, the jostling entrance of the Americans (and, subsequently, the British, the French, the Russians) could be assimilated only within the context of this other, older source of contention. For many Japanese, the two great political turmoils of the age—one new and international, the other ancient and domestic—were sensibly resolved in the popular slogan "Revere the Emperor, Expel the Barbarians." The two demands seemed philosophically of a piece. But if the first was soon to be fulfilled, with the Meiji Restoration of 1868, the second became more dreamily unworkable with each passing year, as Western customs and fashions, laws and ideologies, penetrated ever deeper into Japanese society. Poor Hanzo cannot compass this necessary process of interchange and reconciliation on the international level; his earnest, occluded outlook is limited to "straightforwardness and wholesomeness." If the West *must* be admitted, Hanzo would ask that each of its aspects be given fervent scrutiny and only those compatible with innate Japanese values be granted adoption. As becomes clearer with each chapter, he is unsuited to the indiscriminate, lumping approximations of daily life, and his inability to cope with the hybrid developments of a modernizing Japan nudges him incrementally toward madness.

Hanzo enters intellectual life as an optimist and an activist. In his mid-twenties he becomes a disciple of the Hirata school of National Learning, an intellectual movement that, according to Naff's glossary, "strove to recover through philological study and religious speculation the presumably pristine character of early Japan." It pitted itself against "Chinese-mindedness," which it perceived as a legacy of Japan's middle ages, and as being variously responsible for the ascendancy of the shogun over the emperor, the substitution of imported Buddhist practices for indigenous Shinto rites, and the acceptance of "empty verbalizations." According to Hanzo's beliefs, any resumption of what was "open and generous" in the national character can come only with the reinstatement of the emperor in the sacrosanct position that Jimmu, the first emperor, enjoyed; the fallacies of a millennium need to be swept entirely away. Hanzo's "rejection of the middle ages" and "return to antiquity" are not meant to support a blind return to ancient ways, however; he seeks an enlightened, consciously chosen program of cultural rescue, by which a "new past" may be found.

The first half of the novel mounts step by step toward the fulfillment of Hanzo's elevated vision. Out for a walk one snowy morning in the winter of 1867, Hanzo stops in a teahouse, where he meets Kozo, a friend and fellow-disciple of the National Learning movement, who has some astonishing news. In a room suffused with morning light, Kozo informs Hanzo that the shogun has agreed to relinquish his power to the emperor. Dizzy with jubilation, the two friends exchange cups of sunlit sake. To Hanzo and Kozo it seems that their country is about to be spiritually reborn at last. To the reader it seems that a threshold has been crossed—that the dawn of the novel's title has arrived. But Hanzo's delirious joy is recurringly darkened by an insight that he has first expressed during a doctrinal debate: "I was just twenty-two when the Black Ships first came here. But it is a mistake to think that those were the first Black Ships. If you think about it, you will realize that there is no way to count all the Black Ships that have come to this country since the beginning." It seems the taint of the foreign has been with the Japanese all along. And by now it may be ineradicable.

Hanzo eventually discovers that the villagers of Magome are curiously unmoved by the Restoration. He wants them to "begin living by completely new rules." But earthbound, daily life, with all its old pettinesses and dissatisfactions, goes on. And although Hanzo cannot share the villagers' outlook, he empathizes sufficiently to see that for them what has occurred is a mere exchange of tyrants. The shogun's knowingly brutal exactions have been supplanted by the decrees of an ignorant bureaucracy that likewise impoverishes them, this time in the name of the emperor. In the eyes of the villagers, most questions of the spirit, including even that of national regeneration, are an extravagance reserved for those with time on their hands—the priests, say, or those rare men, like Hanzo, who have the wealth to indulge themselves in schemes of universal betterment.

According to Naff, Japanese literary authorities disagree about the import of the novel's title. Any allusion to the rising sun must, of course, evoke the nation as a whole, and the emperor, who symbolizes it, but some readers have speculated that the title also refers, less weightily, to the early-rising author's work habits. Others have detected in it a glimpse of the shadowed era of the novel's composition—those increasingly militaristic years during which Japan was inching toward global conflict. Naff favors a more cheerful interpretation: "The most important source is probably the term *reimeiki* or 'period of dawning,' which Japanese cultural historians often date from around 1887. It was then that the first desperate rush of almost indiscriminate foreign borrowing . . . was superseded by years still tense and perilous but marked by the emergence of a new generation that had both the time and the training to think more critically about the problem of European influence." That the book's epilogue takes place a year before the "period of dawning" argues strongly in Naff's favor. Still, readers may wish to regard the title as darkly ironic—for this novel is, in the end, a heartbreaking story. The illumination that the title promises may be only that of a false dawn. Almost the last words the reader hears from Hanzo are "I am going to die without ever seeing the sun again." The cry expresses the running anguish of his final two months, which he spends immured in a cramped, frigid, filthy hut. Hanzo's own son Sota has locked him up, in response to the villagers' conviction that Hanzo's gathering madness imperils them all. The reader will probably grow to feel that, however misguided its impulses, Hanzo's spiritual restlessness—which propels him into a job in the Ministry of Religion in Edo, and eventually into a lonely four-year stint as a Shinto priest—distinguishes and ennobles him. But Hanzo himself, shortly before his final mental disintegration, becomes convinced that "his insignificant life simply did not amount to much." The sunlit sake he once shared with Kozo now becomes a dark, treacherous fluid as Hanzo floats toward alcoholism. In his descent into hallucination and madness he is spared no pain or indignity. And, in a sudden shift, this vast novel, heretofore marked by spotless decorum in its handling of sexual and bodily matters, turns graphically revolting at its close. The reader, too, is spared nothing: Hanzo, his "hair and nails . . . grotesquely long," is seen hurling his own excrement at those who would visit him. When this gentle, unrealistic man loses all sense of reality, he becomes a savage animal.

The ambiguity of the title sets the tone for a novel in which motivations are often obscure. Critical events in the lives of the characters are often obliquely reported, in the form of hearsay, rather than directly portrayed. The narrative method is unassertive, insinuative. Time and again, when the author presents some small revelation—a memorandum, a letter, a snatch of dialogue—he offers the reader no initial identification or preamble. One is momentarily compelled to sift and analyze without the mediating assistance of the author. For all Toson's forthrightly didactic intentions, in depicting personal dealings he relies on a characteristically Japanese subtlety and restraint.

The book's plotting, by contrast, is often a loosely disciplined, and even vagrant, affair. Hanzo sometimes disappears for thirty or forty pages at a stretch while Toson supplies the reader with "historical reflections." This interplay between an individual and a nation, both of them struggling and confused, works dynamically at times, with each side complementing and enriching the other. But there are moments when the story threatens to collapse altogether under the double weight. Toson handicaps himself further by failing to create deep, tiered characters. The critic and translator Edwin McClellan hardly overstates the case when, in his book *Two Japanese Novelists,* he observes of *Before the Dawn* that "of the many characters that appear in it, not one, not even the hero, seems to emerge as a fully rounded personality." Hanzo's questing hunger does come through, and so does the mute, inadequately squelched despair of his daughter Okume (who, ominously, is described as "exactly like her father"). But for the most part the farmers, priests, merchants, scholars, and innkeepers of this novel bustle about in a flat, two-dimensional world. The reader is likely to feel unreasonably overworked as he tries to keep track of the constantly growing cast of characters (a task enlarged by Toson's decision to introduce at various points women named Otami, Otama, Otomi, and Omaki).

Before the Dawn is, then, a crowded tale, but one happily rendered into a clean, idiomatic English. The reader may come away from it regretting that no very distinct impression of Toson's writing style is conveyed (perhaps an inevitable shortcoming, for, according to McClellan, Toson chose to work in a style "bereft of ornament"), but he will nevertheless delight in the easy fluency of Naff's lines. Punctuation is kept to a minimum, and the reader can travel for pages without encountering a parenthesis, a dash, or a semicolon. Commas, too, are often nimbly deleted, thanks to a sure ear for speech rhythms, as first displayed in the prologue: "The rule of the Tokugawa had still been secure when a mound topped by a stone inscribed with a verse by Basho was set up beside the road in Shinjaya hamlet at the western edge of Magome." In its sheer length, its detailed forays into political history, and its emphasis on ideology and the life of the mind, *Before the Dawn* clearly imposed heavy burdens upon Naff—who, by serving Toson unobtrusively, has served him well.

McClellan notes that all of Toson's novels except his first, *Broken Commandment,* had firm autobiographical underpinnings. Throughout his career, Toson transferred the events of his turbulent life—which included three years of self-imposed exile in Paris after he had, scandalously, impregnated his niece—directly into his fiction. As Japanese readers would be likely to know, Hanzo was based squarely upon Toson's father, Masaki Shimazaki, who had both served on the Kiso Road and pledged himself to the National Learning movement. A profusion of Hanzo's writings—poems, letters, petitions, journal entries—appears in the novel, and all were originally Masaki Shimazaki's. But if uncertainties about Toson the stylist may hamper the Western reader slightly, an ignorance about Toson the man in no way impedes an enjoyment of *Before the Dawn*. Everything the reader might need to know about Toson's life can be gleaned from the novel itself.

Rooted firmly in dates and itineraries, rich with convincingly quirky particulars, the portrait of Hanzo bears the unmistakable stamp of actuality; remote as Hanzo's heart may sometimes seem, especially in his dealings with his wife, there is never a doubt that behind him stands a historical person as model and inspiration. And toward the close of the novel another actual person teasingly, transformatively emerges. In the reader's mind, a suspicion hardens into a certainty that Hanzo's bookish son Wasuke, a peripheral but winsome character who "is fond of learning," must be based on Toson himself. With this revelation, the book is converted into an intimate family monument—one whose heft and grandeur are the more poignant for being erected in honor of an undiscerning, often foolish, ultimately demented man.

Perry's Black Ships of 1853, and the character of that determinedly indrawn nation whose waters they breached, present questions that Japanese novelists and historians will be reevaluating for centuries. Perry's steamships—which were capable of crossing the Pacific in less time than a procession normally required to negotiate the Kiso Road—introduced a heady new age. Working as both novelist and historian, Toson Shimazaki sought to illustrate how that age affected a solitary man, his father—whom, as the Hanzo-Wasuke relationship suggests, he had scarcely known. Like Wasuke, Toson left home to study in Tokyo while still a young boy, and rarely saw his father afterward. Unfamiliarity in no way hindered him, however, in drawing a sweeping, sympathetic portrait of a man who had "lost his way in his journey through this world." Hanzo himself was left believing that "everything that had accumulated in Japan over the centuries was being treated as though it had no value." But the very existence of *Before the Dawn* attests to the persistence of one traditional virtue: ancestral piety, the devotion accorded a father by his son.

(1987)

IRRESISTIBLE DEMONS
Junichiro Tanizaki's *Naomi*

Although a brief, uncluttered, and happily accessible novel, Junichiro Tanizaki's *Naomi* arrives from somewhat tangled origins. A reader making Tanizaki's acquaintance through this book—and there's probably no better gateway into the dense, haunting world of this man who may have been Japan's finest modern novelist—might well keep these in mind as a sort of warning. For *Naomi*'s plot, too, comes with hidden complexities.

The book was serialized in the Osaka *Asahi* newspaper from March until June of 1924, when it was dropped after eighty-seven installments in response to protests from conservative readers and government censors. When, while working on another novel a few years before, Tanizaki had found it difficult to meet the demands of serialization, he simply abandoned the book altogether. *Naomi* was different, though, as he explained in a note to his unexpectedly interrupted readers: "This novel is my favorite of recent years, and my inspiration is at its peak. As soon as I can, I shall find another magazine or newspaper in which to publish the remainder." Tanizaki proved true to his word. Five months later, publication was resumed in a magazine called *Josei* and—despite the story's increasingly lurid revelations, far more shocking than those which triggered the original banning—continued without incident to the book's conclusion. Although *Naomi* remains in Japan one of Tanizaki's most popular books, and is so commonly known as his "first important novel" among his Western critics that the phrase seems to have affixed itself as a kind of subtitle, it has until now gone unpublished in America. Readers here may have seen references to it under either of two titles, *A Fool's Love* or *An Idiot's Love*. Anthony H. Chambers, an associate professor at Wesleyan University, has chosen to resolve this confusion by taking an inspired liberty and calling his clean, flowing translation *Naomi*. But even this title is less simple than would appear, for the heroine's name is not pronounced with the long "a" customary in America. She is a Japanese girl whose name is written in ideographic characters and spoken with the soft *ah* of a Japanese "a"— one of the few softnesses to be found in the person of the book's beautiful, predatory heroine.

Like so many other Tanizaki novels, *Naomi* is a tale of deception. Its narrator, Joji Kawai, a provincial farmer's son whose career as an electrical engineer has landed him in Tokyo, seems in no hurry to explain the "undreamt-of misfortunes" resulting from his marriage to a very young café hostess named Naomi. Only slowly does the reader see the extent to which Kawai has been lied to, and has lied to himself.

A reader acquainted with Tanizaki's books will find much that is familiar in *Naomi*. In this novel, too, one yields immediately to a narrative deftness, a sense of being in the hands of someone who knows a good story when he finds one and delights in its telling. And like so many of Tanizaki's protagonists, Kawai is a feckless man given to self-mockery—a self-described "country bumpkin," "idiot," and "oaf." Again one encounters a fascination with the trappings of Western civilization, as well as misgivings about their suitability to the Japanese temperament; a love of the movies (not long before writing *Naomi*, Tanizaki worked for a time as a screenwriter); and a keen eye for furniture, architecture, food, and women's clothing. Above all, one meets again what Kawai himself calls a "terrifying enchantress"—another manifestation of that cruel yet irresistible woman who seems to have figured as the largest archetype in Tanizaki's imagination.

This enchantress began to brew her sorcery early in Tanizaki's career. In 1910, while still a university student, he established his reputation with a short story entitled "The Tattooer." An ugly fable, at once unsatisfying in its construction and unforgettable in its grisliness, it recounts the story of Seikichi, a tattooer who longs to display his art on the body of a flawlessly beautiful woman. When at last he meets the perfect woman, he lures her into his apartment, drugs her, and, working unrelentingly through the day and night, realizes his masterwork: a hideous spider perched indelibly on the milky whiteness of her back. The woman gradually wakes to a double revelation. She discovers not only her frightening new appearance but also, at Seikichi's prompting, a corresponding internal malevolence. Seikichi unveils for her his secret collection of paintings that depict torture and slaughter, and she (with rather unconvincing rapidity) acknowledges the thrill they bring her. She has found her fate, and will now go forth to enslave and punish men. Although Seikichi has in a sense created her, he proves no less her slave for that; the spider on her back has ensnared him, too. Tanizaki often returned, over the years, to variations on this twisted tale of Pygmalion and Galatea, and one might view *Naomi,* as well as the later novel *The Key,* as expansions of "The Tattooer."

Naomi is only fourteen when Kawai spots her working in a seedy café. Quiet and tractable, she would seem to present the perfect clay from which an idealistic young man of twenty-seven might mold a mate. Kawai soon liberates her from her job, sets her up in his house, and marries her, vowing to make her "a diamond," a lady of such polish that she "won't even be ashamed to mix with Westerners." Kawai keeps a diary entitled "Naomi Grows Up," in which he records her progress and pastes her photographs. This little girl's appetites prove colossal, however, and Kawai is soon bankrolling an endless line of steak dinners and Western-style dresses, as well as lessons in music, dancing, and English. Eventually, Kawai must lie to his mother in order to stave off bankruptcy with a loan. Meanwhile, it turns out that he is no match, either on or off the dance floor, for an assortment of boorish young men whom Naomi has somehow befriended. A plodding fellow, Kawai proves remarkably slow to reach the truth, and the reader is no doubt meant to chafe with impatience at his bottomless gullibility.

Like much of Tanizaki's other fiction, *Naomi* induces a sense of claustrophobia. While Tanizaki is hardly unique among novelists in frequently compelling his readers to witness a slow, predictable, and hopeless decline—slowness, predictability, and hopelessness being elements common to most tragedy—he manages to lend disaster an additional, constrictive poignance. Time and again, it is not simple ignorance that makes his characters behave so stupidly. They march knowingly for Hell. By the time Kawai admits to himself that Naomi has been exploiting and cuckolding him, he is so thoroughly her sexual and psychological prisoner that he seeks only to ensure that she will find him worthy of continued mistreatment; the one fate he cannot endure is abandonment. By the book's close, he has become her slave. The reader has been longing to have Kawai see the truth, but it turns out (as so often for Tanizaki's characters) that the truth will not set him free.

Tanizaki relieves the book's suffocating atmosphere in a couple of ways. Here and there he inserts aerating hints of surrealism, of a world lying well removed from Tokyo in the twenties. Naomi is repeatedly compared to an animal, initially to a bird and mouse, then to a colt, and finally to that creature so rich to the Japanese imagination, a fox. Japan's folklore abounds in tales wherein foxes are transformed into human beings, and the reader almost comes to believe that this puzzling, protean creature, this Naomi who is both café hostess and enchantress, is not quite human. Such possibilities are subtly invoked, as in Kawai's reflections when Naomi, who has left him for, among others, an American, returns to the house briefly:

> My nose detected a faint but familiar scent. Aah, that scent—it evoked in me thoughts of lands across the sea, of exquisite, exotic flower gardens. It was the scent of the dance teacher, Countess Shlemskaya. Naomi was wearing the same perfume.
>
> Whatever Naomi said, I could only nod in response. Even after her form had vanished again into the darkness of night, my sharp sense of smell pursued her gradually fading fragrance as one pursues a phantom.

Tanizaki also dilutes the book's confining air in an unsettling way, through hints of some purgative act of violence. Halfway through the novel, Kawai comes home to find Naomi peacefully asleep. The reader is treated to a lovely but disturbing description that suggests the possibility of an eventual murder:

> As I sat gazing, her breast, in the shadow thrown by the lampshade, loomed vividly, like an object lying in the depths of pellucid water. Her face, too, radiant and kaleidoscopic by day, now wore a mysterious cast, a melancholy frown, like that of one who's just swallowed bitter medicine, or of one who's been strangled. I loved her sleeping face. "You look like a different person when you're asleep," I often told her, "as though you're having a terrible dream." "Her death-face would be beautiful, too," I often told myself.

On the following page, Naomi's limbs "dangle limp as a corpse." While the reader has good reason to doubt that Kawai, a pathetically timid figure, could ever commit a murder even if he overcame his formidable indecisiveness, these presentiments of violence at least leave the possibility open. And even in the book's last chapters, when Kawai seems hopelessly subjugated, the reader may feel both queasy and tantalized when Naomi asks Kawai to shave the nape of her neck in preparation for the low-cut gown she plans to wear to a dance that evening:

> Spellbound, she seemed to be savoring the pleasurable sensation of the razor's caress. I could hear her steady, drowsy breathing, and I could see the carotid artery pulsing beneath her chin.

It is a testament to the book's evocation of entrapment that murder could seem to promise some workable escape. The reader may almost hope to see Kawai trade his psychological prison for a physical one.

Naomi was the first novel Tanizaki published after moving from the cosmopolitan hubbub of Tokyo-Yokohama to the more traditional Osaka-Kyoto region of western Japan. Tanizaki left Tokyo after the great earthquake of 1923. He was thirty-seven. He planned a brief sojourn, just long enough to let Tokyo rebuild itself, but he stayed on in western Japan until his death in 1965. The move appears to have been a happy one for Tanizaki personally, as well as a great boon for his readers: nearly all of Tanizaki's best work emerged after his resettlement.

Today the differences between Osaka and Tokyo—those two thriving industrial megalopolises that lie only a few hours apart by bullet train—can seem almost negligible. Both were largely razed by bombs in the war, and in either city one can walk the gleaming streets for block upon block without meeting a single structure that looks weathered. But in the twenties, the disparities in pace and outlook must have been vast. Tanizaki was born in Tokyo, into a merchant family of failing finances, and one might view his move to Osaka as a further repudiation of his parents, who had hoped to see their bright son enter business. Yet one might also regard the move as a pursuit of profound familial loyalties. What seems to have drawn Tanizaki to Osaka were its provincial vestiges of a vanishing world—that of his childhood—and in particular a somewhat outmoded standard of feminine beauty. In western Japan, one still commonly found women who cultivated the delicate refinement and manner he had known in the Tokyo women of his mother's and grandmother's generations.

At some point after his move, Tanizaki the combative literary iconoclast became Tanizaki the mournful social conservative. He began to treasure what he'd previously reviled. He himself presented this transformation in the starkest terms when describing his first response on learning of the vastness of the earthquake's destruction:

> Joy welled up inside me. . . . Various scenes of Tokyo after the reconstruction passed before my eyes like flashes from a film. Scenes of parties where champagne glasses floated like jellyfish among the evening dresses, tailcoats and tuxedos, the congestion late at night before theaters where many strands of headlights criss-crossed in the darkly glowing streets.

This account, written eleven years after the earthquake, probably should not be deemed wholly trustworthy, given Tanizaki's penchant for dramatic overstatement, but his books themselves leave no doubt that he underwent some permanent change in the twenties. The belated arrival of *Naomi* should make clear to Western readers that for Tanizaki the allure of Europe and America faded quite soon after he left Tokyo—if not before. The book lampoons the Japanese eagerness to adopt Western styles of dining, dancing, dress, and architecture. And for all her beauty, the book's heroine, with her Western-sounding name and "Mary Pickford expressions," finally proves shallow, insecure, meretricious—and a force of destruction.

One perhaps would not expect Tanizaki, who showed so little interest in politics, commerce, and science, and whose best books were often historical fictions submerged deep in a shogunate past, to clarify for Western readers much about the metamorphosis of modern Japan. But his books prove remarkably enlightening on the subject of modernization, which in Japan has been an especially complicated process. As Tanizaki pointed out in a celebrated essay published in 1933, "In Praise of Shadows," Japanese society in this century has been struck by two not always separable tidal waves. The Japanese have been required not only to adapt themselves to the technological miracles that have uprooted and dizzied societies all over the globe but also to absorb that sweeping mass of enticements and priorities which goes under the heading of Westernization. Tanizaki's dynamic blend of dissatisfaction and openness, his heightened sense of the contrary pulls of tradition and innovation, gave him an ideal vantage for analyzing the shifting of his own culture. "In Praise of Shadows" is a long, hyperbolic, rambling (an anecdote about Albert Einstein set beside a highly detailed recipe for persimmon-leaf sushi), sometimes illogical, and unflaggingly fascinating essay. It ambitiously seeks to isolate the essence of Japanese aesthetics, which Tanizaki thought partly a result of architectural and climatic conditions:

> The fact that we did not use glass, concrete, and bricks, for instance, made a low roof necessary to keep off the driving wind and rain. . . . The quality that we call beauty . . . must always grow from the realities of life, and our ancestors, forced to live in dark rooms, presently came to discover beauty in shadows, ultimately to guide shadows towards beauty's ends. . . . Westerners are amazed at the simplicity of Japanese rooms, perceiving in them no more than ashen walls bereft of ornament. Their reaction is understandable, but it betrays a failure to comprehend the mystery of shadows.

For Tanizaki, the power and mystery of shadows ultimately lay in their elusive alliances with the past. Through their very obscurities, they seem to offer liberation from the brutal fixity of the present moment. He praised the "elegance of age" in tin tableware that has become tarnished, the "sheen of antiquity" in Oriental pottery, the "accumulation of the long Chinese past" discernible in the cloudiness of jade. Not surprisingly, given the torment found in so much of his writing, this invitation to a kind of time travel held for Tanizaki a bit of terror:

> In temple architecture the main room stands at a considerable distance from the garden; so dilute is the light there that no matter what the season . . . the pale, white glow scarcely varies. . . . Have you not yourselves sensed a difference in the light that suffuses such a room, a rare tranquility not found in ordinary light? Have you never felt a sort of fear in the face of the ageless, a fear that in that room you might lose all consciousness of the passage of time, that untold years might pass and upon emerging you should find you had grown old and gray?

Tanizaki was content to keep the past a mysterious, shadowy place. Unlike his contemporary Mori Ogai, who strove for rigorous accuracy in his historical fiction, Tanizaki relished the freedom to invent, to create a past that wasn't limited merely to what had occurred. He especially delighted in creating sham historical documents. In a preface to one of his historical fictions, he explained he had set his tale in the remote sixteenth century because it was a period that neither he nor his countrymen knew much about.

For all the powers of the traditional Japanese shadow world, it proved curiously vulnerable. Tanizaki saw no way in which it could endure exposure to a bolder, light-loving Western aesthetic. Indeed the shadow's beauty, like that of the cherry blossom, resides in its fragility:

> There can be no harm in considering how unlucky we have been, what losses we have suffered, in comparison with the Westerner. The Westerner has been able to move forward in ordered steps, while we have met superior civilization and have had to surrender to it, and we have had to leave a road we have followed for thousands of years.

While acceding to this "surrender," Tanizaki found himself haunted by the notion of an alternative world, one in which present and future would be shaped by Asians:

> I always think how different everything would be if we in the Orient had developed our own science. Suppose for instance that we had developed our own physics and chemistry: would not the techniques and industries based on them have taken a different form, would not our myriads of everyday gadgets, our medicines, the products of our industrial art—would they not have suited our national temper better than they do?

The stunning emergence of Japan in the last few decades as a world leader in technological innovation, as well as the recent industrial awakening of Taiwan and Korea, exposes the idealism of Tanizaki's notions. Those processes and products which so discomfited him would now seem to spring from economic imperatives that know no national boundaries. It was not Western, but modern, technology—with its demands for assembly-line production and fungible goods—that left him feeling so woeful.

Whether working as iconoclast or conservative, Tanizaki in book after book revealed a dislocated soul. Much of his fiction sprang from a nostalgia for a past that he freely admitted had never quite existed, and from yearnings for a future that never could. Fervent, fertile illusions, and they served him well.

. . .

Tanizaki needed, perhaps more than other novelists, to draw on whatever creative resources he could. For he appears to have been artistically handicapped from the outset by virtue of an idiosyncratic and in many ways straitened temperament. He suffered from severe blindspots. As a child of the merchant class, he developed a precociously rebellious aversion to business which never left him. Almost no one in Tanizaki's novels seems to hold a real job. A character may be assigned some nominal employment, like Kawai's position as an "electrical engineer," but the actual place of work—and, beyond it, that whole tiered structure of loyalties and tensions which composes the world of Japanese commerce—never engages Tanizaki's imagination. Kawai's colleagues are so peripheral that they've become mere initials (the only characters so designated in the novel), and they serve no narrative function except to offer an outside source from which to cast doubts on Naomi's chastity.

It would probably be fair to extend this generalization and say that Tanizaki's writing shows little interest in men, or at least in their dealings with each other. The whole polychromatic palette of male friendship, and of father-son relations, rarely colors his work. His men appear to take on a purpose, and animation, only in the presence of women. The typical Tanizaki hero walks timorously through a world of pallid, uninteresting men and irresistible but painfully indifferent—or, worse, painfully attentive—women.

An even graver artistic handicap may have been Tanizaki's inability, or stubborn unwillingness, to distance himself from his personal obsessions. One would not expect to have to launch this criticism at an artist who fought so splendidly against the close-to-home, autobiographical tendencies of so much Japanese fiction, and whose own books strike off with such boldness across the densely wooded hills of Japanese history. But even the most accommodating reader eventually must grow weary of Tanizaki's sexual preoccupations—particularly the foot fetishism which appears unabashedly in book after book. The reader will find himself at some point wishing that Tanizaki would bend the powers of his imagination over a wider range of human anatomy.

Any investigation of Tanizaki's artistic shortcomings must inevitably, if hesitantly, lead to an examination of his personality in the aggregate, and to the conclusion that he could be a very unlikeable man. His books make it hard to maintain that laudable, civilized critical convention which supposes that an author stands wholly apart from his books and that the blindnesses and cruelties they record are not to be imputed to the author himself. An unignorable streak of sadism runs through Tanizaki's books, and a reader can hardly escape a sense at times that their author delights more than he should in piling misfortunes on his characters. Admittedly, Tanizaki's personality seems to have little troubled his American reviewers (his books have been often greeted as masterpieces here, even *The Secret History of the Lord of Musashi,* that gleeful tale of human mutilation which is surely one of the most vicious books anyone ever wrote), but one suspects what may be coming into play here is an admirable, if slightly misguided, attempt to avoid ethnocentricity through the suspension of moral judgments. Among literary people in Japan, the mention of Tanizaki's name is apt to provoke vehement, head-shaking censure. This is not to suggest that in his own country Tanizaki lacks a wide and devoted readership; but if it is reasonable to call him "much loved" in Japan, it's probably also fair to call him "much disliked"—a mix of responses he himself seems to have striven for.

Tanizaki is best known, and rightfully so, for *The Makioka Sisters,* his voluminous portrait of the four sisters of a declining Osaka merchant family in the years before Japan entered the Second World War. It is not merely the family fortunes but the very world the Makioka family embodies—an aristocratic and artistic, insular, and introverted world—that trembles on the rim of extinction. The book is a muted but profoundly affectionate elegy. It is also one of the world's great shaggy dog stories. It recounts in unstinting detail the search for a husband for Yukiko, the pretty but paralyzingly shy third sister. The reader gradually perceives that the book will proceed in cycles: first a potential suitor will materialize, then an elaborate courtship will ensue, to continue chapter after chapter, as investigations are made and negotiations are carried out, until—until, perhaps for some trifling reason, the courtship collapses, often in a page or two, and the suitor disappears forever. Meanwhile, a new Mr. Almost Right stands in the wings. . . .

Impressive in a variety of ways, *The Makioka Sisters* perhaps makes its deepest impressions through a masterful evocation of passing time. Tanizaki had a rare talent for making a book's internal calendar seem palpable. One comes to feel almost physically the seasonal flow through which the four sisters so charmingly pursue their lives—the weighty heat of an Osaka summer, the flaring of a poignantly late fall.

The arrival of *Naomi*, his "first important novel," should make clear to Western readers that Tanizaki possessed this talent early on. Naomi is just fourteen when the story opens. When it closes, some two hundred pages later, she is twenty-two. The reader is asked to believe that eight eventful, erosive years of married life are encompassed in this short book. And the reader believes it without question. To follow this sad, engrossing, unsettling little tale to its conclusion is to feel that one has traversed some considerable distance.

(1985)

SEVERED FUTURES
Kobo Abe's *The Ark Sakura*

"None," Kobo Abe replied when an American journalist asked him, not long ago, which of his fellow Japanese novelists had influenced his work. For all its terseness, Abe's answer represented a show of two-pronged defiance. It was a reproach to a West that often regards Japanese literature as exclusively inbred and indrawn. And it was an act of subversion against literary traditions in Japan, where artistic discipleship continues to be viewed as a source not only of creative vigor but of spiritual merit. In his interviews and books alike, Abe aspires to confound, and a reader puzzled by one of his mulling, enigmatic novels—including the newest, *The Ark Sakura*—can take consolation in the notion that puzzlement just might be what the author is after.

Among that loose-knit aristocracy of contemporary writers who could be termed "world-class novelists"—those elevated men and women whose failures no less than their successes demand translation and international scrutiny—probably none is more vexatious than Abe. Or, at times, more downright irritating. His novels can seem matchlessly uninviting, both for their mysteries of motivation (Abe rarely explains why anyone does anything) and for their grotesqueries of conduct (which include necromancy, human vivisection, incarceration, rape, kidnapping, murder, suicide, and a stubborn refusal to bury the dead). He tends to punctuate long stretches of murky uneventfulness with sharp moments of extraordinary grisliness, in an uneasy stylistic alliance usually subsumed, in dust-jacket copy and critical discourse, under the catchall designation "psychological thriller." But as is true of Poe and Kafka—two writers whose influence does seem apparent—Abe creates on the page an unexpected impulsion. One continues reading, on and on, while an internal voice alternately announces "This book is ghastly" and "This book is good."

Abe was an insect collector as a child, and bugs of every outlandish description, factual and ideal, flutter and scuttle and whirr and click from chapter to chapter. Even when insects are not his subject matter, or his vehicles of metaphor, he exudes the taxonomic coolness one associates with the entomologist; in the earlier novel *The Box Man,* for instance, the desperate, constrained movements of his characters— starkly identified as A, B, C, D—suggest the wrigglings of pin-impaled specimens. Had Kafka never written *The Metamorphosis,* Abe would seem the planet's likeliest candidate to compose something closely akin to it. Gruesome transformations abound in his work—including, unforgettably, the genetic tamperings of *Inter Ice Age 4,* in which aborted human fetuses become free-swimming, gill-equipped "aquans." In that novel, as in Kafka's masterwork, much of the reader's satisfaction springs from a victory over his own squeamishness: one thrills to that gingerly, tender extension of sensibility whereby pathos and sympathy and beauty come to reside in what was deemed purely repellent.

Abe's elusiveness, his avoidance of generalization and summary, at times may foster—particularly at the typically abrupt close of one of his novels—a sense of incompletion and frustration. His books linger in the mind like obscure reprimands. One recalls an unspoken grief, the author's manifest dismay over the injustice around him, but little sense of where or how he would see it remedied.

Of the seven Abe novels so far translated into English, one can say, with remarkably little stretching of a point, that all concern missing persons. In *The Woman in the Dunes,* which was published in this country in 1964 and which for Western readers remains his first book (some earlier novels have not yet been translated), the hero disappears, like Wonderland-bound Alice, into a hole in the ground—where he is condemned to spend the remainder of his days shovelling and transporting the down-drifting sand that threatens to smother his hellish new home. *The Woman in the Dunes* was followed, in 1966, by *The Face of Another,* in which a scientist whose face has been grievously disfigured (in a laboratory accident, although his keloid scars inevitably evoke Hiroshima and Nagasaki) painstakingly constructs a resinous mask that promises him a new life. Like Dr. Jekyll in Stevenson's novella (a tale that *The Face of Another* echoes in numerous ways), Abe's unnamed scientist "vanishes" in order that an alternate, ascendant self can run amok. The hero of *The Ruined Map* (translated in 1969) is a detective on the trail of a fugitive who may have been murdered. *Inter Ice Age 4* (1970) centers on the shadow—glimpsed fleetingly through a window—of a man or woman who has killed an accountant. In *The Box Man* (1974), the hero retreats into a cardboard container (suggestive of an insect's carapace), which renders him indistinguishable from the "fake Box Man," a similarly outfitted acquaintance, who becomes his rival in what must be one of literature's most bizarre love triangles. The protagonist of *Secret Rendezvous* (1979) spends most of the novel wandering through a hospital in search of his wife, who has been spirited away from home early one morning by a mysterious, unrequested ambulance. (He finally locates her inside a secret amphitheater, where she is a formidable contender in an Orgasm Contest, and promptly abandons her for a teen-age girl suffering from a bone disease that, by the novel's close, reduces her skeleton to putty.)

In the new book, *The Ark Sakura,* the missing eventually come to outnumber the present. Early on, a man disappears by the banks of a subterranean river; later, a party of junior high school girls vanishes (hotly pursued by a band of lecherous retirees); finally, in a visionary, sunblasted coda, the world itself seems to shimmer into invisibility. The novel is labyrinthine in both method and setting: its piecemeal revelations are disclosed mostly under the earth, within the echoing vaults of a colossal and only partially mapped abandoned quarry.

Pig is the grossly overweight narrator's nickname, but he yearns to be addressed as Mole. As ambitions go, this drive to be perceived as a cousin to a rodent may seem pathetically modest, but it proves touching as well, since Mole reveals in time a winsome temperament. He calls the quarry an ark and designates himself its captain, although he has no crew; he passes his troglodytic life in solitude, studying aerial maps of Japan. The novel retails his attempts to enlist a suitable crew with whom to "set sail." But it turns out that few are prepared to exchange the pleasures of life aboveground for a dubious Ticket to Survival.

Like Noah's flood, the apocalypse that Mole envisions is a deluge—the radioactive rain of nuclear holocaust. "We're teetering on the brink of disaster," he announces amiably. Mole's ark is, of course, immovable, and the voyage he envisions will be temporal rather than geographical; snug in their subterranean chambers, captain and crew will float into the future. Unfortunately for Mole, the crew he winds up with is a supremely unreliable bunch. It includes an aging mountebank, who peddles an insect that "thrives on a peculiar diet—its own feces"; a young man who has committed extensive credit-card fraud; and the young man's skittish and manipulative girlfriend. Mole quickly succumbs to the tarty charms of the girl—who, in order to soften his disapproval of her boyfriend, confides that the latter unknowingly suffers from cancer and has only six months to live. Later, the young man informs Mole that the girl does not yet realize that she is a cancer victim; she, too, has only six months left. Meanwhile, it transpires that the ark may be not only infiltrated by stowaways but also riddled with toxic chemical wastes.

Step by sinking step, Mole's pristine passenger ship comes to resemble human intestines. In time, he renders the equation explicit: "Until now these walls had seemed a second skin to me. They had seemed the inner walls of my own bowels, turned inside out for my contemplation." The novel is pervadingly scatological. Mole—who in early adolescence was chained for a week to the pipes of a toilet after falsely being accused of rape—spends the last quarter of the novel with one foot wedged inextricably in a toilet bowl. As the leg swells up, the reader begins to sense that the toilet, like some primitive deity, may exact a dire sacrifice—that amputation alone can win his liberty.

Lest all this sound hopelessly unsavory and contrived, I should hastily add that, as such vessels go, Abe's *Ark* is a buoyant, weathertight construction—clearly his strongest novel since *Inter Ice Age 4,* and perhaps since *The Woman in the Dunes,* which might credibly be judged a masterpiece. Humor isn't something one always associates with Abe, even though he has been called a Japanese Beckett—if he shares the Irishman's flair for rendering metaphysical confrontation in honed, visually dramatic forms, he often lacks the inspired loopiness that repeatedly save *Waiting for Godot* or *Endgame* from ponderousness. But *The Ark Sakura,* for all its grimness, reveals a droll, slapstick imagination. And one is heartened to discover, deep in the bowels of the earth, where a bickering, misfit crew awaits the world's end, intermittent bursts of belly laughter.

. . .

What makes the book's triumph so fascinating is that most of the limitations one identifies with Kobo Abe are on display here. If funnier than its predecessors, *The Ark Sakura* departs very little from the obsessions and occlusions that have shaped his work from the outset. In this novel, too, adult affection and love—as well as all the novelistically fertile dissemblings, tensions, dares, and deliverances that accompany sexual desire—are virtually absent. Mole may be enamored of his one female crew member, but so adolescent are his yearnings (culminating, as they do, in an urge to swat her leather-miniskirted bottom) that one views their unfulfillment as amusing rather than desolating. And when minimal physical contacts do occur, a clinically detached, physiological exactitude renders them profoundly unromantic: "My voice was thick, as if spread with glue. The girl's continued massaging of the back of my hand had swollen the mucous membranes of my throat."

An even more significant absence is that of history. Japanese literature in this century has, in the main, been suffused by a grandly impersonal, elegiac nostalgia. A number of masterly writers—one thinks especially of Tanizaki and Kawabata—have taken as their core theme the submergence of traditional ways and outlooks by that ongoing torrent of influences which is called, for lack of an even more inclusive term, Westernization. Book after book glances back toward a society that, like a mountain village in a *sumi-e* watercolor, mists into a lovely obscurity. In Abe's world, by contrast, people seem to lack both a national and a personal history (a blankness turned absolute in *The Ruined Map,* whose hero ultimately becomes an amnesiac). Abe's singular childhood—as a Japanese boy growing up in Manchuria, where his father was on the staff of a medical school—may explain why his books are so frequently set in an unlocalized Anywhere: the sterile, fortresslike hospital of *Secret Rendezvous,* the city "where every block bears exactly the same number" of *The Ruined Map,* the derelict quarry of *The Ark Sakura.* Abe once described himself as a "man without a home town." Naturally, one can descry traditional themes in his work (his obsession with electronic surveillance, for instance, might be linked to the porous, perilous households of the Kabuki stage, where an eavesdropper is forever poised beneath the floor or behind the shoji screens), but one does so at the risk of distorting the degree to which he has managed to deracinate himself.

Abe's indifference to the past is balanced by, and perhaps largely justified by, an obsession with the future. Each of his books seems to take up anew the task of extrapolation; each freshly investigates emergent aspects of modern life—nuclear proliferation, environmental spoliation, cybernetics, overpopulation, bioengineering, statistical prediction. He has a marvellous talent for conveying the dizzying welter of contemporary society, as where the Box Man reflects upon his addiction to radio bulletins:

> I couldn't stand it if there weren't fresh news reports coming in one after the other all the time. Battlefield situations go on changing minute by minute. Moving picture stars and singers keep marrying and divorcing. Rockets go shooting off to Mars, and a fishing boat sends off an SOS and blacks out. A pyromaniacal fire chief is apprehended. When a venomous serpent escapes from a load of bananas and an employee of the Ministry of International Trade and Industry commits suicide and a little girl of three is raped, an international conference achieves great success and ends by collapsing, a society is formed to breed sterilized mice, a child is discovered buried in cement at the construction site of a supermarket, the total number of deserters from troops throughout the world sets a new record, the world seems to be boiling over like a tea-kettle. The globe's capable of changing shape the minute you take your eyes off it even for a second.

Detail builds upon detail, all of it memorable—and all, finally, unassimilable. If this is our present world, the Box Man seems to be asking, what is our future?

In a postscript to *Inter Ice Age 4,* Abe offered some observations about that novel's genesis which might also serve as a sketchy artistic credo:

> Thus I decided to grasp the image of a future that intrudes on the present, a future that sits in judgment. Our usual sense of continuity must give way the instant it faces the future. In order to understand the future, it is not enough simply to be living in the present. We must be clearly aware that there is real evil in the very commonplace order of things we call everyday living.
>
> Perhaps there is no such thing as a cruel future. The future, properly speaking, is already cruel by virtue of being the future. The responsibility for this cruelty lies not on the side of the future, but on that of a present unable to accept the abyss that separates the two. . . .

Yet I shall have fulfilled one of the purposes of this novel if I have been able to make the reader confront the cruelty of the future, produce within him anguish and strain, and bring about a dialogue with himself.

Like his Polish contemporary Stanislaw Lem, or his Italian contemporary Italo Calvino, Abe is a writer so obsessed with technology and its social impact that these can become a central artistic presence, to which mere characters seem subordinate. Lem is almost always grouped with science-fiction writers, Calvino and Abe are only occasionally so, but the three men evince a kindred impatience with the conventions of literary realism, particularly in regard to social change and technological expansion. The "real" world, each would remind us, is moving with breathtaking speed toward evolutions and upheavals that its inhabitants cannot begin to compass. And, given our velocity, what lies behind us increasingly blurs.

The Japanese reading public that composes Abe's primary audience no doubt has a heightened appreciation of the dislocation that comes from living in proximity to a future that threatens to engorge the past. Anyone familiar with modern Tokyo knows the giddy, befuddling feeling that derives from a gleaming, unweathered architecture. Although the city's mapped outlines may still reflect—as the guidebooks tell us—the careful, concentric encampments by which both shogun and emperor protected themselves from insurrection, what strikes the stroller's eye is the unbroken newness of it all: block after high-tech block of buildings erected in the last few decades.

Abe's latest novel extends the challenge he posed in *Inter Ice Age 4*, where he asked the reader to contemplate "a rapidly evolving future, one which may well destroy, deny the present—a severed future." In *The Ark Sakura* he urges us to ponder a further—a final—dislocation: one brought about by nuclear devastation. He implies that in conceiving a world whose past has been reduced to deadly, glowing rubble we might see ourselves without any distorting overlay of pretension or sentiment. Although he once observed that "it is extremely doubtful whether one has the right to sit in judgment of the values of the future," the truth is that his projections are unrelievedly harrowing. Unlike Lem or Calvino, he seems unwilling to entertain, even occasionally, the possibility of a roseate future.

Abe's books threaten us with loss—of government, of the environment, of those values which sustain the dignity of humankind. One is left, dimly, with a sense of the sweet, vulnerable virtues of the past—and a suspicion that this implicit affirmation of historical values may approach as close to nostalgia as this dour and challenging novelist will permit himself to go. Anguish and loneliness, he suggests, must reside in the national soul that is severed from its past. And must reside, one is tempted to add, in the soul of any novelist who would answer "None" when asked which of his countrymen had influenced him. *The Woman in the Dunes, The Face of Another, The Ruined Map, Inter Ice Age 4, The Box Man, Secret Rendezvous,* and now *The Ark Sakura*—these are not the offspring of a happy man. But what else would one expect, given the vision that obsesses Abe? It's an abyss that lies before us, and a wall behind.

(1988)

AN EAR FOR THE UNSPOKEN
Saiichi Maruya's *Singular Rebellion*
and Shusaku Endo's *Scandal*

Common sense suggests that the comedy of manners ought to flourish in Japan. What more fertile ground could there be for that gentle, slightly quaint literary genre than a country whose etiquette is ancient, embracing, lovely, and, at times, quite paralyzing? But, reasonable though such expectations may be, few novels that fulfill them have surfaced in the West. The modern Japanese writers who have some following in our country—principally Yukio Mishima, Yasunari Kawabata, Junichiro Tanizaki, Kobo Abe, and Shusaku Endo—are capable of amusing us in diverse ways, but none could be thought of (even after allowances are made for the perishability of humor in translation) as a comic novelist.

The arrival of Saiichi Maruya's *Singular Rebellion* therefore comes as something of a surprise, and it urges us to ponder the degree to which an unwritten connivance of social and commercial forces may skew our vision at the outset by determining which works are translated. Could it be that the novel of delicacy, taciturnity, elusiveness, and languishing melancholy—traits we have come to think of as characteristically Japanese—is less characteristic than we thought? *Singular Rebellion* is a big, gregarious, boisterous book. Maruya, who was born in 1925, has been a popular writer in Japan for two decades; he has been a notable translator, introducing his countrymen to some of Graham Greene's "entertainments" and to Jerome K. Jerome's *Three Men in a Boat;* and he has received significant literary prizes. Nonetheless, *Singular Rebellion* is the first book of his to find its way into English, and required fourteen years to do so. Given its charm—at a number of points it made me laugh aloud—one can only suspect that the Japanese humorist faces considerable international resistance.

Literary absences are often difficult to isolate and identify, and not until I came across *Singular Rebellion* did I realize that here was a tone—bantering, chummy, exaggeratedly and playfully levelheaded—unlike anything I'd ever heard in a Japanese novel. From its opening lines, the book presupposes an informal, comfortable sharing of assumptions between reader and writer:

> There's a lot to be said for having a girl fall in love with you because she's mad about your good looks, or—if your looks aren't up to much—your friendly, cheerful personality. There's even more to be said for having her succumb to a protracted campaign of pure attrition. But for her to take a liking to you on account of your great-grandfather is surely eccentric; and yet I can't help feeling it wasn't until we got on to the subject of that grand old man that Yukari started showing any interest in me.

With remarkable speed, the reader comes to look on the book's hero, a widower named Eisuke Mabuchi, as a friend.

Since reticence is both the method and the theme of a large number of Japanese novels, readers may consider Mabuchi's easy garrulity an act of rebellion. If they do, they will be in accord with most of Mabuchi's acquaintances, who are forever ascribing more rebelliousness to him than he will admit to. In 1969, when the story opens, Mabuchi is an ex-civil servant: he left his job a few years before, upon being asked to transfer to the Ministry of Defense, and now works for a company that manufactures electrical appliances. This spurning of the military seems, especially to the young people he meets, a symbolic blow against the establishment—an action no less insurrectionary for his having subsequently become a businessman. Mabuchi himself sees little daring in his stand, and stresses that he is "very much an establishment person." He makes a great point of his ordinariness. And yet this ordinary man's life grows more outlandish with every page. He marries a young fashion model (the aforementioned Yukari); accepts as a boarder Yukari's grandmother upon her release from prison, where she has spent thirteen years for murdering her husband; befriends a politically radical free-lance photographer who specializes in student riots and street disturbances; and, in the end, forgives Yukari for committing a flagrant act of adultery. After a good deal of rumination, Mabuchi determines that, if no revolutionary, he is indeed an unconventional man:

I don't suppose there can be all that many people in whom the solid virtues of the citizen seem to coexist in exactly equal proportions with their opposites. My wish to rebel balanced my desire to conform.

Mabuchi may have no use for reticence, but it provides, just the same, some of the book's most telling moments. He is surrounded by people of few words. Near the novel's close, Tsuru, the consummately devoted, "feudalistic" servant who has been with him for decades, announces that she is leaving his service, and takes this opportunity to extend some understated but unmistakably bitter advice: "Master Eisuke, I strongly recommend that you do not refer to the next person who comes here as 'the maid.'" And when Yukari, who has never previously pitched any serious complaint against her husband, seeks to explain her infidelity she blurts out a cryptic protest about "the bed problem"—words from which Mabuchi, who hears in them a challenge to his virility, recoils. But it turns out that what is bothering Yukari is her husband's simple failure to buy a new bed; she resents the ghost of Mabuchi's first wife in their bedroom, and one of her reasons for taking a lover may have been to amend the imbalance of a spiritual ménage à trois. Her abrupt complaint sets Mabuchi wondering about his first wife:

> In the dim light of the taxi I thought how women got upset by such peculiar things and then kept quiet about them, and I suddenly remembered my first wife and wondered if she too had been dissatisfied in various ways like Yukari, and whether she'd died without ever mentioning them. And if she had, then what things had she hated in me, I wondered, feeling again close to her and yet sensing what a mystery she'd been essentially, something unfathomed, eventually unknown.

The poignance of this moment proves all the more intense because of Mabuchi's fundamental decency; he is a likeable and loving man. But it appears that he has little ear for the unspoken. Day by day—the author seems to be telling us—even the kindliest head of a household may be squelching the life of his servant or his spouse.

"I'm confused, I'm sad, I'm bewildered . . . that's how it is," Mabuchi explains when he confronts his wife and her lover. He has every right to feel confused, since guardian angels have heretofore rescued him at every misstep. Benign forces are astir throughout the novel, making altogether plausible, for instance, the evolution by which Yukari's homicidal grandmother settles down in cozy domesticity with another former jailbird—a man who, she confesses with mixed pride and illogic, is intelligent enough to have been twice convicted of fraud. In the long run, then, Mabuchi doesn't have anything to worry about—nor, in this sunny-spirited book, does anybody else.

But if *Singular Rebellion* has the enchanted, sheltered feel of a fairy tale, it also boasts a rich, lived-in density; the rooms and streets through which Mabuchi moves have nothing attenuated or sketchy—nothing of the traditional Japanese watercolor—about them. Rather, the landscape is satisfyingly weighted and cluttered, as in this reflection, prompted by a business trip:

> When I stepped out of the plane at Manila into the velvet darkness and the sweltering heat, I regretted not having remained behind on the aircraft. This was partly due to the heat, but the main reason was that I remembered how nasty the duty-free shop in the transit lounge had been some years ago, all they had on sale being local products such as Philippine cigars and some "artless" (or, to be brutally frank, barbaric) pieces of native handicraft, crude trays, boxes, and ornaments made of wood. I'd found them distinctly unattractive, feeling that in these primitive objects all the poverty and wretchedness of Asia was on blatant display.

Even in Mabuchi's moments of perceptual nicety, his world seems tactile, solid—as when, in a blending of reverie and desire, he arrives at Yukari's apartment for their first real date, and she retreats into her bedroom to change her clothes:

> I was surprised it could be as quiet as this in Tokyo. She hadn't closed the door to her room all that efficiently (which may have been on purpose, I don't know), and there was a fairly large gap through which I could hear her taking her things off one by one, a much more emphatically erotic sound than if the door had been wide open. The fact that I thought I could hear the rustling sound as she slid off her stockings probably only indicates how the lack of a visual object will stimulate the imagination to more vigorous activity, and now I was seeing Yukari as she approached stage by stage the state of total nudity, pricking up my ears in the silence that this perverse, usually clamorous town had decided to preserve for me, forever it seemed, and smoking my cigarette.

While there is something pleasingly improbable in Mabuchi's successful juggling of his duties as a "salaryman" and his growing loyalty to a demimonde of fashion models, murderesses, con men, and door-to-door peddlers of aphrodisiacs, his feat is but an emblem of the novel's larger meshing of stylistic incongruities. Perhaps chief among the multiple pleasures of *Singular Rebellion* is its way of harmonizing the workaday and the numinous. The book offers those who have never visited Japan a foretaste of a similar reconciliation—one to be found throughout Japanese towns and cities, but perhaps most strikingly in the floodlit shopping emporiums that are stacked beneath some of the major train stations. The first-time tourist who wanders there, with all the technological miracles of an emerging world arrayed in tight, glittering profusion before him, might swear that the world of the fairy tale and the world of commerce are one.

Shusaku Endo's *Scandal,* his eighth book of fiction to the published in this country, may not elicit, as *Singular Rebellion* does, audible laughter, but it is in many ways the most high-spirited volume we have seen from him so far. Endo is often called a Japanese Graham Greene, and though, like most such border-crossing equivalences, this comparison carries a danger of reductionism, it does prove illuminating. Both men are not merely Catholics but Catholic writers, whose books are an open, ongoing meditation on the meaning of their faith. Both are obsessed with physical pain and the ways in which the body—that mere envelope of the everlasting soul—can distort or canker our spiritual convictions. In selecting a hero, both show a penchant for loners who undertake long journeys that quickly become spiritual pilgrimages. And in bidding their heroes farewell both can be unsentimental to the point of coolness. But in the case of *Scandal,* the English Catholic writer whom Endo most tellingly evokes is not Greene but the Evelyn Waugh of *The Ordeal of Gilbert Pinfold.* In *Scandal,* as in *Pinfold,* we encounter cheerfully undisguised self-portraiture: the author's counterpart is a happily married, aging, eminent Catholic writer who temporarily slips into confusions that may signal a bout of madness.

With the possible exception of Kobo Abe, Endo is Japan's best-known living writer. His books have been translated into more than twenty languages, and he has grown to seem a plausible candidate for the Nobel Prize. For some Western readers, Endo's appeal may stem less from his literary gifts than from his Catholicism, which provides a familiar doorway into an otherwise insular culture. Those who have previously found Japanese novels intractable or remote will surely take heart at Endo's patent sense of being, by virtue of his faith, an outsider in his own country. But Endo's literary attractions reach far beyond matters of faith. He is a craftsman of organization. Pick up any of his books and you are likely to discover that the narrative proportions feel right, that subplots tuck neatly into the larger plot, that the story advances with the surefootedness of someone who understands pacing. He can also be admirably relentless; he does not blink or flinch when handling cruelty, selfishness, or betrayal. At the same time, he exhibits an endearing and somewhat old-fashioned complaisance. Unmistakably, he wishes to accommodate his readers and will do anything in his power to keep them interested or to help them understand. It is typical of Endo to have begun a novel—*When I Whistle*—with the words "Excuse me."

Such virtues having been tallied, it must be pointed out that he displays a number of fundamental shortcomings that might not be expected in a writer of his international renown. He is an artist of finite inventiveness, and especially along a story's edges—in its minor characters and tangential incidents—creative energies seep away. His work rarely surprises. On both the small scale (choice of similes, treatment of dialogue, evocations of place) and the large (revelation of plot, character, theme), Endo's fiction usually proceeds along foreseeable lines. And at times—as in his early novel *Volcano,* in which a smoking mountain represents buried human passion, the struggling human spirit, the indifference of nature, God's anger, and much more—he will invest an object with a greater weight of symbolism than his characters themselves merit; he can be heavy-handed.

Most of his virtues are on display in *Scandal*—as are his weaknesses, although in diluted enough form to seem more illustrative than irksome. The book is a variation on the doppelgänger theme, which has fascinated many twentieth-century writers (including Nabokov, Borges, Calvino, and Lem) and whose nineteenth-century dual forefather is Dr. Jekyll/Mr. Hyde. The story opens as its hero, Suguro, is about to receive a major literary prize. During the ceremony, he spots someone who looks a good deal like himself, who wears an expression that "could be taken either as a grin or a sneer," and who disappears before Suguro can speak to him. Unfortunately, this disappearance is not complete; Suguro's double goes underground, where he consorts with louche young women and generally misbehaves in a Hyde-like fashion. Suguro's double, it becomes clear, is in the heady position of having his public misdeeds attributed to another—to, ironically, the esteemed Catholic novelist Suguro, who has built his literary reputation on investigations into the concept of sin.

The book has its menacing overtones (including the revelation that a seemingly angelic middle-aged woman is a sexual sadomasochist) and its profound theological questions, but in its tone and in the antic improbabilities of its plot it offers a levity all the more welcome in the light of the grimness pervading so much of Endo's work. His novels have seemed at times like sermons of unrelieved bleakness. He is clearly obsessed with what he perceives as a characteristically Japanese tendency to retreat from national disgraces and disasters; in particular, he has asked his readers, throughout his career, to contemplate the tortures that the seventeenth-century shoguns imposed upon Christians—Japanese converts and European missionaries alike—in order to compel recantation. When not dealing with religious persecution and martyrdom, he has often turned to another cheerless subject—the modern hospital, where he has spent, all told, years of his life. Endo, who was born in 1923, has suffered from grave health problems during most of his adulthood and has had to undergo some risky lung operations. It is tempting to suppose that while he was lying in a crowded ward, listening nightly to the sound of torment that was, blessedly, softened by modern anesthetics, he became haunted by the way the torturer employs his intellect not to mitigate pain but to enhance it. In any case, Endo's is an imagination that paces between the torture chamber and the sickroom and a reader cannot help delighting in the unwonted breeziness of *Scandal*. Endo seems to be having fun.

A good argument might be made, though, that fun isn't Endo's métier. Here and there *Scandal* shows signs of strain—in its occasionally forced dialogue, its stereotyped lowlife, and its repetitions that do not deepen but merely rephrase what has come before. What is unquestionably his darkest novel, *Silence*—translated twenty years ago—is almost as unquestionably his finest. It is a hearteningly bold novel in many ways, the most striking being that its hero is not a contemporary Japanese but a seventeenth-century Portuguese, a Jesuit missionary named Rodrigues. Endo has sought, from book to book, to envision his country from the outside, and in the annals of Japanese letters probably no one has made comparable efforts to see the world from a foreigner's point of view. Here is how Japan appears to Rodrigues, from his monastery in Portugal: "As one opened the map one saw the shape of Africa, then India, and then the innumerable islands and countries of Asia were all spread out. And then, at the northeast extremity, looking just like a caterpillar, was the tiny shape of Japan."

In moral terms, *Silence* is as complex and instructive as almost any novel I know. Its title is something of an indictment. Why, Rodrigues wonders, does God refuse to speak to us, even in our moments of mortal need? For the bulk of the story, as Rodrigues travels from Portugal to India, from India to Macao, and from Macao to southern Japan, where he performs clandestine Masses and baptisms, he foresees his eventual capture by the shogun's agents, and his overriding concern is whether or not he will be able to hold steadfast to his Christianity under torture. The book promises a gruesome test of faith. But after his capture Rodrigues is put to no test. He chooses, for reasons that seem influenced but not dominated by fear, to apostatize—a decision that leaves the reader feeling let down. Where is the struggle that we have been promised? A hunger inside us for combat and adventure has been stirred but not sated. Only when we step back from the book do we recognize that our letdown is, in truth, disappointment at seeing a courageous, noble man released from unthinkable agonies—that, in short, we have been made spiritual confederates of Rodrigues' persecutors. In our urge for conflict we have become complicitous with the barbarians.

A lingering puzzle in Endo's œuvre is whether his ascetic temperament derives from his Christianity or he finds Christianity congenial because of an innate asceticism. What is clear, in either case, is that Endo is the least sensuous of major modern Japanese writers. His renunciation of bodily pleasures encompasses the sexual act but extends well beyond it to the smells, tastes, and tactile beguilements of everyday life. In his eight books of translated fiction, many meals are served, but there is never a moment when the reader's mouth waters. Many sounds ring out, but never one that hovers musically in the ear. Endo proves an anomaly in a country whose novelists have generally extolled the virtues of a finely calibrated physical existence. In Tanizaki's *The Makioka Sisters,* for instance, the reader may entertain doubts about how well Sachiko, one of the novel's heroines, would perform in a blind taste-test involving sea bream taken from Osaka waters, which she relishes, and sea bream caught elsewhere, which she dismisses—but one never questions either her faith in her discernment or Tanizaki's admiration for it. One feels a similar authorial approbation in the talk about variations of dye and silk in Kawabata's *The Old Capital,* and in the discussions about the essence of sand in Abe's *The Woman in the Dunes.* All this fussing over minuscule differentiations uplifts a Western reader; it acts as a counterweight to the down-dragging melancholy of so much Japanese fiction. Even when a book ends sadly, one may still feel cheered by the company of people who seem pricklingly alive to the material nuances of the world.

Endo is looking and listening elsewhere. Compared with, say, Tanizaki, who turns with such avid, infectious joy to the fulfillments of music, food, sex, theater, gardens, Endo seems like only half a writer. Endo himself would perhaps not dispute the accusation. However, he would surely add that by forsaking in his fiction the body for the spirit he has chosen the right half.

(1987)

A HOOK SOMEWHERE
Haruki Murakami's *A Wild Sheep Chase*

Haruki Murakami's *A Wild Sheep Chase* lingers in the mind with the
special glow that attends an improbable success. Its lusters are the
brighter for their unlikelihood. The book's pointedly nondescript hero
(who eventually announces, "I've made no name for myself, have no
social credibility, no sex appeal, no talent") is a twenty-nine-year-old
businessman who is sent, under mysterious threats and inducements,
to the snowy reaches of the northernmost of Japan's main islands, Hokkaido, in search of what may be a mutant sheep. He fails to find it.
This comes as no surprise to the reader, who has already watched him
lose by turns an old girlfriend (she is hit by a truck), a wife (she leaves
him for a guitar-playing friend of his), and a new girlfriend (she simply
disappears). In short, this shaggy-dog-story-about-a-sheep is a tale of
severed connections—and, as such, traverses somewhat overfamiliar
ground. Nonetheless, the unfamiliar manages, at each new bend in the
tale, to assert itself: the reader, no less than the book's never-named
hero, is repeatedly hoodwinked. *A Wild Sheep Chase* is a book flush
with satisfying revelations.

Our hero's life is upended from the moment when a cryptic
stranger—a forbiddingly dour man in an impeccable black suit—
makes two demands: that the hero's small public-relations firm stop
distributing a promotional bulletin it had issued on behalf of a life-
insurance company; and that an interview be arranged with whoever
was responsible for supplying the bulletin with a photograph of some
grazing sheep. We soon learn that the man in the black suit—who,
also, remains nameless—works for a figure known only as the Boss.
The man in the black suit makes it clear that, when crossed, the Boss
can display an untempered severity. What he wants done gets done.
And what he wants in this instance is to locate one of the sheep in
the photograph—an irregular creature, belonging to no recognizable

breed, with a star-shaped pattern on its fleece. Before long, our hero
has entered an underworld in two senses: he has not only descended
into a demimonde of blackmail and thuggery but taken an Alice-style
tumble into a Wonderland of loopy transposals and incongruities, in
which a solicitous chauffeur offers to provide him with God's telephone number, and a man in sheep's costume raises no reflection in a
mirror. His only certainty, in a life gone topsy-turvy, is that there must
be "a hook somewhere"—that he is being conned.

With the figures of the Boss and his minions Murakami appears to
be making sport of the popular perception of his country as a power
network at once monolithic and impenetrable: here we encounter, in
a heightened form, that hierarchical, minutely cogged society which
we in the West, with a mixture of awe and disparagement, have dubbed
Japan, Inc. The Boss could well have sprung out of the dark, beery
daydreams of an American businessman who was having trouble gain-
ing access to Japanese markets: he is a wheeler-dealer without scruples,
a man with an unslakable urge for self-aggrandizement. He lives in
imposing isolation, within a sort of fortress, and it turns out that, in his
anonymity and utter lack of accountability, he may be the most powerful man on earth:

> He used his money to corner the market on both politics *and* advertis-
> ing, setting up a power base that thrives to this day. He never surfaces
> because he doesn't need to. So long as he keeps a grip on certain centers
> of political authority and on the core sectors of the public relations in-
> dustry, there's nothing he can't do. . . . Stocks. They're his principal
> source of revenue. Manipulating the market, forcing hands, takeovers,
> the works. His newsboys gather all the necessary information, and he
> picks and chooses according to his fancy. Only a minuscule slice of what
> really goes on ever hits the wires. All the other news is set aside for
> the Boss.

We later discover, though, that the Boss is a mere pawn, an impotent
stand-in. And with the unfolding of this mystery it grows apparent
that business success—the "Inc." in Japan, Inc.—is but the physical
embodiment of spiritual ends beyond the reach of human agency. In
its literary methods, the book quietly exchanges the hard-packed
ground of naturalism for the boggy, fog-wrapped terrain of the surreal.
Bit by bit, the peculiar evolves into the unreckonable. What initially
looks like feminine intuition becomes irrefutable demonstrations of

E.S.P.; a nonsensical dream about a talking cow reveals itself as a har-
binger of danger; the dead begin to speak. And while it would be a
spoiling shame to spell out the novel's final, far-flung illuminations, it
seems permissible to say, by way of confirming the bitter envisionings
of our hypothetical American businessman, that Murakami advances
firm evidence of a link between the Boss and Genghis Khan.

It is not only the hero, the Boss, and the Boss's black-suited henchman
who lack names. Almost no one and nothing afloat on the waterways
of this fluid narrative is anchored to a solid label. Neither the hero's
business partner nor his wife nor his two girlfriends are named; his
home town is merely "the town." Characters are distinguished by their
functions (the chauffeur, the secretary, the proprietor) or by nicknames
(the Rat, J, the Sheep Professor). The hero's cat has attained a tottery
old age without having been given a name, and a scene in which he is
belatedly christened Kipper is presented as an occasion of moment.
Murakami's withholding of personal and place names deracinates his
characters, making them less Japanese and more universal. It also serves
to highlight the shift in tone that arises when, in Hokkaido, the countryside emerges in painstaking detail. Abruptly, place names and dates
come streaming forth, courtesy of a book of local history. The little
northern town the hero has arrived in—which I take to be fictitious—
feels far more substantial and lived-in than the Tokyo he left behind.
Still, names do have their proven uses—having been around since
before the arrival of Eve—and whatever artistic benefits Murakami
derives from their deletion are probably not worth the reader's
consequent hesitancies and confusions. At a number of points in this
otherwise limpid translation, I came upon a "he" or "she" that mis-
led me.

Food provides Murakami with the material for another little game.
If our hero is coyly reluctant to name names, he is scrupulously exhaustive about what he and others eat and drink: cheese crackers, Campbell's soup, omelettes, spaghetti, shrimp au gratin, sandwiches, Caesar
salad, Salisbury steak, foie de baudroie à crème fraîche, rôti de veau
avec garni persil, cheesecake, hazelnut ice cream with Cointreau, fancy
cocktails, Cutty Sark. No one ever seems to sit down to a Japanese
meal.

Murakami's handling of names and food is emblematic of his overall portrait of his homeland. The hero's parents are, significantly, never mentioned—not even when he volunteers a brief summary of his youth and upbringing. The ancestral past feels not repudiated so much as expunged. Murakami budgets few of his resources to the depiction of traditional dress, scenes, customs, diversions. The result is an acute contrast to the spate of recent books—fiction and nonfiction—in which we have seen a broad range of Western authors, sharing the raptness of vision that comes with initial exposure to the exotic, take exquisite pains to reproduce sushi bars, kimono shops, tea ceremonies, moss gardens, painted screens, temple gongs, sumo matches, tatami mats. It is as though Murakami had happily left such things to the foreigners.

Not that he has no eye for a vibrant detail. His mind has a bright analogical bent, and time and again his similes are triumphs of rightness and good humor: "The elevator shook like a large dog with lung disease," or "The pilots and stewardesses, strutting back and forth in the lobby with heads held high, seemed quaintly planar, like little girls' cardboard cutouts," or "I was about to speak when the maître d'hôtel advanced on our table. He showed me the wine label, all smiles as if showing me a photo of his only son." But most such little felicities are inspired by imported practices or modern machinery. On those rare occasions when he trains his eye upon his native landscape, he's apt to treat it with an antic irreverence: "On one edge, the meadow adjoined a birch wood. Huge birch trees of the kind you find up in Hokkaido, not the puny stunted variety that flank the entrance to your neighborhood dentist's office. These were birches that four bears could have sharpened their claws on simultaneously."

By and large, Murakami's world is an interchange of hotels and bars and coffee shops, and the music that continually trips over their loudspeakers is Western: the Doors, Boz Scaggs, Bill Withers, the Brothers Johnson, the Rolling Stones. (Incidentally, the book's dust jacket tells us that Murakami managed a jazz bar in Tokyo from 1974 to 1981.) The plot unfolds to the buzzing strains of an electric guitar. Where are the traditional stringed instruments of Japan—the samisen, the koto? The hero does not ask. What he does ask—poignantly, a third of the way through the novel—is *Where is the ocean?* He returns to his home town and finds that the sea has vanished: buildings now stand where breakers once dragged to and fro. A friendly bartender offers some clarification: "They bulldoze the hills to put up houses, haul the dirt to the sea for landfill, then go and build there too." As the novel's core image (it appears once more on the final page), this vision of an artificial landscape could hardly be bettered. Why should Murakami fuss over the minutiae of a dissolving past? Instead, he has winningly seized upon a single, sweeping symbol for a world that, programmatically, is being levelled.

It is difficult not to regard *A Wild Sheep Chase* as an event larger even than its considerable virtues merit. Many years have elapsed, after all, since any Japanese novelist was enthusiastically taken up by the American reading public—and this may soon be Murakami's destiny. The last writer so treated may have been the Catholic novelist Shusaku Endo, but his finest book, *Silence,* reached the States twenty years ago, and his subsequent career has been patchy. Something similar might be said of Kobo Abe, whose best and most famous work, *The Woman in the Dunes* (its fame enhanced by Hiroshi Teshigahara's internationally acclaimed film), appeared here in 1964. Specialists in Japanese literature often complain that American interest in their field fell away with the passing of the "Big Three"—Junichiro Tanizaki, Yukio Mishima, and the Nobel laureate Yasunari Kawabata, whose deaths all came within a decade of each other, in the mid-sixties and early seventies. At a time when Japan is impinging on our lives as never before—on how we eat and dress and do business and entertain ourselves—its new fiction stirs little excitement outside academe. We are certainly ripe to be won over by a lively debut.

Murakami has already won over his compatriots. *A Wild Sheep Chase* is his first book to cross the Pacific, but he has published half a dozen novels in Japan, one of which, *Norwegian Wood,* has sold an astounding four million copies. Born in 1949, a quarter century after Endo and Abe, Murakami has evidently been adopted as the voice of a new generation—which seems fitting, since his is clearly a youthful sensibility steeped not only in jazz and rock music but in the disillusionments and dispersions of the student movements of twenty years ago. Just as clearly, when Murakami alludes to Western writers—something he does repeatedly, in an ever-growing list that includes Melville, Dostoyevski, Proust, Sholokhov, Conrad, Ellery Queen, and Arthur Conan Doyle—he is not being showily exotic; he feels at home with them.

What is less clear is where Murakami stands in connection with the literature of his own culture. *A Wild Sheep Chase* seems to flirt, here and there, with long-standing literary traditions, such as the notion of the Japanese as "connoisseurs of silence." He throws considerable energy and invention into a cataloguing of various species of quiet. There is "aquariumlike silence," and silence that hovers "fine as dust"; the "perfect" silence after a snowslide, and a brief silence that is compared to "a pebble sent plunging down a fathomless well"; silence "strong enough to make your ears hurt," and silence that is "a viscous fluid filling every opening," and a "ponderous silence such as follows a massacre." But what begins in subtlety ends in levity, and the more hairsplitting he becomes, the more one suspects him of rumpling tradition, of having us on: "The room was utterly silent. Now there is the silence you encounter on entering a grand manor. And there is the silence that comes of too few people in too big a space. But this was a different quality of silence altogether. A ponderous, oppressive silence. A silence reminiscent, though it took me a while to put my finger on it, of the silence that hangs around a terminal patient." Finally, there is this: "The man cleared his throat, then fell silent. This was a definitive silence, one you could judge the qualities of other silences by."

The novel also has a good deal of innocent fun with sexual fetishism (the hero's otherwise plain Jane of a girlfriend has ears so alluring that when she exposes them in a restaurant the "white plaster wall seemed to ripple" and a waiter "who came over with more espresso couldn't pour properly"), which may be a nod at Tanizaki, whose notorious foot fetishism found its way into book after book. But if it *is* a nod it's a fleeting one; there's little in the ambience of this novel to suggest that the creation of particularized parodies was among the author's principal objectives.

No, the book is notable more for shrugging off the past than for hailing it. In a symbolic gesture of severance and estrangement, Murakami launches his prologue on November 25, 1970—the day of Mishima's suicide. The old literary guard is dying off, and their governing aesthetic with them. In one way or another, many of the books they produced echoed Kawabata's famous avowal that he would, in the aftermath of Japan's defeat in the Second World War, henceforward compose nothing but elegies. The fictions of the Big Three often represented a retreat or retrenchment. Theirs was the novel as sanctuary, constructed for the preservation of whatever beauties of landscape and quiddities of national temper might be vaster than war or politics. In a similar vein, Kawabata wrote, "All that is left is for me to return alone to the old mountains and rivers. I consider that I have already died, and I do not expect to write even one line in the future except about the beauty of Japan"—an especially interesting observation in the light of the zippy bravado that Murakami brings to the "old mountains and rivers." Murakami's autumnal Hokkaido is vividly realized—the reader experiences nakedly the encroaching cold, the imminent blizzards—but with a jocularity that seems unmistakably youthful. It is a place where "snow was fluffy, like stuffing spilling out of a torn cloud"—which almost sounds like the result of a pillow fight.

Stylistically, this book about the quest for a mutant sheep is itself something of a mutation or hybrid. It begins as a detective novel, dips before long into screwball comedy, and at its close—when the dead speak—becomes a tale of possession. That such unruly, disjunctive elements mingle harmoniously within it is perhaps the signal feat in a highly accomplished piece of craftsmanship. If *A Wild Sheep Chase* is not in itself an unqualified success—it has its longueurs, its labored whimsies—it may be something more heartening still for the Japanese novel: a presentiment of fresh outlooks and impulses. It would be a choice irony, of a sort that Murakami might relish, if a tale about a missing sheep proved to be a bellwether.

(1989)

Introduction: Far North

Does the world offer a solitary person any pleasure more sweetly vexing than that of standing at a fork in the road and longing to venture down both branches simultaneously? It's the great goal of travel, it seems to me: not the destination but the calculated inducement of that avid, inquisitive, slightly jittery intimation that marvelous things are close at hand and profound consequences may hinge on the route you select.

This feeling was often with me when my wife and I first moved to Japan, in the summer of 1980, and persisted throughout our three years in Kyoto. Time and again its streets contrarily tugged at me. I'd reach an intersection and sense that something beautiful or illuminating or piercingly odd was on display just round the corner; I was always about to miss something I very much didn't want to miss. It was a feeling potent enough to convert my daily bicycle commute from home to office—some two or three miles—into an exhilarating, exhausting series of impulsive veerings and wistful second-guesses.

Robert Frost had an uncommon genius for illuminating common states of mind and his "The Road Not Taken"—perhaps his best-loved poem—captures the fervent paradoxes of this condition. Although Frost's walker clearly relishes his solitude, he soon finds himself craving company of a sort. His singleness is troubling to him:

> Two roads diverged in a yellow wood
> and sorry I could not travel both
> and be one traveler, long I stood
> and looked down each as far as I could
> to where it bent in the undergrowth.

He would "be one traveler" and yet undertake plural adventures; he yearns for variant lives.

In one of the multiple lives that a less stingy cosmos would have granted me, I would have remained in Japan—a place that doubtless could have fed indefinitely an untutored gaijin's appetite for wonders. It was unnerving for me, when my wife and I moved to Washington, D.C., in 1983, to discover that the streets of our new neighborhood failed to tug at me. Many of them were lovely, particularly on warm summer evenings, when the big golden rooms behind the leafy trees unmistakably held lives as rich as anyone's, and yet my walks produced what might be called intersectional indifference; this way or that, it was all the same. The hushed streets of Amherst, Massachusetts, to which we moved the following year, were likewise slack, as were—surprisingly, and somewhat alarmingly—the echoing stone streets of Rome, to which we moved a year later. As were those of London, the year after that. Mournfully, I was coming around to the notion that my Kyoto experiences had had less to do with the charms of Japan than with the ardent susceptibilities of youth.

But when we moved to Iceland in the depths of what everyone told us was an unusually severe winter—moved to Reykjavik, in January of 1989, for another one-year sojourn—the old feelings came over me. I was again a man besotted, and like anyone newly in love I longed to prove my passion by having stiff trials imposed on me. Were the days dark, was the wind strong? Bring on darker days, fiercer winds! In those first weeks of January, the sun didn't actually climb above the hills that ringed the city until about noon. I remember sitting in a coffeeshop one morning and feeling regret steal over me as a languorous rosy glow began to soften the horizon. I wanted to say to that sky, *You don't have to doll yourself up for me!*

I'd come to fresh territory. In Italy I'd been dogged by a feeling that there wasn't a church or a fountain or a ruin not already haunted by some Poet of Visits Past. England was even worse; before each inspiring shrine the spirits actually gathered into a well-bred, respectful queue. Of course, Iceland had its own extended literary tradition—many centuries older than America's—but it was, blessedly, remote from mine. I had a feeling from the outset that this was a place where the ghosts and I could get on.

And yet it wasn't merely a matter of effectively having located a sort of spiritual Rooms to Let, a vacancy in one of the hilltowns on the lower slopes of Parnassus. No, I *liked* this place. Liked the dark snowy unshovelled streets, the square gray houses with their incongruous lacy curtains and roofs painted bright kindergarten colors, the stunted doing-the-best-we-can birches, the cacti in the windows that spoke of antithetical climatic hardships. I liked the smell of the ocean as I walked down Reykjavik's main street—the bay's urgent nearness. For all its killing coldness, the sea was our protector, a fact confirmed by any map. Iceland was inhabited only along its watery edges. In the lifeless Interior, wind cohabited with snow.

Increasingly, those maps drew my eye toward Vatnajokull: the country's (and Europe's) largest glacier. That a mass of ice in this country was large and durable enough to be a concern for cartographers—along with mountains and rivers and harbors—appealed to me hugely.

On a brief visit to Iceland, Richard Nixon once was overheard to remark, probably while being driven through one of the lava fields that cover some eleven percent of the entire country, that the land was "god-forsaken." He was referring to its desolation, perhaps, although this aspect of the landscape has always seemed to me more praiseworthy than lamentable. NASA once brought its astronauts to Iceland to acclimatize them to the moon. For me, having grown up under the long shadow thrown by little Sputnik, the race to the moon had been a contest to take quite seriously. I was sixteen years old when Apollo landed (and Nixon was President), and back then it seemed reasonable to suppose—oh dear dream!—I might make that journey myself someday. The moon has since drifted farther away. I suppose the lava fields of Iceland are as close as I'll ever come to a lunar constitutional. I'm grateful for the approximations they have provided me.

But President Nixon's remark was to be quarrelled with on another level. The land might be lifeless, but it was far from forsaken. No, it was inspiriting to see how it evidenced the same providential eye for detail and fineness of touch manifest in a life-teeming rain forest or a coral reef. I drove one very cold December day to some lava fields west of Reykjavik. It was dusk, though I suppose it wasn't yet three o'clock. The sun was low and pink and distant—I might almost have been contemplating it from a tableland on Mars. The air was pristine. The stone fields, overspread with moss, were a pale green in the light, and everything underfoot—stone and dirt and moss—lay under heavy frost.

In its rich thickness the frost gave off a sense of multilayered stars, a superabundance that spoke—as the Milky Way does—to the eye's bounded frailty; more was to be seen than could be seen, clearly, and to stoop low before this cracked and pitted terrain was to behold how every bump and burr of stone carried its own astral encrustations, and it may be that the lava fields of Iceland are as close as I'll ever get to heaven, too.

—A heaven, to be sure, that had its perils. As I made my meandering way, shivering through the fading light, I entertained visions of a tumble into a fissure—a not unheard-of occurrence—from which I would be unable to climb out. I was going to freeze to death out here before anybody found me. . . . Such fantasies have the benefit, anyway, of leading one to marvel anew at how, for more than a millennium, people have scraped out a livelihood from so inhospitable an island.

This sense of having triumphed over long odds may help explain something deeply winsome about the Icelanders: their sense of the attainability of grand accomplishment. In *Northern Sphinx,* Sigurdur A. Magnusson, one of the country's leading men of letters, puzzled over why his countrymen had produced no significant philosopher:

> It is noteworthy that they have never produced any original or profound thinker. Philosophy is almost nonexistent, whereas poetry flourishes. In literature their preference is for the epic style, the descriptive passage, the flowing narrative, to the exclusion of the analytical, the philosophical or the psychological approach.

What is so appealing in this is the assumption that Iceland by rights *should* have produced a world-class philosopher—that its failure to do so needs to be explained. This is a nation whose aggregate population is smaller than that of, say, Birmingham, Alabama, or Mississauga, Ontario, or Querétaro, Mexico. Imagine ourselves placed in a world where someone might plausibly wonder why Birmingham or Mississauga or Querétaro, although having produced literary masterworks and world-famous explorers and the greatest per capita level of chess expertise in the world, had never produced a "first-rate thinker." Imagine, for that matter, the Birminghamites or Mississaugans or Querétarans accepting as a matter of course that they should produce their own currency, own system of jurisprudence, own representatives to the U.N., own trade policies, own film industry, own international airline, own educational system . . .

If the forbidding climate and landscape have fostered a sense of proficiency, they have probably also contributed to a welcome, complementary humility. In a country whose internal roads are sometimes snow-blocked until June or July, no one rises far above the weather. By chance, I was in Iceland when the Reykjavik Summit was announced; in a few days' time, Reagan and Gorbachev, as well as hundreds of reporters and officials and photographers and interpreters, would be arriving. The eyes of the world would be focussed on this small island nation as never before. To a professor friend of mine, a soft-spoken and gentle man, I expressed a hope of good weather. October in Reykjavik can be lovely and a stretch of lucid, mild days might dispel worldwide illusions about the unremitting fierceness of the place. My friend considered for a moment and said happily, "I hope it's utterly hellish. Those bastards need to learn there are things out there bigger than they are."

A NONESUCH PEOPLE

2

Iceland is a place that seems to generate both superlatives and a people with an appetite for documenting them. Everywhere a visitor goes, he meets statistical boasts and curiosities. Reykjavik is the world's northernmost capital. Its average winter temperature is higher than New York City's. Iceland contains Europe's largest glacier, Vatnajokull, which is as big as Rhode Island and Delaware combined. Iceland was the last country in Europe to be settled. (The first settlers are believed to have been troglodytic Irish monks who arrived around the sixth century A.D. and mysteriously vanished before the year 1000.) Politically, it is one of the newest countries in Europe. (Full independence from Denmark was not achieved until 1944.) It is geographically the newest country in Europe: roughly one third of the lava that has spilled from the earth in the past five hundred years has emerged from Icelandic volcanoes. Iceland has the highest per capita number of chess grandmasters in the world. It has the highest proportion of VCRs to households in the world. Icelanders have the highest life expectancy of any nationality (a contention disputed by many, including the Japanese). Icelanders have the highest literacy rate in the world (again disputed by the Japanese). And—a superlative evidently not open to question—Iceland publishes more books per capita than any other country.

I came across the statistic about VCRs a few years ago in an airline magazine, while I was descending toward an empty, scarred landscape that included a glint from the distant Snaefellsnes peninsula, to whose glaciered steeps and fissures Jules Verne sent Professor Liedenbrock and his nephew Axel in search of the crater that would start them on their journey to the center of the earth. The statistic about book publishing, on the other hand, is one that I have encountered many times during my visits to Iceland, and not merely from travel brochures or the staffs at tourist-information centers. One hears it from shopkeepers, farmers, businessmen. Icelanders are manifestly proud of their literary tradition, and protective of it. Sigurdur A. Magnusson, a poet and novelist, and the author of numerous books about Iceland, exults in being a harsh critic of the trends of modern life. "I worry all the time," he told me recently, as we sat in the living room of his Reykjavik apartment. "You know, I see the French, and how zealous they are about protecting their culture, and I get angry at my countrymen. We need to be equally zealous—more so. When I see the French talking about 'cultural imperialism,' I say to myself, Why aren't we fighting that more vigorously in my own country?"

"Cultural imperialism" is a phrase I have heard frequently in Iceland, along with various calls for resistance to it. What gives this situation special poignance and drama is the smallness of the country that would protect itself. In France, say, any invasion by the English language, or the American fast-food chain, or the Hollywood movie, must come up against the bulwarks of a culture whose resources are deep, multiple, and long-standing. And France's population—of fifty-five million—is more than two hundred times greater than Iceland's. Just how tiny Iceland's population actually is may go unperceived by the average tourist, who is likely to while away a brief stay within the clogged streets of Reykjavik. Although Iceland is one of the world's largest islands (it is about the size of Kentucky), its population numbers only some quarter of a million.

Iceland seems to have accumulated only barely enough people and affluence to participate fully in the cultural and social activities that characterize modern European life. Were it much less populous, or poorer, its people probably could not hope to speak of full "cultural independence" at all. But unlike its two nearest neighbors—Greenland, to the west, with a population of about fifty-three thousand, and the Faroe Islands, to the east, with a population of about forty-five thousand—Iceland has the cultural and commercial wherewithal to support a professional symphony orchestra, an opera company, a number of public theaters and a pool of playwrights to nourish them, a university, an extensive state broadcasting system, a busy international airline, and a national film company. Inevitably, such cultural breadth in so small a country has meant that many of the arts are, in Sigurdur Magnusson's words, "a bit thinly spread." Until this century Iceland had almost no tradition of painting, sculpture, architecture, instrumental music, or theater. It is no wonder, then, that Icelanders feel so vulnerable to what they sometimes call the Anglo-Saxon invasion—that stream of American and British television programs which spills into their homes night after night.

This is an invasion that has occurred in distinct, controversial waves. In the early 1960s, Reykjavik residents began buying televisions in order to pick up broadcasts from the military base at nearby Keflavik. Although technically a NATO installation, Keflavik is often called the American base, since the vast preponderance of its soldiers have always been Americans. The presence of foreign soldiers on Icelandic soil has itself been a source of fierce debate ever since the end of the Second World War, when many Icelanders had hoped to see all foreign military personnel withdrawn. The unchecked presence of American television was therefore perceived in some quarters as an additional incursion, and the State Broadcasting Service (SBS) was inaugurated largely as a defensive response to it. Although its broadcasting hours were quite limited (with no daytime and no Thursday offerings), the state-run channel proved widely popular. The Keflavik channel was eventually confined to the base, and so for a time SBS enjoyed a virtual monopoly on broadcasting. Then, in the 1980s, videocassette rental outlets began to spring up, not only in Reykjavik but also in every tiny fishing village in the country. The government's television monopoly was effectively broken, and an onrush of American movies, crime shows, and situation comedies followed. The state monopoly was formally dismantled in October 1986, with the advent of Channel Two, the first private television station in Iceland. Daytime and Thursday broadcasting had arrived.

Given the country's long, sunless winters and frequently impassable roads, television was destined to have an enormous impact on Icelandic society, and the debate between the advocates of "freedom of the airways" and those of "protection from cultural imperialism" has been bellicose. But in Sigurdur Magnusson's mind, the choices are one in their most significant effect: "*Any* sort of television viewing is going to take people further and further from the Sagas."

· · ·

The variegated collection of anonymous tales grouped under the heading "Sagas" (literally, "things said") is a central, defining element of Icelandic culture. The earliest of the Sagas were written in the first three decades of the thirteenth century; most originated during Iceland's literary renaissance, which came a little later, from about 1270 to 1300. The Sagas have bequeathed to the modern Icelander much otherwise unavailable historical information as well as a feel for his culture's medieval past. They have also provided a pool of shared anecdote and expression; modern Icelandic conversation is sprinkled with aphorisms and descriptive phrases drawn from the Sagas. To the writer, they serve as a perpetual summons to creation. Sigurdur Magnusson says, "There are days when I ask myself, Why the *hell* am I writing in Icelandic? I write English tolerably well, and have even written books in it. Icelandic will be dead in a hundred years. But there are other days when I think, No, it will change a lot, but the language of the Sagas will survive."

There are those who argue that the Sagas are in fact more often alluded to than read. One American I met, who had worked in Iceland for a number of years, was quite skeptical: "They'd have you thinking that in the evenings they're all reading Sagas by candlelight. Well, that's just not so." Other visitors to Iceland have come away, often ecstatically, with quite a different impression. Travel books about Iceland abound with picturesque accounts of sheep farmers observed in huddled discussion of Grettir the Strong, who beheaded the ghost Glam but suffered ever after from a fear of the dark; or of fishermen observed in good-natured, schnapps-fueled disputation as to why, in the year 1011, Njal resisted so little when his house was razed with him and his family inside it. Whatever the truth as to how frequently the average Icelander turns for pleasure to the Sagas, they remain a source of national pride. An Icelander admits to ignorance about Grettir or Njal only with reluctance.

The Sagas were written in Old Norse, the language of Iceland's first permanent settlers, the Norwegians, who arrived in their Viking ships in the ninth century. The bold reach of the Viking conquests for many centuries gave Old Norse a farflung currency, and probably fostered among the anonymous authors of the Sagas, geographically dispersed as they were, a sense of being part of an extended literary community.

Sigurdur Magnusson writes in his book *Northern Sphinx:* "The Norse language, which is spoken in Iceland today with very slight modifications, was thus for a time a 'world language.' It was spoken all over Scandinavia, and at the courts of the Scandinavian rulers in England, Scotland, Ireland, France and Russia. It was the recognized language of the Emperor's bodyguard in Byzantium. And it was the first European language spoken on the shores of America." While Old Norse underwent upheavals and transformations elsewhere in Europe, in Iceland it was passed along intact from generation to generation. The result is that the Sagas, masterpieces written in a world language when it was already somewhat past its meridian, are now directly accessible only to some quarter of a million people whose mother tongue is the oldest living language in Europe.

Iceland officially converted to Christianity in the year 1000—two or three centuries before the Sagas were written. But many of the events they chronicle antedate the conversion, and in their atmosphere and language, as well, they often recall the earlier, pagan world of Thor and Odin and Loki. Iceland's medieval poetry and Sagas provide us with our only substantial body of pre-Christian Teutonic lore and belief, and in their various translations and transmutations they have shaped culture throughout Europe. It appears that Shakespeare, for example, borrowed the tale of Hamlet from the Danish historian Saxo Grammaticus, whose source must have been Icelandic. So much of Wagner's *Ring of the Nibelungen* draws on Icelandic sources that one has difficulty envisioning its existence without them.

The Sagas stand in Iceland as a surprisingly proximate and yet poignantly unreachable monument. Theirs is an apical greatness—born of the one irrecoverable moment in the nation's history when it was a literary center of Europe. The modern citizen of Reykjavik, no less than his counterpart in Rome or Athens, knows the thrilling reverberations of a distant golden age—even if, in the Icelander's case, it is one whose monuments endure not in marble and alabaster but in heaps of inscribed, age-darkened calfskins.

This sense of a vanished cultural heyday may be connected to a common impression in Iceland of a more recent decline. Among literary people one finds a pervasive suspicion that earlier generations manipulated the language with greater agility and freshness. Sigurdur Magnusson, who links linguistic decline to the growing influence of film and television, says, "Ours is a very difficult language, and a very intricate one, and people don't have the command of it they used to. They are losing control of its intricacy and they are simplifying it." Thorbjorn Broddasson, the country's leading expert on the media, says, "If you read what people, often people without formal education, were writing around the turn of the century, you often find an extremely beautiful, fluent, and rich language. You see much less of this now. The language is becoming flattened and less varied."

Much as the Sagas clarify and enrich Iceland's past, the works of Halldor Laxness animate its present. Well before he won the Nobel Prize for Literature, in 1955, Laxness had become a figure of towering importance to the Icelandic nation. Steinunn Sigurdardottir, one of the country's best-known younger poets, says of Laxness, "He really is a kind of god here. His effect is everywhere. Not just in our books but in little things, like dress. Among our artists we haven't had much of a tradition of bohemian dress, and that's just because of Laxness—because he is such a dandy."

An elderly man, born in 1902, Laxness lives a few miles outside Reykjavik, not far from where his family farmed when he was a child. He has stopped writing in the past few years, and his speech has slowed, but he still conveys a sense of great authority—though it is cushioned these days by a beaming affability. He has reconciled himself to a number of things that once enraged him, including the Keflavik military base. His anecdotes range over the globe, for he was a peripatetic man in youth and middle age. Denmark, Sweden, Luxembourg (where he lived in a Catholic monastery), Italy, the Soviet Union (where he wrote of communism with an enthusiasm he later regretted), the Far East, the United States. . . . He is fond of recalling his friend Upton Sinclair, a "good man but a very bad writer," and Ernest Hemingway, whose *A Farewell to Arms* Laxness translated into Icelandic. The two men never met, but, according to Laxness, Hemingway would occasionally telephone from thousands of miles away to impart some choice gossip about the workings of the Nobel selection committee. And Laxness remembers W. H. Auden, who first visited Iceland in 1936, sauntering around Reykjavik with a piece of shark in his pocket, because he "wanted to smell fishy."

A penchant for the outrageous and a joyful urge to shock still enliven Laxness' conversation. He has described himself as "the most hated man in Iceland." He had been resented for years, he boasted, for revealing the rude facts about Icelandic life not only to his countrymen, who wish to romanticize themselves, but, worse still, to the rest of the world. (Laxness has been translated into thirty-five languages.) Although he wrote of the countryside, there is little of the conventionally pastoral in Laxness' work: there is certainly nothing swainlike about his coarse, blaspheming shepherds. He sought to represent life as it was actually lived, or endured, in the farmers' cold, dark, low-ceilinged, tubercular turf houses.

In his epic novel *Independent People* (which, for all of his happy claims to being execrated, is probably the best-loved novel in Iceland) he recounts the tale of a proud, doomed farmer, Bjartur of Summerhouses, whose almost impenetrable brusqueness is tempered by a taste for composing *rimur*—traditional verse that, at least in Bjartur's hands, is "technically so complex that it could never attain any noteworthy content." Bjartur lives in the twentieth century, but the modern era, with its world wars, hardly impinges upon him, save in the fluctuating demand for wool and mutton. In Bjartur's household lives an ancient woman who cooks over a fire (she has never seen a stove) and whose voice, as she chants snippets of verse, goes back to the age of the Sagas. In the course of his long life Halldor Laxness has had the chance—a rare and wonderful opportunity for a writer, and especially singular for a European—to record his country's passage out of the Middle Ages into an era of supersonic military planes and home computers.

The signs of modern life perch lightly on Iceland. From downtown Reykjavik, with its luxury hotels and hamburger stands, its international franchises like Benetton and Laura Ashley and Mothercare, one need drive for only a few minutes to reach an uninhabited and all but uninhabitable terrain of fiercely contorted lava fields. Much of the interior of Iceland is an unrelievedly gray desert.

Iceland has always been peopled only along its edges. Its fishermen may venture out upon the sea, and its farmers pursue their flocks deep into the interior, but in the end Icelandic communities hug the island's rocky shore. The economy has lately expanded beyond fish and wool to encompass a range of high-tech industries, but life is still lived on the sites of the old coastal villages. The interior, with its glaciers and lava fields, its deserts, volcanoes, crevasses, and flash-flooding rivers, supports little human life—and almost no animal life. On my first trip to Iceland, in the summer of 1984, I hiked for a week and a half in the interior and was amazed to pass whole days without spying a single animal larger than a spider. No rodents, no fish, not even a cruising bird in the limpid sky.

The interior's fascinations are diverse—rhyolite hills, ice caverns, black-snouted glaciers, echoing cataracts, steaming sulfuric hot springs—but they share an elemental ruggedness. If dulcified here and there by sugary patches of cottonweed and low-lying clumps of pink moss campion, and everywhere by a pure, unstinting northern light that Auden thought "the most magical light of anywhere on earth," Iceland remains a pretty spooky place. The landscape may help to ex-plain why Icelandic lore abounds in supernatural beings—trolls, elves, ghosts, water cows. And perhaps because the island lies just south of the Arctic Circle, where it endures some twenty hours of unbroken darkness during the shortest days of winter, the pull of the supernatural remains strong. Farmers still routinely leave patches of hay unmown where "hidden folk" are thought to live, and a few years ago a road was rerouted in order to leave an elf colony undisturbed. Palmistry thrives. Mediums and spiritualists fill Reykjavik auditoriums.

A sense of rapid turnover, so prominent an aspect of modern Icelandic life, is encouraged by climatic and soil conditions that ferociously con-spire to raze whatever buildings one erects. Because the country pos-sesses no easily workable building stone, and almost no timber except driftwood, traditionally the only practicable home for most farmers was the turf house, which requires constant upkeep. An abandoned farm— of which there are many in this rapidly urbanizing nation—dissolves speedily into the earth. As the towns began to flourish, houses were constructed first of corrugated metal and then of concrete. Either way, the effect is often dreary. But if Icelandic architecture is far from hand-some, its severity and newness create a faintly surreal and oddly satis-fying contrast to the terrain. In Reykjavik one finds little visual suggestion of historical continuity or of harmony between community and landscape. All of it might well have been set down in the past few months—the clean-angled, boxy houses with their painted, particolored roofs; the seaside warehouses; the red bus shelters; the strings of yellow streetlights. To the Icelander this environmental contrast is rendered still more pointed by the durability of his language.

In the midst of dizzying cultural and social change, the fixity of the language provides constant reassurance that life is not changing *too* quickly. According to Sverrir Hermannsson, the Minister of Culture and Education, "These things—affluence, technology, American films and music—have transformed our society in the last fifty years, but not dangerously, since we have kept our language." Hermannsson became Minister of Culture and Education only two years ago, and at once established himself as an activist—particularly in the area of language preservation. Among the first regulations he worked to implement was one requiring every television broadcast of foreign material to carry either Icelandic subtitles or an overlaid Icelandic commentary. So proficient are most Icelanders in English that a television station might otherwise choose to forgo the expense of subtitling or dubbing. The new regulation was required, Hermannsson says, "because otherwise we would be overrun by English."

The broadcasting regulations are but one of a range of rules designed to protect the language. The most controversial of these are the "name laws." In Iceland patronymics are traditional, and first names are so pervasively employed that even the phone books are organized around them. Icelandic surnames are unstable from one generation to the next. Sverrir Hermannsson's surname is Hermannsson because he is the son of a man whose first name was Hermann; if Sverrir had a daughter named Asta, she would become Asta Sverrirsdottir. The name laws stipulate, among other things, that a newborn child must be christened with a traditional Icelandic name before its birth can be registered. The adoption of a family name—a once popular "Danish" fashion— is proscribed, although those that were in existence before the law's promulgation are permitted. In addition, foreigners granted Icelandic citizenship must renounce their original names and take new, Icelandic ones.

That regulations like these, which would be regarded as infringements of civil liberties in our own country, have been accepted suggests a cluster of attitudes quite divergent from ours in regard to governmental intrusions into everyday life. It is as though Icelanders perceive the most baneful threats to their society as external rather than internal. In any case, Icelanders seem remarkably acquiescent—given the general liberality of their country—about what Hermannsson calls "culture-strengthening" regulations. The laws about liquor, for example, are uncompromisingly strict, perhaps in recognition of the heightened dangers of alcoholism in a land of long arctic nights. The state, which holds a monopoly on the retailing of alcoholic beverages, ensures that sales outlets are few, their hours short, and their prices high.

The tolerance, even approval, of regulation is especially in evidence with regard to the Icelandic language. The name laws, for example, extend to the commercial field. A proprietor of a shop or restaurant is generally prohibited from giving his establishment a non-Icelandic name. "But," Gudrun Erlendsdottir told me last summer, "we have not been quite so firm in this area." Formerly an attorney and professor specializing in family law, Erlendsdottir recently became the first woman appointed to Iceland's Supreme Court. "You will notice that we have these discothèques—like Broadway and Hollywood—and of course these are not Icelandic names. And every week or so, it seems, you see an article in the newspaper saying that such exceptions should not be allowed." Her court appointment was all the more notable in light of her political beliefs; Erlendsdottir is one of the country's most prominent feminists. The changes that feminism has brought to Iceland come vividly to life (as does, once again, the smallness of the population) in some of the statistics she cites. "I was only the fifth woman to become a lawyer in Iceland. The first came in 1934, the second in about 1942, and third and fourth in 1958, and I in 1961. At the university now, between a fourth and a third of the law students are women. And, by the way, not one of Iceland's women lawyers has yet passed away. We're all alive."

"Laws may be useful, but in this field they really cannot do so much," Baldur Jonsson explained to me when I visited him recently. "It must be done by the people themselves."

Baldur Jonsson is the chairman of the Icelandic Language Committee. If the country's diverse efforts to preserve its language have any single center, it is his neat, unimposing office in a one-story house on the campus of the University of Iceland. Jonsson has taught at the university since 1963, although he has had to curtail his teaching duties since he came to the Language Committee, in 1978. He is, he explained, a "philologist, although you might say my field is language planning."

Even in English, his second language (or third or fourth, for he is fluent in Danish and Swedish as well), Jonsson conveys an exceptional precision. A soft-spoken, gray-haired man in his mid-fifties, he commonly meets any inquiry about Iceland or Icelandic with a deliberative pause and a prefatory, slightly apologetic "That's a very difficult question." What he says next, however, shows that he has thought about the question in depth, and has a number of tentatively offered but quite plausible answers.

"No one can explain why Icelandic has remained so stable," he told me. "I suppose there are several factors. First, we had this very rich literature in common at such an early date. From the twelfth century we've had great written literature in both poetry and prose. And we're geographically separate. You can call it isolation if you want, although I dislike that word, I think it causes misunderstandings. After all, we have not been isolated in the sense of not knowing about other people. It's other people who have been isolated in the sense of not knowing about us. Think about the Viking voyages to North America, which no one 'knew' about for so long. Well, for centuries now every child in this country has known all about them. Another factor is our great social stability. In the year 1800 the inhabitants of Reykjavik numbered about three hundred, and this was the largest town in the country. People lived on farms, century after century, in the same way. And lastly, there has been long-term stability in the population. Of course, this was subject to all sorts of short-term fluctuations."

In the streamlined, cool way that numbers have, the population statistics for Iceland tell a heartbreaking story of recurrent want and disaster. The country grew steadily in its first few centuries. By the year 1100, a little more than two hundred years after the arrival of the first Norwegian settlers, the population had reached about seventy thousand. Six centuries later it stood at half that figure. Smallpox, the Black Death, famine, and volcanic eruptions had ravaged the settlements. It wasn't until well into the twentieth century that the population reached one hundred thousand. Neither the decline nor the eventual growth owed much to migration.

Over the years the Icelandic language has been protected also by what Jonsson called its "naturally conservative character." He gave two examples. The language is highly inflected, which means that only those foreign words that are adaptable to a variety of suffixes can be imported. And nearly all Icelandic words are accented on the first syllable, which often makes direct borrowing an impossibility. But if the full extent of the language's conservatism must remain obscure to the English-speaking visitor who knows little or no Icelandic, its effect can plainly be seen in a newspaper: I was amazed at how few words I could pick out. Unlike most European languages, which have borrowed large numbers of English words and cognates in recent decades, Icelandic has continued to turn to native roots when new words were needed.

With the country's increasingly technological economy and cosmopolitan culture, this has meant that thousands of neologisms have had to be found and catalogued. "Often somebody will telephone here and ask for an Icelandic translation of a word, usually an English word, and if I don't know one, we start to discuss possibilities," Jonsson said. "Frequently the result is that the caller will suggest something that seems good. And eventually it may get picked up by the public—or it may not. But in any case, the Language Committee is basically a coordinating organ. We don't make many words. That's often the job of various technological committees, who collect words and discuss them. In many cases they have found themselves in time with a large glossary, which we have helped to publish.

"These questions can be very complicated. Let's take the word *skjar,* which is now used to designate a computer screen. The word originally referred to a window—a certain type of obsolete window in a turf house. So somebody got the idea of using the word for this new sort of window." Jonsson nods at the personal computer that stands beside his desk. "The danger is that the new word will swamp the old, and alter our literature in the process. Some people think we shouldn't have taken this *skjar* and used it in this modern sense. We terminologize— as it is called—words from the common language. But in certain cases we have to make sure we don't go too far, throwing unwanted associations into our old poetry, for example. This word *skjar* wasn't completely dead. It remained an active word that people knew from poetry, and from songs that we still sing. One must be careful with living words. One must be careful not to do too much of this.

"Incidentally," Jonsson said, "all of our publishing work is done on computers." I observed that there is a fine irony in using new technology for such a conservative function—to which Jonsson responded with another meditative pause. "Conservative? Well, yes and no. I am a modern person. Before I started at the Language Committee, I had worked more or less as a pioneer in linguistic computing. I am working on the improvements of a tool—the tool of the Icelandic language—and the better that tool is, the better the nation. I sometimes compare our language to a tree. Let the tree grow, but without changing so much that the very structure is different. Let it remain the same tree. If we lose our contacts with the Sagas, if we can't read them anymore, then we can't read this morning's newspaper, because it is written in the same language.

"When the struggle for independence began, in the last century, the purity of the language became a big issue. Always these two things—political independence and linguistic purity—have gone together. We are independent now, and yet we still feel threatened. Perhaps a small nation is always struggling for its independence.

"Actually, Icelanders have always been this way. If you go back to a text we call the First Grammatical Treatise, which was written in the twelfth century, and which is the first phonology in any Germanic language, you find that it's written in Icelandic. It is anonymous, but we can see that its author was a learned man who knew languages and knew what was going on in neighboring countries. But he never used Latin terminology. He made up his own. So we must ask ourselves, Why in heaven did he do that?

"Now *this* is the sort of person," Jonsson added, and his soft voice, turning wistful, became softer still, "there should be television programs about."

Jonsson's pride in the cosmopolitan outlook of the anonymous author of the First Grammatical Treatise seems characteristically Icelandic. More than once in my visits I was informed that Icelanders have always been great travelers—that in the Sagas they wandered the world over, from North America to Russia, Turkey, Africa: it is perhaps one more datum in support of a widely favored image of themselves as a nonesuch people. This small native vanity, and a natural eagerness to dress themselves in mystery, may explain the continuing allure of a bizarre account of their origins. Until recently the orthodox view was that most Icelanders were of Scandinavian extraction, with a small admixture of Celtic blood. Modern anthropological research, taking into account blood types and skull measurements, has suggested that the Irish component may be much greater than previously supposed. A radically different claim based on literary evidence is that modern Icelanders are the descendants of a fair-skinned nomadic people who lived long ago around the Black Sea. This theory was propounded by a professor at the University of Iceland, the late Bardi Gudmundsson, and according to Sigurdur Magnusson, there is at least some linguistic evidence to buttress it. Whether valid or not, the hypothesis creates a beguiling historical symmetry. By means of it, those voyages that Icelanders like Leif Ericsson made to the coasts of North America are balanced by earlier wanderings that led the Icelander back to the Middle East and "the cradle of civilization"; Iceland is given a mediating role in history, a fulcral position between the Old World and the New. The message for the modern visitor, much as it was for Verne's Professor Liedenbrock and his nephew Axel, is that one comes to Iceland to reach the center of the earth.

(1987)

THE BOOK OF MY LIFE

Halldor Laxness' *Independent People*

There are good books and there are great books and there may be a
book that is something still more: it is the book of your life. If you're
quite lucky, you may at some point chance upon a novel which inspires
so close a kinship that questions of evaluation (Is this book better than
merely good? Does it achieve true universal greatness?) become a nig-
gling irrelevance. Luck has everything to do with it. For this sensation
has its roots in a poignant, tantalizing notion that this marvelous new
addition to your existence, this indelible and invaluable Presence, has
arrived by mere serendipity. Anyone who cares seriously about fiction
will eventually get around to *The Brothers Karamazov* or *Madame Bovary*
or *Pride and Prejudice* or *Moby Dick* or *Don Quixote,* and if you're somebody whose closest literary attachment is to a book of this staple sort,
the satisfaction you take from it will not be graced by the particular
haunted feeling of good fortune I'm talking about; you will have,
instead, the assurance of knowing that your keenest literary pleasures
were preordained. One looks differently on the book of genius that,
even in a long bookworm's life, one might never have stumbled
upon.

The feeling I'm describing may account for Henry Miller's pronouncement about Knut Hamsun's *Mysteries,* about which he declared
that it "is closer to me than any other book I have read. . . . Reading
this book, I always feel as though I am reading another version of my
own life. . . ." Or John Fowles' reverence toward Alain-Fournier's *Le
Grand Meaulnes:* "all those of us who were entranced, almost literally
tranced, by the book from the beginning have never, whatever the
colder and sterner judgements of adulthood, lost our intense love for
it." And: "I am, in short, a besotted fan, and still feel closer to Fournier
than to any other novelist, living or dead." Or Randall Jarrell's obsession with Christina Stead's *The Man Who Loved Children,* which even-

tually precipitated the longest essay he ever wrote. (It concluded: "*The Man Who Loved Children* makes you a part of one family's immediate existence as no other book quite does. When you have read it you have been, for a few hours, a Pollit; it will take you many years to get the sound of the Pollits out of your ears, the sight of the Pollits out of your eyes, the smell of the Pollits out of your nostrils.") Or what Rilke felt about Jacobsen ("Of all my books, I find only a few indispensable . . . the Bible, and the books of the great Danish author Jens Peter Jacobsen"), particularly his *Niels Lyhne:* "the more often one reads it, the more everything seems to be contained within it, from life's most imperceptible fragrances to the full, enormous taste of its heaviest fruits."

No doubt Rilke and Fowles and Miller and Jarrell recognized that greater novels were to be found than the objects of their devotion. But after all, what does greatness signify once you have stumbled into love's dizzy province? For what we are talking about is a sort of imperishable romance, in which the flaws of a book are as endearing—as treasurable—as the flaws in the face of one's sole beloved. This is the real thing: a head-over-heels incredulity that there exists in the universe so perfect an imperfection.

I don't suppose it's any accident that in three of these four cases the book was written in a language foreign to its admirer, or that in every case the novel's author and its admirer came from different countries. Distance naturally enhances a sense of mystical unity—adds to it the wonderment of experiencing such intimate ties with somebody who worked at various removes from you.

And the book of my own life? I remember vividly my initial encounter with it. I finished its last chapters one late afternoon in Rome, seated in an all-but-deserted café. Outside, a storm had abruptly blown in and a chill autumn rain was lashing the streets, and I read as though furtively, hunched over the pages. I did this for two reasons. The light had turned dim. And I didn't want anyone happening to glance my way to notice I was steadily weeping.

The novel was Halldor Laxness' *Independent People*. It always strikes me as a bitter irony that, in urging the book on someone, I often must first identify its author. Of what other living Nobel Prize–winning novelist would this be true? But the fact is that Laxness won the Nobel many years ago, in 1955, and that he represents the smallest country ever to produce a laureate: Iceland, with its population of a quarter of a million. All of Laxness' books are out of print in English.

Still, *Independent People* is not hard to come by in the States. When it was published here, in 1946, it was a Book-of-the-Month Club Main Selection, and copies regularly turn up in used-book stores. Provided the price is ten dollars or less, I snap them up whenever I come across them. They make an ideal gift—though some explanation may be in order when, arriving at someone's home for dinner, you hand your host not a bottle of wine but a dusty, almost fifty-year-old book, translated from Icelandic, about sheep farmers. At one point, I'd accumulated over twenty copies; I rarely have on hand fewer than ten.

I might never have read *Independent People* had I not, in the summer of 1984, spent two weeks hiking in Iceland. However obscure a figure Laxness may be to us, in his native land he is a colossus without peer or parallel, and anyone drawn to Iceland will get around to him before long. The Icelandic literary tradition is of course illustrious, but nearly all the medieval Sagas and poems that are its capital glory remain anonymous. Before Laxness emerged, prodigiously and prolifically (his career began in 1920, when he published his first novel, *Child of Nature,* at the age of eighteen), Iceland had never produced a modern writer of anything like international reputation. He has been translated into more than thirty languages.

Even so, despite a readership extending across the globe, I maintain a belief that I alone in the world am *Independent People*'s ideal reader. It's an indefensible attitude, I know, but an understandable one: for surely one of the defining traits of this feeling of having come improbably upon the book of your life is an illusory, heady sense that the two of you, book and reader, were "made for each other." To an American reader, who may not have heard of Laxness, my boast may look pathetically meager. To an Icelander, the notion that the book's ideal reader is a foreigner who knows the novel only in translation would sound absurd. But whether my claim represents a small or an overweening triumph, it is something I, infatuatedly, cling to.

Like *One Hundred Years of Solitude,* with which it shares all sorts of family resemblances, *Independent People* in its opening pages evokes the dawn of time. Marquez' novel commences on a blue morning when the boulders in a streambed look like dinosaur eggs. *Independent People's* first chapter summons up the days when the world was first settled, in 874 A.D.—for that is the year when the Norsemen arrived in Iceland, and one of the book's wry conceits is that no other world but Iceland exists. The tale takes place among farmers habitually so impoverished that they "died without ever having transacted a business deal involving more than a few dollars at a time." These are men who might venture outside their valleys once or twice a year, hiking to a little fishing village to purchase a few provisions; for them, even Reykjavik is a misty dream. Meanwhile, their children dispute whether "foreign lands" exist, exploring the question with the same eager intensity with which kids elsewhere might probe the reality of Santa Claus.

The book is set in the early decades of the twentieth century, but the dates of individual events within it are hazy. *Independent People* is a pointedly timeless tale. It reminds us that life on an Icelandic croft had scarcely altered over a millennium; the season shifted, but the overall pattern of want and hardship and stoicism endured. Midway through the novel, however, off at an unimaginable distance, something called the Great War erupts. Normally, there would be nothing new or noteworthy in this (on the Continent, people were forever "hacking one another to pieces like suet in a trough"), but this time the conflict lifts to unprecedented heights the prices for Icelandic mutton and wool. Even the poorest of farmers begin dreaming of an emancipation from their tight, tethered poverty.

War or no war, freedom has always been the aim of the book's hero, Bjartur. When the story begins, he has just finished slaving for eighteen years for a man he despises, the bailiff of the district, in order to save money enough to purchase a pitifully modest holding, Summerhouses, and a handful of sheep. Bjartur of Summerhouses views the Great War coldly and gratefully: "I only hope they keep it up as long as they can." Ultimately, though, he cannot concern himself with the "madmen" in the South—indeed, can hardly concern himself with the affairs of the people around him. Of far more significance are the sheep around him. On their welfare his world depends. He is fighting his own world war, at once the most significant and the most risible conflict on the globe— the smallest war ever fought. He is a "generalissimo" whose troops consist purely of a dog that helps him round up his sheep. He tends to be much more comfortable with animals than with people.

Bjartur's combat is two-tiered. He contends with the hostility of nature—a terrain so cold and forbidding that starvation has always threatened the Icelandic subsistence farmer. And he contends with supernature—a curse. Long ago, the valley in which Summerhouses lies was inhabited by a murderous, blood-drinking witch, the fiend Gunnvor, who formed an unholy alliance with the infernal spirit Kolumkilli. She was eventually brought to justice (she was dismembered), but her scheming spirit still blights the valley. To propitiate her, it is customary for passersby to "give Gunnvor a stone"—to place a rock on the cairn devoted to her memory. But this, characteristically, Bjartur refuses to do. He scorns the "nonsense these old wives let their heads be stuffed with."

Gunnvor and Kolumkilli embody an unholy—an infernal—marriage, and it would seem that one legacy of their union is the withering of all romantic alliances in the valley. Bjartur marries twice. His first wife, a furtively miserable woman, evidently agreed to move into the hovel at Summerhouses only because she was, unbeknownst to him, pregnant by the son of the hateful bailiff. She dies in childbirth, alone. His second wife, a sickly, broken-spirited woman who during the dark arctic winters scarcely rises from her bed, eventually collapses and dies after a horrific, famished spring.

Occasionally it is borne in upon Bjartur that his women are torturously unhappy. He senses uneasily (his relationships with women are never easy) that they, perhaps in response to his crushing ruthless drive for self-sufficiency, have reserved to themselves some sector of their minds he cannot reach. But in time there comes to Bjartur a different sort of romance, a new form of "marriage." The child of his first wife survives its mother's death and Bjartur agrees to rear it as his own. This child, granddaughter to the bailiff, belongs to the "enemy." But it turns out that Bjartur, for all his aloofness, harbors a clumsy warmth toward infants; he views them with some of the same tenderness he feels toward baby lambs. Looking down for the first time at this newborn girl, he

> marvelled that it could be so small and delicate. "You can't really expect it to be much of a thing," he added apologetically, "the way mankind is such a sorry affair when you come to look at it as it actually is."

He bestows on her, just the same, a lofty name: Asta Sollilja. Asta the Sun-lily. She becomes his soul's "one flower."

In time, Bjartur's sun-lily reaches the gangling verge of womanhood. When she is about thirteen, he guides her for the first time across the downs. After hours of trudging, she beholds, far off, a "strange blue color" that "seemed to embrace all the mysteries of distance." She has to ask her father what it might be. It is the ocean, he tells her.

> "Isn't there anything on the other side, then?" she asked finally.
> "The foreign countries are on the other side," replied her father, proud of being able to explain such a vista. "The countries that they talk about in books," he went on, "the kingdoms."

They enter a fishing village and put up in a raucous and squalid lodging house, where they must share a bed. In the night, the frightened girl reaches innocently for her father and he, for a moment, responds to her sexually—he places a hand on her bare leg.

Aghast at himself, Bjartur leaps from bed and insists they strike off immediately for home. His daughter, having sensed nothing sexual in his touch, is thoroughly mystified. But Bjartur will henceforth see to it that nothing like a sexual exchange arises between them. Their "marriage" must be altogether virtuous.

Asta's virtue soon crumbles, though. Wh' n she's fifteen, she is impregnated by a whimsical scholar who tut' rs her and her brothers (the man is also, it transpires, a "notorious drunkard and jailbird who is not only a parish pauper with a horde of children but also rotten with consumption"). On learning of the girl's condition, Bjartur strikes her and expels her from his home. He informs her that she has "shamed" him—which may be true, but of course he's also ravaged by displaced guilt and an unacknowledgeable jealousy.

So Asta sets out on her own, in an icy rain, in the middle of the night. She's a fanciful child even yet, who will discover before the dawn that her papery shoes are ripped to shreds and that she is penniless and friendless in the wide world. Still, she never thinks of retreating, of begging Bjartur for another chance. For it turns out that she, no less than this father of hers who is not her true father, nurtures within her a proud independence. Somehow she will get by.

Years pass. Bjartur and Asta never meet. Neither will approach the other. Neither will relent, even after Asta contracts tuberculosis.

Bjartur has always perceived himself as a soldier whose "war" concerns sheep, but it turns out that the true conflict of the book is between father and daughter. And the two of them are so evenly, formidably matched that it almost seems the novel can never arrive at any sort of satisfying resolution. Asta is the only person in the world who has ever managed to penetrate Bjartur's leatherlike skin. She is an irresistible force. But he is an immovable object. And how (the reader is left continually wondering) can two such ever be reconciled?

I first picked up *Independent People* with faint misgivings, somewhat put off by both its title and its subtitle, *An Epic*. (In the original, the book is called *Sjoelstaett Folk*—literally, "Self-standing Folk"—which doubtless is more inviting.) I feared I was about to encounter an uplifting story composed in a firm nationalistic tenor—a rousing testament to the valiant and indomitable Icelandic temperament. Was this going to be a land of too much steeliness and too little irony?

But one needn't read very far to perceive Bjartur's utter unsuitability as any symbol of a nation's virtues. He's far too quirky and crusty for that. And too big a fool. The book is as much mock as genuine epic. When Bjartur and his dog first stride into the valley, and he utters the first word of the novel—"No"—it's clear that he's a poor man's Odysseus and his worm- and lice-infested dog is a cut-rate Argos.

Partly because I'd so fallen for the book, I've now spent, all told, a year and a half in Iceland and I've met Laxness a few times. The first occasion was in 1986. He was then in his mid-eighties and growing confused and forgetful. When I spoke of my admiration for Bjartur, a look of perplexity gave way to one of alarm. "Oh, but he's so stupid!" he objected.

"Oh, but he's so *wonderfully* stupid!" I replied, and the old man peered at me, and pondered darkly a moment; then his features cleared, and he abruptly laughed with pleasure.

Bjartur is a man who seemingly can hold in his head but one ideal—financial independence—which looms so large he scarcely has room to entertain another thought. In his eyes, abstract speculation is a pastime for layabouts. At the rim of his thinking, though, other notions—strange ideas with arresting cadences—are forever seething. Bjartur turns out to be something of a poet. His verses, not surprisingly, have little to say. He's a man in a perpetual muddle, who can scarcely be expected to find any clarity in his lines. No, Bjartur comes to poetry, as to everything else, in search of a task to be fulfilled. He is enamored of the old *rímur* of traditional Icelandic verse, with its obscure kennings and intricate forms: "His poetry was technically so complex that it could never attain any noteworthy content; and thus it was with his life itself."

Bjartur is for me one of the great twentieth-century literary characters—one of the immortals, like Humbert Humbert or Jay Gatz/ Gatsby or Gregor Samsa or the four Makioka sisters. He is petty-minded and heroic; brutal and poetic; cynical and childlike. All these traits crystallize magnificently in the book's great storm-scene, in which Bjartur, gone off in search of a missing lamb, gets caught in a blizzard. Before it's over, the story will impose on Bjartur near-legendary trials. And yet, typically, these are interwoven with the absurd, for Bjartur's real problems begin when he seeks to capture a reindeer with his bare hands and the beast, its would-be captor slung over its back, plunges into a furious, icy river: "Here he was sitting neither more nor less than up to the waist in Glacier River, and that on no ordinary steed, but on the only steed that is considered suitable for the most renowned of adventures."

This journey deposits Bjartur on the far—the wrong—side of the river, miles from any shelter. In the dead of the howling night, seeking to stay conscious, he turns to a characteristic refuge:

> Seldom had he recited so much poetry in any one night; he had recited all his father's poetry, all the ballads he could remember, all his own palindromes backwards and forwards in forty-eight different ways, whole processions of dirty poems, one hymn that he had learned from his mother, and all the lampoons that had been known in the Fourthing from time immemorial about bailiffs, merchants, and sheriffs. At intervals he struggled up out of the snow and thumped himself from top to toe till he was out of breath.

Ultimately, it's a question of whether poetry—in combination with sheer cantankerousness—will suffice to keep Bjartur alive. The storm keeps raging. And Bjartur keeps fighting, and reciting. In the end, he is reduced to all fours, like the sheep he has searched for in vain:

> He forced his way at first with lowered head against the storm, but when he reached the ridge above the gully, he could no longer make any head-

way in this fashion, so he slumped forward on to his hands and knees and made his way through the blizzard on all fours, crawling over stony slopes and ridges like an animal, rolling down the gullies like a peg; bareheaded, without feeling.

At this moment, Bjartur might well consider himself alone in all the world. No one knows where he is, and were he to succumb to the blizzard, no one would know even where to search for his body. Indeed, he is still more alone than he realizes, since his wife—his first wife—is lying dead at home; she has bled to death in giving birth to Asta Sollilja.

Nonetheless, there *is* someone who has Bjartur uppermost in his mind—his maker, Laxness, who feels toward his creation so potent, so tempestuous a blend of affection and exasperation that the book's every page reverberates with the tension. And the reader, too, is tracking Bjartur's every struggling step. For by the time you've passed through the storm with him, it's almost impossible not to be rooting for that monomaniacal, unkillable, wonderfully stupid old bastard, Bjartur of Summerhouses.

When I tell people I meet that my favorite book by a living novelist is Halldor Laxness' *Independent People* and am asked what it's about, my reply is, "Sheep." This is a story (I continue) in which farmers are forever analyzing sheep and examining sheep: it's about tapeworm in sheep and lungworm in sheep and diarrhea in sheep. Whatever virtues the novel boasts, it's bereft of glamor.

My reply is actually less facetious than might first appear, for while the book does keep large issues constantly in mind (the largest: mortality and memory and love and duty), it is also very much about dung and sheep-parasites; it sets the reader vividly, unforgettably upon a farm. The book is about scything hay and rounding up stray lambs and hauling stones—all of it conveyed so painstakingly that you come away almost feeling that your hands and feet are callused with its tasks. In Bjartur's household there are no separate quarters for the animals, whose stinks and bleatings infiltrate even the dreams of the family. Before you discourse on the novel's grander intentions, *Independent People* calls on you to acknowledge the total, tactile claims of the land.

What is *Independent People* about? Like any big, great novel, it encourages a reader, earnestly wrestling with its scope, to encapsulate it into a single overarching theme. And like most big, great novels, it is varied enough that all such attempts are soon undone by the need for expansion and qualification. I've already said that at the heart of the book lies a war between father and daughter. But perhaps there is a still more pivotal subject: the war waged within a single spirit. *Independent People* presents the most gripping depiction I've ever encountered of the gradual, daily contraction of a human soul and its eventual redemption.

For in his victory over multiple adversity, in his slow and carefully husbanded prosperity, Bjartur somehow loses everything of import in his life. Near the close of the novel, he finds that he has attained what has always struck him as the summit of life—he has become wealthy enough to build a "proper home"—and he discovers his triumph is empty. Not only are both of his wives dead, but his children have died as well, or moved off. Finally, Gvendur, his middle son—the boy he feels closest to—announces that he is emigrating to America. Bjartur is so disgusted he does not even bother to rise from the trench where he's working in order to bid a final farewell to his son.

And Bjartur is still standing in the mud when, a moment later, the entire novel realigns itself. Infinitesimally, everything turns. The book has presented the reader with cataclysmic events—deaths, betrayals, storms, love affairs—but when it reaches its climacteric, the narrative could hardly be quieter:

> Thus did he lose his last child as he stood deep in a ditch at the stage in his career when prosperity and full sovereignty were in sight, after the long struggle for independence that had cost him all his other children. Let those go who wish to go, probably it's all for the best. The strongest man is he who stands alone. . . . He had taken to his digging again. Then all at once some new thought struck him; throwing down his spade, he swung himself on to the bank; the boy had got a short distance away over the marshes.
>
> "Hey," cried the father, and hurried after him until he caught up with him. "Didn't you say something about Asta Sollilja last night?"
>
> "I was talking about giving her my sheep if you didn't want to buy them."
>
> "Oh, I see," said his father, as if he had not remembered the connection. "Oh well, good-bye then. . . ."

Bjartur may not yet realize it, but his life's underpinnings have been removed. He had vowed to have nothing more to do with Asta Sollilja (Hasn't she betrayed his trust? What matters it to him if she's dying of consumption?), and he is a man who holds to his word absolutely. And yet he has, minutely, given way. He doesn't quite know what is the nature of that irresistible force Asta Sollilja embodies (it is love), but the immovable object that is his own soul has been budged. The remainder of the novel conspires to humble him. He must lose his wealth. He must lose his pride. He must lose himself to find himself.

This process is protracted. Bjartur's soul dilates as slowly as it has heretofore narrowed. He is a man of resolute obliquity, who could never bring himself directly to admit that he was wrong to have rejected Asta when she most needed him. So, as any wooer might, Bjartur begins his overtures toward Asta with a poem, which is delivered by Gvendur. It is an impacted verse of just the sort that Bjartur admires—tightly rhymed and alliterated—in which he speaks of a stone and of a flower that has "fled." Asta Sollilja disdains the verses: "And tell him that I also know the empty, drivelling doggerel that he cudgels into shape with hands and feet. But I, I am engaged to a young man who loves me. He has been to school, and he is a modern poet."

Modern poetry? Contemptibly lax in Bjartur's eyes: "It's just like diarrhea. End-rhymes and nothing more." But merely so "no one shall say of me that I couldn't write in these simple modern measures," he prepares a second, more plainspoken poem for Asta, again to be delivered by Gvendur, and adds a postscript, "No, while there's a breath of life left in me, nothing will make me go to her." And a second postscript: "But if I die, you can tell her from me that she may gladly lay me out."

Asta declares that she "can't be bothered to listen to it," and yet attends to it all the same. She then flies into a tirade—"while there's a breath of life left in me, nothing will ever make me go back to Bjartur of Summerhouses"—but she, too, has an afterthought: "when I'm dead he may gladly bury my carrion for all that I care."

Well, the two warring spirits already are largely reconciled. They are united eternally; they have pledged themselves to each other in the hereafter. It is merely in the little, fleeting business of life that they are unworkably at odds—and the generous, ingenious way in which Lax-

ness renders the unworkable workable, effecting a reconciliation between father and daughter, constitutes the most intricate and moving
scene in this most intricate and moving novel.

So brilliantly drawn are Bjartur and Asta that they risk overshadowing
the book's every other character. But with each rereading of the novel
(six, and counting), I find myself marveling at just how accomplished
is the entire supporting cast. There's the credulous, book-loving Olafur
of Yztidale, whose idolization of the printed word is such that he cannot conceive of a misprint; he confidently announces to a group of
fellow farmers, having read this fact in an almanac, that next year's
Easter will fall on a Saturday. And there's the querulous Reverend Gud-
mundur, who "had bigoted opinions on every subject, but changed
them immediately if anyone agreed with him." Here he is bargaining
with Bjartur over the funeral oration for Bjartur's first wife:

> "And how much do you think you can give for a speech?"
> "Well, that was really one of the things I wanted to arrange. Actually
> I consider that you owe me a speech from last spring and I think I might
> as well have it now. It won't improve with keeping."
> "No," said the minister decisively. "I will hold no sermon over a
> woman who lives in marriage for one summer only, then dies. You can
> think yourself lucky that I don't have the matter inquired into. There
> might be ways and means of letting you have your next marriage sermon
> for nothing, but to trade a funeral sermon for a wedding sermon is a
> type of jobbery that I'll have nothing to do with."

Even better—as good, in their way, as Bjartur and Asta—are Bjartur's third son, Little Nonni, and Nonni's grandmother. They are creatures straight out of a fairy tale: he the enchanted third son, the
dreamer, the one whose destiny is threaded with magic; and she the
timeless, ageless crone, given to queer, perhaps vatic, pronouncements,
who serves as fairy godmother.

They, too, have a "marriage" of sorts. They are not merely sleeping
companions; they complete each other—give to each other some quality without which life would be lacking. For Nonni, the old woman
represents a feminine clemency and a patient approval which he lost
catastrophically with the death of his mother. For the old woman, there

is the suspicion that Nonni alone hears her, as she mumbles and maunders through her day. It isn't as though Nonni is actively listening to her prayers and her chants and her aphorisms. But the sounds of her voice are shaping him; her cadences will be with him forever. Nonni ties her, in her floundering old age, to the land of the living.

How do we know her voice will stay with him? You might think Nonni's future would be a blank, given that he emigrates to America while still a boy, vanishing from our story. But as befits his status as the enchanted child of the fairy tale, Nonni is accorded special treatment within the narrative. Toward him alone, the novel repeatedly looks forward: "And when later in life he thought of those days . . ." "all his life through he remembered it, meditating upon it in secret . . ." ". . . the boy knew it well enough to remember it his whole life through." "In years that were yet to come he relived this memory in song. . . ." "It was a sound that was never afterwards to forsake his soul, however far he travelled and however resplendent the halls in which he was later received. . . ."

Before she died, Nonni's mother invested her son with a task whose implications neither he nor she fully understood:

> "Listen, my dear," she said then, "I dreamed something about you the other night."
> "Me?"
> "I dreamed that the elf-lady took me into the big rock and gave me a bowl of milk and told me to drink it, and when I had drunk it the elf-lady said: 'Be good to little Nonni, because when he grows older he will sing for the whole world.'"

But what can these stirring words, *sing for the whole world,* possibly mean to a little, ignorant Icelandic farm boy and his miserable, landlocked mother? Nonni knows only that this quest involves foreign countries, and when the opportunity to emigrate arises he seizes it without hesitation. Slip of a boy though he may be, he approaches with gravity his maternal elf-duty.

So Nonni disappears—only to remain. For he manages, present or absent, to suffuse the novel's every page: he is the presiding genius of the book. He departs from the valley that he might learn to sing—and though the authorial hints are subtle, they also look unmistakable: Nonni has ventured forth in the world in order to write books like . . .

like *Independent People.* Whether or not Nonni's boyhood circumstances mesh with Laxness', he is a clear stand-in for the author. Quietly, almost parenthetically, Laxness remarks of Nonni that he is fated to become "greater than all other Icelanders." It's a roundabout and comely act of self-assertion.

Nonni's personality is set off strikingly by his older brother, Helgi, his soul's dark twin. Any male reader who grew up with brothers will surely appreciate the nuanced rightness of their dealings; *Independent People* offers one of the best portrayals I know of the tribal richness—the ritual tussles and the acts of obeisance and the reciprocal manipulations—that bond older and younger sons. The two boys are "complementary antitheses." They are both philosophers, given to elongated musings about religion and what would happen if time were to stop. But while the older boy is the unquestioned leader, a seeming tower of physical strength, it is he and not Nonni who will crack and shatter in the end. Nonni's softness will, paradoxically, protect him, for in his dreaminess lies his refuge from life's cruelty and rapacity. Helgi comes undone at his mother's death. Nothing, not even prayer to the elves in the rocks, will restore her, and he arrives, in his earnest boy-philosopher's way, at a terrifying nihilism. He claims to have seen Kolumkilli, the ghost-spirit who haunts the valley:

> "And do you know why I see him?" continued the other. Gripping little Nonni's wrists, he held them fast as he whispered into his face: "It's because I'm dead too. Nonni, look at me closely, look into my eyes. You see a dead man."

Helgi will nearly destroy the farm—bring ruination upon them all—before committing a murky act of suicide. The presiding witch of the valley, Kolumkilli's bloodthirsty mate Gunnvor, has claimed another victim. It seems the cycle is never to be broken. And yet little Nonni carries within himself the seeds of a magic greater than that of any fiend: he is, dawningly, the poet, the tale-bearer, the bard. The independent people of Nonni's family will be redeemed by *Independent People.* He will rescue them all through the high-soaring sorcery of Art.

When Laxness buoyantly referred to himself, by way of a stand-in, as "greater than all other Icelanders," he was making a claim that in time would become so overwhelmingly true as to look like an under-statement. Given Iceland's tiny size and its subordinate role in modern history (it did not receive full independence from Denmark until 1944), it's hardly surprising that Laxness is generally perceived not only as the country's foremost artist of the century but its most influential citizen. He looms larger than any modern statesman or religious figure. Not merely through his fiction but through his journalism and essays and political stands he has shaped the mores of his rapidly changing nation.

I've met a number of younger Icelandic writers who consider him a baleful presence. (One has to sympathize if some of them feel that the mountain range which Laxness erected blocks the sunlight from the gardens they themselves would tend. . . .) And I've met Icelanders of various walks of life who deplore his social influence. Laxness has been an impassioned and mercurial political thinker who, over time, has embraced and censured both communism and established religion. As a satirist, too, he has offended many of his countrymen over his long career. But even those who would disparage him, as artist or thinker, first accord him primacy.

These days, sadly, he's a much-diminished figure. When an Icelandic friend took me to visit him in 1992, I encountered a man who still looked hale but was in perilous shape. He was nearly ninety, and fuzzi-ness of thought had given way to a thoroughgoing disorientation. He almost never left his home anymore, being constantly ministered to by his wife. He had become increasingly uncomfortable with strangers—a group whose ranks were sadly multiplying, for he recognized fewer and fewer people. His speech drifted in and out of coherence.

I sat beside him. He couldn't recall from one moment to the next what my name was or where I was from. It no longer seemed possible to speak to him, even in the broadest terms, about literature. Still, gratitude prodded at me, and so I declared to him, loudly and slowly, "I love your book *Independent People*. I love Bjartur and Asta Sollilja."

Laxness looked befuddled—and, hunching, eyed me suspiciously.

"You have written a great book," I continued.

And still he peered at me. *Who,* his glance seemed nervously to ask, *is this stranger in my home?*

"In America," I went on, "I have more than twenty copies of *Inde-pendent People* on my bookshelf."

At this remark, an unexpected and unforgettable thing occurred. The venerable head lifted, the brow unknitted itself, and every feature in his face was aglow. He'd been touched once more with what is, perhaps, the most beautiful egotism in the world—that of the artist who exults in having kindled love and delight in the heart of a stranger.

This man who, these days, struggled so hard to express so little, now proudly protested, "Ah, you have left me with nothing to say! You have struck me speechless!"

Struck him speechless? If I had, there was in this a gorgeous irony. For sitting at my side was somebody who had already said to me everything he ever needed to say.

(1994)

A NOTE ON THE TYPE

This text of this book was set in a film version of a typeface named Bembo. The roman is a copy of a letter cut for the celebrated Venetian printer Aldus Manutius by Francesco Griffo. It was first used in Cardinal Bembo's De Aetna of 1495—hence the name of the revival. Griffo's type is now generally recognized, thanks to the research of Stanley Morison, to be the first of the old-face group of types. The companion italic is an adaptation of the chancery script type designed by the Roman calligrapher and printer Lodovico degli Arrighi, called Vincentino, and used by him during the 1520s.

Composed by Graphic Composition, Inc.,
Athens, Georgia

Printed and bound by Quebecor Printing,
Martinsburg, West Virginia

Typography and binding design by
Dorothy Schmiderer Baker